CAN ATHEISM

RESCUE GOD?

AND VICE VERSA

MEL THOMPSON

Brimstone Press

ACKNOWLEDGEMENTS

I am indebted to friends and colleagues with whom, over the decades, I have discussed the idea of 'God'. The variety of their views has surprised and encouraged me. They range from atheism that comes from a serious quest to be honest, to spiritual convictions that, while conventional by the standards of the best theology, sit lightly on established doctrines.

But, most of all, I am indebted so someone I never met in person, but whose towering intellect and passion for the truth flies off the page – the German-American philosopher and theologian Paul Tillich. Since I started a research degree on his idea of the religious symbol more than fifty years ago, he has given me the courage to struggle with questions related to the much-misused word 'God', even though I have often despaired at what passes for conventional religious belief.

To preserve the privacy of their views, none – other than Tillich – are named in the text, so they can breathe easy.

First published by Brimstone Press
brimstone-press.com

© Mel Thompson, 2025
ISBN 978-1-906-38596-5 (paperback)

Mel Thompson hereby asserts his right to be identified as the author of this work in accordance with the Copyright, Designs and Patents Act, 1988.

For further information on this and his other publications see:
essexthinker.com

CAN ATHEISM RESCUE GOD?

AND *VICE VERSA*

BY THE SAME AUTHOR

Traditionally published:

Cancer and the God of Love
Buddhist Teaching and Practice
Sikh Belief and Practice
The Christian Faith and its Symbols (with Jan Thompson)
The RE Atlas (with Jan Thompson)
Leading the Way
Guidelines for Life
The Buddhist Experience
Ethics: Teach Yourself
Philosophy: Teach Yourself
Buddhism: a new approach (with Steve Clarke)
Philosophy of Religion: Teach Yourself
Ethical Theory
Eastern Philosophy: Teach Yourself
Religion and Science
Buddhism: 101 Key Ideas
Philosophy of Science: Teach Yourself
World Faiths: Buddhism
World Philosophy (ed)
An Introduction to Philosophy and Ethics
Philosophy of Mind: Teach Yourself
Philosophers Behaving Badly (with Nigel Rodgers)
Political Philosophy: Teach Yourself
Me (The Art of Living Series)
Existentialism: Teach Yourself (with Nigel Rodgers)
The Philosopher's Beach Book
Philosophy for Life
Ethics for Life
AQA A-level Religious Studies, year 2 (with J Frye and D Herring)

Self-published:

Through Mud and Barbed Wire
Home: a philosophy of personal space
Little Baddow: the story of an Essex Village

The Cover

A sunset, of all things! Who in their right mind puts a sunset on the cover of anything but a romance?

For me this is no ordinary sunset. It is early April and we are muffled up against the cold. The snow is crisp; crunching under our boots. We are in Arizona. The sun dips lower through the icy air, and below us the ominous void of Grand Canyon loses its contours. The vertical cliffs, barren screes and, below them, a hint of the Colorado River, are gradually losing their pale orange tinges and are vanishing into blackness. Turning westwards and leaning on the guardrail, we look out over the canyon to the desert beyond, still touched by the fading light.

We see the sun more clearly now that it has almost gone. By day we shield our eyes from it, yet its reflected light creates for us a perceptible world of near and far, people and canyons, the familiar and the inhospitable; we find our way around by that which is now slowly being withdrawn. I am reminded of the words of Friedrich Nietzsche 'Do we not stray, as through infinite nothingness? Does not empty space breathe upon us? Has it not become colder? Does not night come on continually darker and darker?' His context: the madman who is mocked for first seeking God and then claiming that he has been killed (*The Joyful Science*, 1882, *section 125*). He fears that the loss of God will bring nihilism, with lack of direction and purpose. But this moment, as the Earth becomes darker and colder, brings its own immediate, chilling beauty.

A sunset is therefore entirely appropriate for the cover of this book. As the day and my life inevitably draw towards their close, I need to write on a subject that has haunted – sometimes tormented – me for more than 60 years: the reality

5

of that to which the ambiguous term 'God' has too often been given. This book is about the madman's quest: about life and misunderstanding, the confusing richness of language about God, and the spiritual attraction of atheism.

Although the words 'God' and 'atheism' are equally mired in confusion, this book explores the possibility that they may be able to rescue one another from a crude literalism that does justice to neither.

As the sun finally turns blood red and appears to sink into the horizon. We bid it farewell and turn to head home, lighting torches to find our way.

Contents

Introduction

As I write, crowds are gathering in St Peter's Square in Rome to file past the body of Pope Francis, with tributes flowing in from across the world, speaking of his humility, his compassion, his care for the poor, his moral seriousness and his friendly disposition. He was a theist. But the Dalai Lama is equally revered for displaying those same spiritual qualities, yet he is an atheist. What they have in common is far more important than whether or not they use the term 'God' in their spirituality or in their description of reality.

In part, this book is an attempt to get beyond the philosophical nonsense in which naïve language about God or uncompromising atheism can so easily become a distraction from engagement with what really matters.

In any case, 'God' appears to be evaporating. That's not the same thing as the general decline in the practice of religion in the Christian West, which has been going on since the middle of the 19th century. No; this is a phenomenon, which seems to be affecting both those who would describe themselves as conventionally religious and the secular majority. In itself it may not be a bad thing, but it leaves behind a vocal minority who cling to a literal idea of God that may prove dangerous and from which 'God' needs to be rescued.

Let me give just one example of thoughtful evaporation. In 2024, during the debate in Britain about the proposal that assisted dying should be legalised for the terminally ill, the Rt. Revd. George Carey was interviewed by a BBC reporter. She suggested that, as a retired Archbishop of Canterbury, he could be expected to be in regular touch with God. So what did God say about the matter? "It doesn't quite work like that" Carey replied, and then launched into serious comments about compassion and respect for those coming to the end of their lives. Her question presupposed that God was an external, supernatural entity. Carey responded by speaking about what seemed to him to be most real and important, with the moral seriousness that was shared equally in that debate by the religious and the non-religious.

At about the same time, an article in *The Guardian* (18th October) included comments by Lord Carey, in which he described life as sacred – 'a gift from God' – and spoke again of compassion, a theme taken up by two Rabbis whose comments were also included in the article. However, a very different approach was taken by an imam from Leeds, who was quoted as saying 'God chooses how long each person will live' and that 'he is not unaware of pain… and he will reward them for their pain and suffering, as he sees appropriate, in the next world.'

Those final comments happened to be made by a Muslim, but could equally be made by conservative representatives of other religions. They exemplify the literal approach to the idea of God, in contrast to the approach of both the retired Archbishop and the Chief Rabbi, who spoke about a level of reality to which the word 'God' can refer, but without using supernatural language. In other words, to make 'God language' real, and to show its relevance, they had allowed potentially misleading supernatural language to evaporate.

When the Assisted Dying Bill was discussed in parliament, superficial political differences were also set aside and MP's spoke of deeply held convictions and with emotion. Party politics had also evaporated that day. No distinction could be made between believers or atheists – all alike were probing the depths of human life and the agonising dilemmas it presents.

Fifty years ago, those training to be ordained were taught the classic arguments for the existence of God, but almost nothing about the social and political implications of religion. Since then, theology has moved on, with the arrival of liberation theology, feminist theology, urban theology and so on. Theology today takes the realities of life and explores their significance. Except among Conservative Evangelicals, its concern with debating the existence of supernatural entities has largely... evaporated.

Today, most of those who appear keen to debate the existence (or non-existence) of God are atheist, for alongside the residue of literal believers there is also a residue of literal atheists. Neither group represents the view of life shared by a majority of people today, but they feed off one another. I suggest that, for intellectual integrity, both 'God' and 'atheism' need to be rescued from such narrow interpretations.

To see the significance of this, let's start by asking...

DOES GOD EXIST?

How is it possible in this 21st century that people still disagree about whether or not God exists?   Can the biggest single question we can ask – a question that clearly shapes our whole view of life and its possibilities – remain without a universally accepted answer?

This unresolved embarrassment is made worse by the fact that the arguments used today are not so different from those found among the radical theologians of the 1960s, or the thinkers of the European Enlightenment, or of the Hellenistic world, or even the playwrights and philosophers of ancient Greece. Has there been no progress?

It would seem obvious, from the way in which most people engage with life today, that they do not believe in God in any literal sense.   We know that science and philosophy cannot give us all the answers to life's dilemmas, comfort us when tragedy strikes or calm our existential angst, but most people find it perfectly natural to face the highs and lows of life

11

without reference to the supernatural. Yet I cannot avoid the fact that many thinking people, including some I personally know and respect, claim to believe in God. Are they wrong? Deluded? I cannot simply dismiss their beliefs because, in discussion, I find that not all believers accept crude supernaturalism and that their view of life is not so different from mine. Yet they come down on the side of nuanced belief, while I come down in favour of an equally nuanced atheism.

The harsh facts of life – war, disease, death, poverty, deliberately inflicted cruelty, the general fragility of all that we cherish – make it all too easy to be atheist, rather than theist. Yet, looking at the past, there were whole eras in which the opposite was true. Faced with equal horrors, a majority appeared to believe in God. Or did they? And what sort of god did they believe in?

Let's start by considering what some ordinary people (i.e. not professional philosophers, theologians, priests or ministers) believe about 'God'.

In *Global Religion 2023*, a survey across 26 countries, published by Ipsos, 40% said they believed in God as described in holy scriptures, 20% believe in a higher spirit, but not as in the scriptures, 21% believe in neither God nor any higher spirit, and 19% were either not sure or refused to say. In 8 of the 10 European countries surveyed, no more than half believed in God or a higher power.

Global averages are misleading. After all, in traditionally Muslim countries, almost everyone will claim to believe in Allah, while in China most will claim to be atheist. But they show a frustratingly balanced range of views.

A rather different approach is to ask about religion. In the 2021 Census in England and Wales, The section on religion was voluntary, but was answered by 56 million people (94% of the surveyed population). To the rather leading question 'What is your religion?' 46.2% described themselves as

Christian (a 13.1% decrease over the previous decade), while 37.2% claimed no religion (a 12% increase). Other religious groups showed a slight increase over the decade. Of the 22.2 million who identified as 'non-religious', only 14,000 people claimed to be atheists. However, the British Social Attitudes Survey, conducted in 2019, asked 'Do you regard yourself as belonging to any particular religion?' Put that way, 53% declared 'none', 12% Anglican, 7% Catholic, 18% other Christian denominations and 9% all other religions.

However, sales of Bibles and books on religion continue to increase in the UK, according to statistics from Nielsen Book Data for 2023 to 2024, and Generation Z, born between 1997 and 2012, are more likely than their parents or grandparents to identify as spiritual, with only 13% identifying as atheist. But that does not translate into the number of people actually taking an active part in any of the major religions.

So, in a nutshell, far more people claim to believe in a god of some sort than actually practice religion, while only a very small fraction of those who are 'non-religious' are prepared to admit to atheism.

In April 2023, the question 'Do you believe in God?' Was posted on Twitter (now X).   Some responded as though the question had been 'Does God exist?' while others tried to answer 'What is the nature of God?' Obviously, I'm not arguing that Tweets represent an accurate view of modern beliefs; that would be naïve. However, they do show that, at the level of *vox pop*, the idea of God is far from clear, particularly among those who claim not to believe in him.

Some responded by offered a definition of what they meant by God…

'an intelligence behind the Universe, but I don't believe it cares about me individually.'

'… greater intelligence beyond our ken.'

'I believe in the power of nature.'

'I believe in a supreme being but I don't know his name.'

'Supernatural being that surpasses human imagination.'

Or they related the question to the practice of religion:

'Maybe, but I don't believe in religion.'

'Spiritual practice helpful. Not trad God.'

And it is clear that while some have no doubts…

'No – idea ridiculous'

Others struggle…

'After six decades of wondering, I am fairly convinced No.'

'Short answer, or the truth?'

'Require extraordinary evidence. Keep open mind.'

'Not in a conventional sense.'

Many believers replied simply 'Yes', some adding…

'We were created in God's image.'

'Any other reason for my existence?'

'We all believe in something.'

When answers vary that much, it suggests to me that there's something wrong with the question.

Possibly half of the population in Britain – and more than that in the USA – claim to believe in some sort of God, or spiritual power, or designer of the universe, but they may not be willing or able to define their belief further. Most will not take part in religious worship on a regular basis, but still want to hold on to the idea that the world makes sense and that it has a purpose in which they can play their part. This, as we shall see, is a modern equivalent of the deism that developed in the 17th and 18th centuries, and it continues to be a popular alternative to traditional theism.

If the results of popular polls suggest that people are confused as to the meaning of 'God', even serious thinkers do not find definitions easy. In the original edition of his *God and the Universe of Faiths* – a well-argued book of essays written almost four decades ago – Professor John Hick (1922-2012) offered the following definition of religion:

> ... an understanding of the universe, together with an appropriate way of living within it, which involves reference beyond the natural world to God or gods or to the Absolute or to a transcendent order or process.

The first part of this causes no problem: religion is about an understanding and response to the world in which we live. But then the confusion starts. How can something 'beyond the natural world' be part of our 'understanding of the universe'? Most people think of the universe as the natural world. What is 'beyond' may involve God or gods, or the Absolute – whatever that means – or 'a transcendent order'. To be blunt, and in spite of having great respect for the work of John Hick, that raises more questions than it answers.

However, in the preface to the 1993 edition of his book, Hick included a far better, inclusive approach to religion, when he suggests that we:

> ... simply accept that the transformation of human existence from destructive self-centredness to a new centring in the ultimate transcendent Reality that we call God is taking place in and through all the great world traditions.

This offers a healthy view of the function of religion, but why should it be limited to one of the 'great world traditions'? Why not see it as a secular possibility for all? And is it wise to identify 'God' with 'Reality' without admitting that it is not what most people mean by 'God'?

You might assume that the Catholic Church, with a global membership of over a billion and a structured and authoritative set of beliefs, should have no problem giving an affirmative answer. Yet Thomas Aquinas, arguably the most influential theologian in the whole history of Catholicism, stated clearly, back in the 13th century, that God is not in the order of existing beings – in other words, he does not exist in the way that everything else exists. Yet, in worship, God is addressed as if he were a separate being in human form, who might well have emotions and wishes, take interest in human activity, and respond by rewarding of punishing people in tangible ways. So, asked if God exists, theologically literate Catholics should really answer 'Yes, but...' and then re-define what they mean by 'exists', to make it clear that it's not what most people mean.

In a very different culture, a Buddhist monk was given the sage advice 'If you meet the Buddha on the road, kill him!' No Buddha you can meet in that way can possibly be Buddha – so best get rid of that idea and keep looking. Does the same thing apply to the word 'God'? If you ask me if God exists, I shall answer 'No', for no God about whom you need to ask that question will do justice to the meaning of that word.

It's not that God ever existed in any literal, physical sense. That's never been a thinking person's option in the monotheistic religions, from the Jewish prohibition of idolatry, through the formulation of the Christian creeds, to Islam's rejection of images.

SAD DEBATES

In part, this book is a reaction to the sad debates that have raged between the more narrowly focused representatives of the atheist and theist communities. I despair of the wriggling of theologians who seek to avoid a rational analysis of their claims, and of philosophers who insist on logical argument while ignoring most of what makes human life worthwhile. You cannot claim to explore the meaning of human life if your questions, along with the only answers you regard as acceptable, are set within a narrowly scientific framework. That is not to denigrate science or empiricism; both are essential and have yielded huge benefits. Rather it is to say that some questions are best approached within the arts, and yield to intuition rather than logic or evidence.

The Buddha argued that, in these matters, conceptual thought was a danger to be avoided. He believed that arguments should be checked against personal experience and that our task is to look realistically at life and ask what is conducive to human flourishing and happiness.

One thing would seem to be clear from the outset, as commonly understood, supernatural religion is out of step with modern thought. We don't live in an enchanted world anymore, as Charles Taylor's *A Secular Age* and other studies of the secularisation of Western culture have shown. But there is a danger that the rejection of the supernatural will lead to a loss of much of personal and cultural value that has been generated by religion.

The universal shedding of the supernatural is not going to be achieved in a single moment of insight – if that were possible, it would have gone centuries ago – but a first step may be to rescue the word 'God' from literalism and superstition.

Many debates between atheists and traditional believers have an 18th century quality about them. Neither side appears to make any significant headway in terms of a global consensus, and both tend to retreat into their own bunkers. Sadly, this level of debate is also reflected in some academic courses on the Philosophy of Religion, and – at its very worst – in unthinking polarisation on social media. This is an impediment both to serious thought and to the spiritual needs of the 21st century. In short, the sooner we get rid of outdated arguments for or against the existence of God the better.

On the other hand, the decline in formal religion raises the challenge of finding direction, meaning and moral seriousness within a secular worldview.

PHILOSOPHY AND THE SHIFTING OF MEANING

Words change over time; their meanings shift, depending on the context in which they are used and the background of thought that gives rise to them. There's nothing unusual about that, it's the basis of all serious academic study in arts subjects. This shifting language makes literature precious and poetry possible, because ideas are blended and meanings shaped to express the author's, playwright's or poet's intentions. If every word had a single, straightforward meaning, life would be so easy and boring!

So, in this book, I'll be exploring a rather strange word whose meaning has shifted beyond recognition over the centuries and about which there have been endless, pointless debates – the word 'God'.

Beyond the scope of this book, we could also look across cultures to ask how the God of theism relates to Eastern concepts of Brahman, or the Tao, or Shunyata. How does the Christian view of God as the Trinity relate to the Jewish idea of Yahweh or the Muslim view of Allah? If you think globally, arguments about whether God 'exists', become parochial and fail to draw out the real significance of that word.

Some philosophers dismiss religious claims, assuming them to be fundamentally linked to a view of the supernatural that is out of step with modern thought and science. They prefer to attend to the analysis of argument rather than intuitions of meaning. That, of course, is not the whole story of philosophy today, since Continental and existentialist philosophy thrive, and at the popular level there are philosophies of everything including, on my bookshelf, coffee and whisky! But philosophy has, in general, kept its distance from the practice of religion, and has preferred to focus on 'The Philosophy of Religion', where religious concepts and propositions have been examined, and generally found wanting, from within parameters set by philosophy.

If religion is seen primarily as a set of factual claims about the supernatural, it is easily dismissed as non-rational. However, Paul Tillich, a philosopher and theologian whose work spans the middle decades of the 20th century, argued that theology – and specifically the idea of 'God' – is not about some external, possible world, but about the depth and the unconditional within human experience. This idea sets an entirely new agenda for the relationship between theology and philosophy, because it sees both as dealing with the same, real world and nourished by the same experience.

Hence, of course, my example of the euthanasia debate in the UK and the metaphor of evaporation. As the debate heats up, supernatural language can evaporate to reveal the real, human and universal issues.

In *Biblical Religion and the Search for Ultimate Reality*, Tillich sees the question of 'Being' as the central one for philosophy, in a tradition that goes back to Aristotle. He argues that 'Man is by nature a philosopher, because he inescapably asks the question of being. He does it in myth and epic, in drama and poetry, in the structure and the vocabulary of any language.'

However, philosophy and theology have generally failed to nourish one another. Why has this come about? Is it intellectually healthy? And might Tillich's approach provide a mutually beneficial reconciliation?

Both 'philosophy' and 'God' are ambiguous. Philosophy can be limited to the examination of rational argument and the nature of language. That has been its main function within professional philosophy. But philosophy can also mean a love of wisdom in a broader sense; a rational explorations of the intuitions about life found in culture. 'God' is equally ambiguous. It can refer to a supernatural being who might or might not exist beyond the universe, but who is able to intervene selectively within it if asked nicely. Belief in such a god is generally superstitious and the very antithesis of philosophy. But the word 'God' is also used for that which is ultimate, or most real. The confusion between these two ideas of 'God', has led to the present irrelevance of much of the

Philosophy of Religion. It has often been assumed that a basic task of the philosophy of religion is to ask whether God exists or not. This is nonsense, and only serves to show that the implied idea of God is inadequate.

'God' needs to be rescued from those who take a narrow and literal definition of that word, not just because many people rejected it, but in order that the word 'God' can continue within human culture as shorthand for a sense of ultimate meaning and value. Equally, atheism needs to be rescued from a caricature that sees it as nihilist, destructive of human intuitions about life, and entranced by scientism. At its best, atheism is liberating, life affirming, and moral.

Without getting too involved in the complexities of theology and philosophy, I shall be arguing that, broadly speaking, there are two very different views of atheism and two very different views of God, and that, for personal integrity and a positive view of life, you need one of each. This book will suggest which you should choose.

I have wasted too much of my life trying to defend the intellectually indefensible. Here I will be honest, but I will also try to be fair and balanced. Above all, I endorse a comment made by Tim Whitmarsh in *Battling the Gods: Atheism in the Ancient World*:

> It is not my aim to prove the truth (or indeed falsehood) of atheism as a philosophical position. I do, however, have a strong conviction – a conviction that has hardened in the course of the researching and writing of this book – that cultural and religious pluralism, and free debate, are indispensable to the good life.

I read that and thought "Exactly!"

Chapter 1

A Legacy of the Gods?

'… before his gods he was never superstitious'
Marcus Aurelius, in praise of his father

Thou shalt have no other gods before me.
First Commandment in *Exodus*

Most gods are functionally dead; that is not in doubt. Who today makes offerings to Thor, Baal, or Anubis? Who now prays in the temple of Zeus, or pays homage to Poseidon before setting sail? We know of such gods now through their stories, images and the remains of their places of worship. We can learn what they stood for and how they were worshipped. We may also appreciate the insights into human nature that these things give. Yet, with respect to the *functioning* of all these deities, we are atheist. If we appreciate them now, it is through their cultural legacy.

Secular museums and galleries are filled with the evidence of humankind's religious quest, and their contents seem quite capable of inspiring without converting. People continue to engage with ancient myths, appreciating their symbolism and the emotions and insights they express; it is a religious heritage that everyone can appreciate, whether or not they would describe themselves as 'believers' or take an active part in a religion. Even a convinced atheist can enjoy the Christmas story or the St Matthew Passion.

Part of the legacy of religion is that it opens up the quest for self-expression and transcendence. So, even if religion appears to be in decline, engagement with religious culture – whether it is listening to Verdi's Requiem, or going to an exhibition of Renaissance art – can stir intuitions about life. You don't have to agree with the idea of judgement at the end of the world to feel your spine tingle as the brass section blasts out the *Dies Irae*; you simply allow yourself become emotionally engaged in the dramatic performance, feeling yourself immersed in life at a depth that evokes a mixture of longing and loss.

That legacy extends to the practical and the popular. Days of the week are named after gods or goddesses without embarrassment. Diana represents the moon for Monday. On Tuesday you have an old German sky god (Tiu), although in French, you swap him with Mardi (from Mars, Roman god of war). Woden is acknowledged on Wednesday and Thor on Thursday. For Friday, we have Frigga, the Germanic goddess of married love. Heading into the weekend, Saturn gives us Saturday, and for Sunday you have a choice of Norse mythology (Sól), Sol Invictus as the sun god, or simply refer to the day as the Sabbath (Saturday for Jews, Sunday for Christians) or use the French Dimanche, or 'Lord's Day.' They are part of our cultural heritage and I do not detect any pressure to eliminate from our calendar names that have a religious origin. At its most popular, Easter eggs, hot cross buns and Santa mark out the great Christian festivals.

It is a rich legacy. Imagine a world in which all references to gods and goddesses were removed. In all their imaginative craziness, the stories of gods have probed the depths of psychology and the accounts of their worship have opened up insights into societies long gone. From a historical perspective, most deities live on as part of human culture, but not as supernatural entities.

The question is whether, before the gods, we are superstitious, or whether we treat them as part of our cultural heritage,

22

while also allowing them to become a source of inspiration, insight, meaning and moral direction.

Gods come to life when they are internalised; in time, most die off or are replaced. But let's look for a moment at the scale of this 'supernatural' phenomenon.

GODS BY THE THOUSAND...

There are many thousands of gods, scattered across the globe and the centuries.

From Egypt, we have the gods of the Old Kingdom, include Ra, the sun god, and Osiris, god of the dead and Atum, who brings order out of chaos. There are gods for every aspect of life and death – Horos, Isis, Nephthys, Nut, Set, Anubis – the turning of the seasons and the chance flooding of the Nile. There was even a brief flirting with monotheism under Akhenaten. In museums today we can stand before their images, read about their iconography, and glimpse a world long past. Did the ancient Egyptians take the stories literally? We cannot tell. Did they use them as a way of interpreting life? Very likely.

One can go north, to the lands ruled by the Norse gods. *Ragnarok*, from the Poetic Edda, written in the 13th century, describes the death of the gods in battle – Odin, Thor, Freyr, and Loki all perish – the burning of the world and finally its submersion. It describes an age of destruction, when the world tree shudders and the sky turns black. The event lives on in modern culture through the music of Richard Wagner, for it is the basis of the *Gotterdammerung*, the 'Twilight of the Gods'. Or we head south to the Aztec gods, or the many gods of African religions, or east to the cultures of Japan, where Shinto gods are supplemented by the many kami, or spirits of place, summoned in temples.

The Greek gods – Apollo, Aphrodite, Dionysus, Hades, Poseidon, Zeus and others – have a massive cultural legacy, not least by appearing as characters in Homer's *Iliad* and *Odyssey*, or by being sculpted in marble. The ruins of their temples provide a backdrop for holiday photographs.

Roman gods, too, are embedded in Western culture – Venus, Diana, Pluto, Mercury Saturn, Neptune, Jupiter. Even those who lack a planet named after them live on, as with Gaia, the creative force of Earth, and it is impossible to escape them when browsing the history of European art.

We cannot hope to trace out the cultural legacy of the thousands of gods who are, or have been worshipped worldwide, so let us reflect for a moment on two groups of gods and goddesses: one dead, the other living.

With more than one thousand *poleis*, or city-states, Ancient Greece was largely held together by a sense of having a common culture and language. Although each polis, had its particular gods, festivals and traditions, with religion used as a way of celebrating local identity, the twelve Olympian gods, along with the literature of Homer and Hesiod, were shared throughout. Indeed, when Greece eventually became part of the Roman Empire, the city-states built temples for the worship of the emperors – thus adding another layer of political loyalty to the earlier, more local ones. This political aspect of religion is illustrated by the fact that the priests were public officials, employed to organise festivals and sacrifices, without any special religious qualification or training.

The gods of ancient Greece appear as supernatural characters in literature. They are human in form and in terms of their loves, hates, jealousies and passions. They have favourites, and punish those who offend them. They intervene to produce storms, or to guide ships to port; they inspire, challenge and manipulate. For Greeks, Homer was the greatest of the theologians – not because he argued for the existence of the gods, but because he told their stories.

Today, the Greek and Roman gods are studied as elements within mythological literature, and sometimes portrayed as symbols, representing features of life – Mars becomes the god of war, Venus the goddess of love. Eros gives us eroticism, and Hermes, protector of travellers and merchants, gives his name to a logistics company. Nobody today asks if Eros exists, but few would deny that the erotic is a fundamental and powerful feature of human life. In his Roman version, Cupid's arrow may still be said to strike when someone falls in love, but nobody debates supernatural archery!

From the gods and goddesses of Greece and Rome, take one thing: that they were vehicles for political allegiance as well as the embodiment of cultural aspects of life, and the variety of gods and goddesses allowed a measure of moral and social flexibility.

In terms of living religions, the greatest plethora of gods is to be found in the Indian sub-continent – starting with Brahma, Vishnu and Shiva, the great triad of creator, preserver and destroyer, and the gods and goddesses of popular mythology and worship, including Ganesha, Krishna, Rama, Hanuman, Lakshmi, Saraswati. Each has its own iconography, stories and forms of worship; each represents an aspect of life. In contrast to the gods of ancient Greece and Rome, the gods of India are functioning deities in the traditions that the West refers to as Hindu. But, although living, they also embody a cultural heritage.

In the *Brihandaranyaka Sutra*, asked how many gods there are, the teasing answer from the sage starts be suggesting that there 300 and 3003, but then reduces that number of 33 (the number given in the *Rig Veda*), then, six, then three, then two then (mischievously?) one and a half, then only one. Asked – no doubt in frustration – how many there are *really*, the sage admits that there are only 33, all the rest being their various manifestations. However, these numbers are dwarfed by the 330 million claimed in the *Skanda Purana*. In other words, beneath their teeming variety there is one absolute reality, which the philosophical tradition of the Upanishads calls Brahman, a reality that is also identified with the self.

God and goddesses are created or adapted within society, take on particular identities and accrue stories (often borrowed from other deities or contexts). For a time they are worshipped, but eventually they die. The Norse gods went out in style, killing one another under a black sky, but most gods simply fade out of existence, their festivals neglected, their temples falling into disuse, repurposed, or destroyed by followers of rival deities.

Their stories may morph from culture to culture. The Epic of Gilgamesh, an early flood narrative from Mesopotamia, finds its way into the Hebrew scriptures and continues to be enacted by children in Sunday School as the story of Noah and his ark, so that the drama becomes popularised and the animals now go in two by two 'for to get out of the rain', as the song goes.

But what sustains this ever-changing pattern of gods? In part, of course, it reflects the social and political contexts within which they developed, but there is also a fundamental human need for which religious culture seemed to provide an answer...

THE QUEST FOR ORDER

The ancient gods are woven into narratives that describe the place of humankind within the world. As the psychologist Karl Jung (among many others) has argued, the myths of the ancients were aspects of a quest for meaning and order.

So, from the first appearance of human culture, the gods have personified aspect of life. As characters within a narrative, they externalised human qualities, providing points of identity and direction in an uncertain world. Religion involves cultural engagement with religious narratives and images and, like medicine, the gods need to be ingested in order to work.

The quest for order also seems to have promoted the idea of monotheism: the idea that there is a single divine reality, either replacing or lying beneath the plethora of individual deities. This was reinforced by philosophy, as we shall see later. But how should philosophy deal with myth and worship? How should it regard the gods? Is reason a more sophisticated way of understanding reality, or merely a more cerebral one? Can thinking yield the same insight as worship or wonder? Is philosophy to be an additional feature of life, an interpretive tool, or a replacement for religion?

The distinction between atheism and theism is not so much an intellectual discussion about the existence of supernatural entities – although, it is often couched in those terms – but about how we engage with religious culture and the quest for meaning.

However, there is one major problem that has fouled up the legacy of the gods – henotheism.

THE PROBLEM OF HENOTHEISM

On the eastern seaboard of the Mediterranean, the Hebrew tribes who infiltrated the region of Palestine in the early part of the first millennium BCE came together to form the small kingdoms of Israel and Judah. Their particular deity, Yahweh, is described as demanding exclusivity and opposing the worship of Baal and the many other gods of the people among whom they lived. The early Hebrew scriptures see Yahweh as battling and triumphing over rival gods, and his followers do battle against the 'people of the land'. The book of Joshua records Yahweh instructing them to carry out genocide against the local tribes, eliminating them entirely before taking over their land. They are told to 'show no mercy' (*Deuteronomy* 7:2) and 'not leave alive anything that breathes' (20:16). Here, political and military action is linked

27

directly to the orders of a god, its morality is based on ruthless, divine self-interest, rather than the more gentle, universal sympathies of both theism and polytheism.

Such religion was not monotheism (the idea that there is only one god) but henotheism – the idea that other gods exist, but that one should be devoted exclusively to only one. Hence, the first commandment became 'Thou shalt have no other gods but me', implying, of course, that other gods existed but were off limits; issued by a god who is jealous and easily offended.

Today, the many gods who were worshipped in Palestine in the early first millennium BCE are best known because they appear in the Hebrew scriptures, and are thus preserved into modern culture through Judaism and Christianity. The biblical God, Yahweh, was known to the Patriarchs as El or El-shaddai, and in *Deuteronomy* 32:8-9 is said to have received an inheritance of people and land from the High God Elyon. Originally, Yahweh was therefore a tribal, rather than a universal god. Within the scriptures we find plenty of El deities (El being a generic term for god), each related to a particular shrine – El Olam (Beersheba), El Elohe-Israel (Shechem), El Bethel (Bethel) El Elyon (Jerusalem), along with the Baal gods, related to fertility, and others such as Gad (fortune) or Mani (destiny). There are nature gods and fertility gods, temples with extensive animal sacrifices – sometimes also human sacrifices, as Abraham finds when ordered to sacrifice his son Isaac, only reprieved at the last moment when a ram is provided to take his place. In the early Hebrew scriptures there is no doubting the reality of other gods, but they are to be foresworn upon pain of death.

Expanding empires are generally faced with the problem of creating loyalty from the disparate nations they conquer. The Assyrian and Babylonian empires had deported leading people in each conquered tribe or nation, and replaced them with their own administrators and rulers. Thus, by the 6th century, leading people from Israel had been carted off to

Assyria and those of Judah ended up in Babylon. The latter struggled to maintain the local religion of Jerusalem while in exile – 'How shall we sing the Lord's song in a strange land?' During their exile they also developed what is known as the 'Deuteronomic' interpretation of their history. This claimed that the invading Hebrew tribes had been given the land of Palestine by Yahweh, and that subsequent rulers of Israel and Judah were to be judged according to the extent to which they separated themselves from the religion of the surrounding people. They saw their exile as a punishment from Yahweh for following other gods, and therefore wrote the historical passages of their scriptures accordingly, promoting an aggressive and confrontational form of henotheism.

The scriptures hint at a more guilty truth – that, in practice, the tribes had integrated to a large extent with the people of the land in which they found themselves, and had shared many of their religious practices. After the Exile, such polytheism was utterly rejected, and even by the time of Jesus, groups such as the Samaritans were shunned for being associated with the earlier religious traditions. As Judaism emerged over the centuries following the exile, henotheism morphed into theism: the belief in a single god, compared with whom other gods lacked reality. But the older tradition lurked with its divisive social and political interpretation.

Within Judaism, the old temple religion of sacrifices gave way to the synagogue and the focus on scriptures. Ritual practices, both at home and in public, including matters of food and dress, became a defining feature of the religion and since Judaism accepted as Jewish anyone who had a Jewish mother, the community as a whole could embrace both those who held traditional religious beliefs about God those who did not. Hence the Jewish community today contains a higher percentage of those who would describe themselves as agnostic or atheist than is the case with members of the other monotheistic religions. Within Judaism, what matters is birth and cultural practice, rather than intellectual agreement on matters of metaphysics.

This is, of course, a simplified sketch of a long and complex process. It is included here to make one essential point: that henotheism can be used to justify political action in the name of religion. If you claim that your god is superior to all others, with you as his or her special object of interest, your beliefs are ripe for political exploitation. The mixture of religion and politics can be lethal. The Roman Empire used public sacrifice to the gods of the city, or to the divine person of the Emperor himself, as a test of loyalty. In Islam, the division between Sunni and Shi'a has likewise taken on a political and military confrontation. Christians launched crusades for what were claimed to be religious reasons, to free the 'Holy Places' from Islam, but quickly degenerated into political and financial enterprises, and the division of Europe between Protestant and Catholic in the 17th century led to slaughter, religious cleansing and political rivalry on a grand scale.

If God is not tolerant of others, human beings will be inclined to follow his example. But these political issues, made much of by those who see religion as the cause of all the world's ills, can only apply to the limited concept of deity that henotheism initiated.

Culture gives religion the emotive power of love or hate, unity or bitter conflict. Neither atheism nor theism is itself likely to become the cause of conflict, were it not for the fact that cultural symbols and ideology make it potent in shaping people's the worldview and the aspirations of those who adopt it. Even an artificially constructed mythology, such as that of Aryan supremacy in Hitler's Third Reich, exerted power through symbols and gatherings that smack of religion – with marching, banners, chanting and gestures. The Third Reich developed a henotheistic cult, centred on the Fürhrer, demanding absolute loyalty, and defining those who were to be excluded.

Henotheism contributed to a desperate problem for Western religion. In polytheism, you may choose a particular god or goddess for your object of worship, but you are not thereby denying the reality of other gods, or the right of other people to choose to worship them. But what happens if you identify your henotheistic, jealous god with 'being-itself'? All other people become heretics, infidels and pagans. Your exclusive god (or 'God') now rules with global reach and encourages you to join him in his tyrannical reign.

If 'God' needs to be rescued, it is from the partisan, literalistic and antagonistic forms of henotheism. If atheism needs to be rescued, it is from the tendency to misidentify theism with henotheism, and thus fail to appreciate the potential of theism's cultural and spiritual legacy.

TRICKS OR CREATIVE CONTROL?

We can engage with stories about God or the gods in order to explore aspects of life, using religious texts as fictions that have a serious purpose and a fair degree of insight. In that way, we accept their language as symbolic and mythological, and we allow them to shape our views.

That's not a bad thing. We all have images of the good life, or stories we'd like to tell about ourselves to make sense of life. It's difficult to get motivated without some sort of fictional narrative – whether it's about progress, growth, marriage, the promises of a political party, or the potential of world domination in a fledgling business. Few are stubborn or superficial enough not to be moved by a good story.

Culture is full of stories, so the question is: Should there be a warning with each story, saying clearly whether or not it claims to be factual? After all, people are happy to buy novels, without having to have a government health warning stamped on them declaring that they are fiction. 'Don't take this story literally', does not mean 'Don't take this story seriously'. The author who labours for years crafting a novel may find the work emotionally exhausting because he or she has to plumb the depths of experience and relationships to find exactly the words needed. No worthwhile fiction should ever be taken literally; it offers far more. So what's wrong with edifying fiction?

In the 17th century, Peter Vavasour, a blunt Yorshireman, was prosecuted for declaring that belief in life after death was 'but a tricke of the clergye, to cause the people to believe… to gett money and to catch fooles withal.' (Quoted from Anexandra Walsham, *Atheists and Atheism before the Enlightenment*, Cambridge, 2023, in a review article, LRB, 25th April, 2024.)

In other words, stories can be use for manipulation or financial gain. Stories of a god who creates and loves, forgives and encourages, can offer comfort and strength. The problem is that people have sometimes wanted more: a god who gives commands and issues threats, a god who will reward those who obey him and condemn to hell fire (or something more moderate for the theologically squeamish) those who do not. When that happens, the person who engages with the story is a danger of being tricked by its narrator for his or her own purposes, or by his or her own projected wishes.

So, before we surrender to a story, we need to ask a few questions…

THE HISTORICAL PERSPECTIVE

We cannot understand the significance of events in history, or the meaning of people's beliefs, hopes or fears without at least attempting to enter imaginatively into their situation. So, we have to ask ourselves: What were they trying to convey by saying, writing, drawing or carving that?

Every term is ambiguous. It reveals its meaning only through a process that the French philosopher Michel Foucault called 'archaeology', digging through layers of understanding and use. Sometimes we short circuit that process, because we intuit that we have had an experience rather like that being described. We therefore jump to the conclusion that we know what it is they were talking about. We may be right about that, or we may be hopelessly wrong. And if we are wrong, we are in danger of re-using their words, and re-telling their stories in a way that distorts them beyond recognition.

The wise judge stories by their credibility and purpose. If you doubt that, just read the Gospel of Thomas or some of the other books that failed to make it into the collection of texts that now make up the Christian New Testament. They offer bizarre wonders and magic, rejected by those who thought scripture should offer serious edification. To appreciate any story or word, you need to do the archaeology. You need to dig down and see the political or psychological forces that have shaped that story, and the purposes to which it has been put. Otherwise you may indeed by tricked into conformity, or whatever else the author intended.

So what of the word 'God'? If the *vox pop* responses in the Introduction above are anything to go by, many ideas of 'God' definitely lack serious archaeology. But the problem is more complicated than that. It is not enough to ask what the term 'God' meant in a particular era, we also need to ask ourselves whether that meaning is still adequate today. If the meaning of 'God' changes, do we simply opt for a particular moment in that process of change? As we shall see later, an idea of god that emerged in the 18th century continues to have destructive popularity.

There are some wonderful books exploring the archaeology of the term 'God' – Karen Armstrong's books particularly spring to mind. Other authors engage with culture and the significance or otherwise of religious ideas – Terry Eagleton would be a great writer with whom to start exploring that. They both show the ambiguity of concepts, the way they change over time, and the subtlety needed to interpret them correctly. But a dilemma remains: an atheist may be perfectly happy to accept that 'God' and religion are aspects of human culture; whether or not they are useful or give some evolutionary advantage is another matter. A theist, on the other hand, while also accepting that all language about God is related to human culture and varies over time, is going to say that there is some reality, external to human culture, that corresponds to the word 'God'.

Belief in God has taken so many different forms over the centuries, and has been used for so many different political as well as religious purposes, that some of us despair at its ambiguity. But that does not necessarily require us to ditch the whole legacy of religion, and much would be lost if we tried to do so. What I am suggesting is that we stand back a little from the narratives that are bound up with belief in God and ask ourselves whether we *need* them – not whether they are beautiful, or comforting, or inspiring, but whether or not they are *necessary* for understanding and living the good life. What happens if we both emotionally and intellectually wipe the slate clean and go for atheism? How then would we understand life and our place within it? What does atheism offer?

Chapter 2

What does Atheism Offer?

> *God is one mortal helping another.*
> *Natural History,* Pliny the Elder

> *To understand the actual world as it is, not as we should*
> *wish it to be, is the beginning of wisdom.*
> *Why I am not a Christian,* Bertrand Russell

> *This is my simple religion. No need for temples. No need for complicated*
> *philosophy. Your own mind, your own heart is the temple.*
> *Your philosophy is simple kindness.*
> The Dalai Lama

For anyone who has struggled to believe, there is something liberating about being told that the supernatural is indeed an illusion and that the world in which we live is – for good or ill – all there is. But with that perspective comes the challenge to come to terms with and appreciate our own finite nature, the fact of change, sickness and death, the tragedy of human behaviour at its worst and the recognition that there is no divine judge to settle the score at the end of time. Atheism, agnosticism, humanism and other non-theistic worldviews are not easy options, but they can provide a view of life that is positive, moral, emotionally and intellectually coherent but challenging.

Professor Marcia Homiak, in a piece entitled *An Aristotelian Life* offers this view of the implications of belief and atheism:

I know many good people who are religious. I consider them to be good people because they are disposed to respond with kindness, comfort, and help when others are in distress or in need. They are warm, outgoing and compassionate, taking a genuine interest in other's lives. They are optimistic, disposed to see the good in others and to see what's right in the world.... And I know that their fine qualities of character are forged in their religious involvement... Now, some people might think that only a religious life can provide these benefits, for only a religious life, they think, can provide proper moral direction, and only God's eternal love can ground human kindness, decency and courage.... But in my view, there are non-religious ways of life that are equally admirable and that contain these same great benefits. These ways of life are principled and coherent. Their values offer sound practical guidance for how to live. These ways of life provide for the important goods of human community, friendship and love. They are not self-centred... And they provide the resources for great psychological strength that will carry us beyond desperation and despair. (In *Philosophers Without Gods*, ed. Louise Antony p133ff)

In other words, both belief and atheism can support a good life. The Dalai Lama, asked whether he thought that Buddhism was better than other religions, replied that different things suited different people, and he could not say that any one religion was better than another.

This recognition of the positive value of both religious and atheist views is far more important than the arguments for or against religious doctrines. The Christian philosopher William Lane Craig, for example, has argued that 'The atheist has to maintain that it's *impossible* that God exists. That is, he has to maintain that the concept of God is *logically incoherent*, like the concept of a married bachelor or a round square. The problem is that the concept of God just doesn't appear to be incoherent in that way.' The fallacy in his argument is that Craig has decided on his own terms for what an atheist needs to prove. In fact, most atheists don't go around arguing that God is logically incoherent, they simply walk away from that concept and get on with examining the world in ways that don't take the idea of God into account. The exceptions, perhaps, are the 'New Atheists', such as Richard Dawkins, who use 18th or 19th century arguments to show that God does not exist, and are therefore suitable opponents for Craig. Neither side can win in that contest, because neither seems to appreciate either the full significance of the idea of God or that of atheism. Theism and atheism are equally trivialised by simplistic argument.

POSITIVE ATHEISM

I was originally going to call this chapter 'Positive Atheism, East and West', but Stephen Bullivant, a Catholic co-editor of *The Oxford Handbook of Atheism*, makes a distinction between positive and negative atheism in a way that is quite different from my intention, so let me explain...

For Bullivant, negative atheists find no evidence for God, while positive atheists hold views that exclude the very possibility of God. What I mean by positive atheism is a view of life that does not require belief in God or gods, but is life-affirming, moral and – in a broad sense – spiritual. I am looking at evidence to counter the accusation that atheism leads to black despair and nihilism. Although the word 'atheism' appears to be defined negatively, it does not imply a negative view of life; indeed, most atheists would argue that it encourages a positive and grown-up approach to life's problems that is both challenging and empowering.

So what can we say about atheism that is both distinctive and positive? I want to argue for three things: that it encourages the free examination of evidence, that it need not be cynical or nihilistic, and that it is possible to be religious without belief in God.

GODLESS REASON

The term 'atheism' comes from the Greek *atheos*, which means 'godless' or 'without the support of the gods'. In his book on atheism in the ancient world, Tim Whitmarsh, explains that it implied that an atheist was not controlled or ruled by gods, just as a lawless person would be *anomos*, or an unjust one *adikos*. An atheist saw no need for gods, and therefore did not take part in their worship.

Being godless has always implied taking responsibility for one's thoughts and decisions. Socrates was said to have followed his own inner convictions rather than the example of the gods and goddesses of his day. Thus Plato, in his dialogue *Euthyphro*, has Socrates posing the fundamental moral question about whether something is good because a god commands it, or whether a god commands it because it is good. If we believe that the latter is the case, it suggests that we have an innate sense of what is good and right, by which even the actions and commands of the gods may be judged.

Hence, atheism challenges people to use their reason, experience, intuitions and emotional responses to shape their view of the world and guide their actions. This is directly counter to the claim made by traditional Protestant Christianity – particularly Calvinism – that human reason is fundamentally 'fallen' and that people are therefore incapable of wisdom and moral insight unless aided by God.

One of the immediately attractive things about atheism is that it puts no limit on what should be examined critically in terms of reason and morality. Scriptures are not to be spared, because they are seen as cultural products like any other. So, if God orders genocide in order to clear the Amalekites from their land and make way for the incoming Israelites, an atheist is free to examine and reject the morality of that order, without having to wriggle to find an alternative and acceptable interpretation. Of course, that is a difficult passage for most religious people and therefore an easy target. But the point is that, if you examine religious documents with a critical eye – even if it is just to try to find an interpretation that makes sense or is morally right – then you have accepted a measure of autonomy for human reason and moral intuition, and that paves the way for a positive interpretation of life without the need for belief in God.

This is not to claim that human reason is always right, nor to denigrate intuition, inspiration and profoundly moving experiences. It simply opens up all human culture – both religious and secular – to the same level of scrutiny.

Simplicity helps. William of Ockham, a 14th century thinker, is famous for an argument known now as 'Ockham's Razor'. Usually summed up as 'Entities must not be multiplied beyond necessity', this is the principle that, if there is a choice of explanations, one should go for the simplest, and the one that requires fewest assumptions. Whereas a theist might feel the need to show to that everything in the world comes about because it is willed by God, the atheist or non-theist, can simply admit that, even though there are many things we do not understand, we can investigate them without also having to factor in an external deity. So atheism may be an easier option intellectually.

If there is no god, we assume that everything has a natural cause. That does not imply that we already know everything there is no know about nature, since all earlier scientific theories have been shown to be inadequate, and it is therefore likely that our present theories will one day be regarded in the same way. It merely suggests that we do not need to think in terms of supernatural agency to explain the unexpected.

Atheism is motivated by naturalism, but this is not the same as materialism, which effectively says that the world comprises physical entities, and nothing else. This is more problematic, because it then has to explain human culture and thought. It needs to account for our own experience of being human, of being more than a physical body. Generally, materialists are prepared to say that, when material objects get to a certain degree of complexity, they take on new sets of characteristics, which build into character, language, culture and so on.

But the problem with a full 'eliminative materialism' is that it argues that minds, thoughts and all other personal and cultural feature of life are *no more than* material operations. It claims that, if I describe myself as 'happy' or 'in love,' there is nothing that corresponds to that happiness or love, other than the corresponding firing of neurons in my brain or the operation of my hormones and various chemical reactions in my body. Of course, nobody would deny that brains and hormones are the physical locus of being happy or in love; they certainly have a lot to do with it. However, in terms of my experience of the world, *what is experienced* is not the same as *a description* of the underlying physical operations. It is this extreme form of materialism that tends to give atheism a reputation for nihilism, since it tends to reduce value, meaning and moral choice to impersonal physical activity.

Suffice to say that atheists are not wedded to eliminative materialism and are as involved in the rich, multi-layered experience of human life as anyone else.

ATHEIST VALUES

Broadly speaking, secular humanism claims to be based on honesty, integrity, altruism and equal respect for all. It recognises that humans have no God-given place within the scheme of things; they are what they are, nothing more but nothing less. But it also includes a sense of wonder at nature, an acceptance of the value of human life, an acknowledgement of the place of humankind within the scheme of evolution, and courage in the face of death and finitude.

However, these humanist values would be shared my most believers, and there is no doubt that atheist humanism, although rejecting its supernatural elements, has been influenced by religious morality and values. Nietzsche saw such humanism as one of the continuing 'shadows' of God, as we shall see in chapter 14. But it is equally possible to argue that these values are fundamental to human flourishing, whether or not linked to any supernatural beliefs, so atheism does not necessarily depend on religion for these values, but simply shares them.

However, in some quarters, atheism continues to have a bad reputation. The assumption is that you cannot trust an atheist, because he or she accepts no divinely ordained moral authority. In a court of law, you were traditionally asked to undertake to tell the truth by swearing on the Bible, on the assumption that you acknowledged it as the absolute symbol of authority. More to the point, atheists have generally been regarded as free spirits, and therefore a danger to the authorities and to those who want to impose conventional moral standards.

So should you trust an atheist? I would argue that, since atheism implies taking responsibility for your own life, including the values by which you live, then atheists are to be trusted (or not) on the same basis as religious believers.

When Nietzsche observed the growing atheism of his day, his major concern – expressed by the 'madman' who proclaims the death of God in his well-known parable – is that the horizon of values and meaning is wiped away by the killing of God, and hence the world becomes darker, colder and sinks towards nihilism. He feared that, without a sense of meaning and purpose, which had previously been seen as given by 'God', we find ourselves in a situation where values and meanings are optional and not open to rational discussion. Nietzsche had his own remedy for that, as we shall see.

In *The Secular Age*, Charles Taylor sees the arrival of postmodernism as a crucial turning point, marking the end of the period in which liberal values and modernism have provided an alternative to traditional theism. There is plenty of evidence to support that suggestion. Our era is given to the multiplicity of explanations and views, with little to distinguish between the rationally valid, the superficially appealing but probably false and the downright bonkers! Conspiracy theories on the internet are 'liked' and spread. For those whose information about the world comes from social media, such theories, however little supported by reason and evidence, become an alternative reality.

Is this new? I doubt it – from the more far-fetched stories about Jesus that abounded in the Early Church but failed to make it into the canonical gospels, to the lurid details of saints and martyrs, to the elaborations of the lineages in Mahayana Buddhism, some people have always been fond of the bizarre, illogical and emotionally appealing. In a world where reality is harsh, miracles have an enduring appeal.

But behind most of the earlier periods in which such fantasies thrived there stood a tradition of philosophy and theology that attempted to hold it in check. That is what is now lacking in a world where metanarratives are unwelcome, reason seen as suspect and data always open to alternative interpretations.

Atheism, in applying a genuinely agnostic approach to all claims, should help us guard against any cultural product – whether it is a modern fantasy game, or an ancient religious text – being taken at face value. At the risk of being boring, it encourages us to check everything out.

Over the years, some atheists have done themselves no favours by presenting their views as a post-Enlightenment phenomenon and an evolutionary development beyond an earlier era of primitive superstition and religion. To assume that religion is all about 'belief in God' is parochial. The evidence for the validity and benefit of non-theistic religions is overwhelming.

In Ancient India, Carvaka (also known as Lokayata) was a school of philosophy that rejected the existence of gods and the concept of karma. It developed at about the time that Gautama and Mahavira were teaching what were to become the Buddhist and Jain worldviews, and was probably well established by 600BCE, although more as a general tendency of thought than a single organised philosophy. The name 'Lokayata' is possibly derived from 'the views of the people' – in other words is was a general assumption of the populace, rather than a school of teaching. If so, we have evidence that atheism, as a practical view of life, was alive and well more than two and a half thousand years ago. Carvaka argued that experience and reasoned evidence were the only valid basis of knowledge, that there was no eternal soul, and therefore no life after death, no need for priests and ceremonies, no heaven or hell. This is pragmatic atheism. It is impossible to know how widespread these ideas were, because they were regarded as non-orthodox, and therefore not promoted by any of the later religious groups.

Against a background of urbanisation in northern India and a wide range of beliefs and practices, Siddhartha Gautama (c563-483), known as The Buddha, taught his radical alternative to the conventional religions of his day. There is a profoundly existential side to Buddhism. The final words of the Buddha to his followers was that they should work out their own salvation with diligence – in other words, that his teaching did not offer a set of beliefs which would lead them to the ultimate goal, but a set of tools with which they should work their way towards it. Above all, personal integrity was seen as the key to its path, along with an attempt to avoid what is, to use Sartre's term, simply 'bad faith'. In addition to this, and as a natural result of its approach, Buddhism is wary of any doctrinal debate. The act of attempting intellectual explanations is itself a hindrance.

Buddhism does not start with beliefs, but with the observation that everything that happens depends upon causes and conditions. Hence, everything and every situation is subject to change and eventual decay. The key to develop wisdom and compassion is to train the mind to see things as they really are, rather than following a fantasy of what we would like them to be. The fundamental attitude of early Buddhism is non-theistic and secular. It is a path to be followed, not a set of doctrines to be accepted.

This approach, taken by early, Theravada and Zen Buddhism, does not automatically imply atheism in a Western sense, but it renders the concept of God *irrelevant* to its spiritual path. As it developed and spread, the *Dhamma* – as the Buddha's teaching is called – took on features of religion, with images, acts of devotion, and a host of different Buddhas and Bodhisattvas. Hence, Buddhists today might sound quite 'religious' in their view, but at its heart the Buddhist tradition is pragmatic and secular. Few would try to deny that Buddhism is a religion, in the sense that it offers an overall view of the world and a set of moral values, but it is certainly not theistic in the Western sense. The Dalai Lama describes himself as an atheist, although he is quite happy to speak about God in the context of other religions.

While Buddhism moved elsewhere, Indian religious thought established itself in different schools, of which I want to mention only one – the Vedanta. Sankara (788 – 880CE) presents a non-dualist approach to the relationship between the self (*Atman*) and underlying reality (*Brahman*). Immediate awareness of the 'ground of being' (in a western sense) is described as the identity of Atman and Brahman in *'sat-chit-ananda'* (being-consciousness-bliss). The idea of Brahman, is possibly the closest we get to the idea of God as 'being-itself' or 'reality-itself' in Western theism. It sees Brahman as impersonal and universal, but also as personally experienced and something with which the self can identify. Expressed in the phrase *Tat Tvam asi* – 'You are that'.

This sense of transcending the self and becoming at one with the 'all', is also found in the Buddhist thinking of Nagarjuna and in Islam with Ibn al Arabi, a 12th century mystic. The crucial thing here is not that these traditions were atheist, Ibn al Arabi was certainly not, but they share a sense of identity between the self and the Absolute that goes beyond description and empirical existence. Ibn al Arabi speaks of the 'supreme reality' (*Al haqq*) of which Allah is a personal manifestation. Like the (niguna) Brahman of Hinduism and the Sunyata (Emptiness) of Buddhism, ultimate reality goes beyond imagery or argument.

Bede Griffiths (in *A New Vision of Reality*, Collins, 1989) makes a very clear distinction between the ordinary world of space and time, which is destined to pass away, and the eternal reality. To be aware of it

> ... means passing from the present mode of consciousness, which is conditioned by time and space, into a deeper level of consciousness which transcends the dualities external and internal, subject and object, conscious and unconscious, and become one with the non-dual Reality, the Brahma, the Atman, the Tao, the Word, the Truth, whatever name we give to that which cannot be named. It is this alone that gives reality to our lives and a meaning to human existence. (*op cit* p226)

This is the key to the mystical tradition in each religious culture, but it is more than that. It is a spirituality that is based on denying exactly the sort of deities that atheism also rejects.

It is talking about a form of awareness, rather than an objective existence. To appreciate Brahman, one needs a good dose of 'atheism' (in the sense that it is 'not this' and 'not that') but to deny the reality to which the word Brahman points is self-contradictory. Atheism here is a necessary correction to a superficial literalism.

We have contrasted atheism with belief in gods, but in terms of these mystical traditions, and much Eastern thought, the gods are no more than a manifestation of a deeper reality. That reality, I will argue, is closer to atheism than what passes as literal or popular theism.   One can certainly follow Buddhist, Taoist or some Hindu traditions while at the same time, in Western terms, remaining atheist.

Some Eastern traditions emphasise practical ethics and social harmony. In ancient China, Mohist thinkers were sceptical of the validity of religious rituals and believed in a pragmatic approach to ethics, emphasizing impartiality and benevolence. In terms of living in harmony with the nature, you have the whole tradition of Taoism, and for social cohesion, the long tradition of Confucianism. There is no scope here to explore these, but in *Understand Eastern Philosophy* I explain why it is possible have a serious moral and social system without the need to believe in 'God' in the Western sense. Living without God does not inevitably lead to chaos, anarchy or nihilism.

Some years ago, on a visit to Japan, I sat for a while before the sand garden in the Kounji temple in Kyoto. The carefully raked lines of sand exactly matched the surrounding landscape and buildings. Sitting there, one could almost breathe in a sense of harmony, and with it an aspiration to internalise it. There is no way to give an adequate rational explanation of that experience, but it seeps into one's consciousness.

Buddhist spirituality is without superstition. There is no magic involved in devotion to a Buddha image, just the quiet recognition and internalisation of certain qualities. Stories, images, actions – all become part of a 'religious' practice, with parallels in Western religions, or in the gods and spirits of Eastern practice, but they are not metaphysical entities separate from the people engaged in the acts of devotion.

This non-theistic experience suggests that there is scope for atheism to encourage theism to go deeper, to recognize that, however valuable and emotionally engaging its imagers and rituals might be, there is the recognition of a reality that is both transcendent and immanent – that within which we 'live, move and have our being' – which goes beyond 'God' in any form that can be defined. Hence theism and atheism can become unlikely partners in the attempt to rescue the religious impulse from those who, by defining it narrowly, deny it credibility in the eyes of those who are not already committed to its doctrines.

Thus, within Buddhist culture, there are images and narratives that depict both wisdom and compassion, and a whole range – for Mahayana Buddhists – of Bodhisattva images, laden with symbols to express values and provide guidance. An atheist, observing this spiritual tradition, is not challenged to believe something on trust, nor to accept propositions without evidence. What happens is… exactly what happens. The action is the action, the moment of quiet counting of the breath is only and simply that. There is no separate, spiritual world to which others have no access; no secret formula to guarantee enlightenment.

There is little difference here between atheist and theist views. Each offers a sense of direction. The Buddhist path builds on the observation of universal change and the dependence of each thing upon its context, whereas the theistic approach, like that of the Stoics – as we shall see later – requires the individual to recognise and align with a universal reason. Both approaches include images as a stimulus to reflection; both engage the emotions as well as the intellect.

A SHRUG OR A WAGER?

Agnosticism – sometimes offered as a halfway house to atheism – is a total copout; little more than a shrug of the shoulders! When Thomas Huxley coined the term 'agnostic' he argued that you should never accept as true anything for which you have insufficient evidence. That's absolutely fine, but does anyone really believe that, with a bit more evidence one way or the other, we'll finally know whether or not God exists? That would make sense only if 'God' were taken to refer to an obscure and distant object that might be identified – and that notion of deity hovers between blasphemy, idolatry and a contradiction in terms. If God is infinite, he has no boundaries and there is nowhere he does not exist. So the demand for evidence is pointless. If you are truly 'agnostic' you should be atheist, even if you feel personally committed to the idea of 'God' or find it culturally useful.

We now come to what I consider one of the saddest and most distasteful of all arguments: Pascal's infamous 'wager'.

Blaise Pascal, a 17th century Catholic mathematician and philosopher, presented belief as a matter of pragmatic choice, based on the assumption that God will reward believers with heaven and consign atheists to hell. He argued that, if you don't believe in God, you gain little (except avoiding the inconvenience of being religious) but run the risk, if you are proved wrong, of God's wrath. However, if you believe in God and he exists, you get heaven as your reward, but if he doesn't you are no worse off. Hence it seemed to Pascal that belief was the safer option. Based on self-interest and the ability to fool an omniscient deity, it represents the worst of all possible worlds – religious belief as insurance against a world controlled by a capricious and vengeful God.

To avoid paralysis, we sometimes have to act upon insufficient evidence – as when we enter into a relationship or marriage. In effect, we have to take a bet. But, please, not Pascal's!

IT REALLY DOESN'T MATTER

There is a moment – whether in silent prayer or meditation or just sitting quietly – when thought evaporates and one is left balanced on nothing, carried forward on the tipping wave of experience, surfing the present moment. At that point, belief in God is irrelevant. You 'know' beyond any doubt; you sense yourself to be fully alive. If you want to use 'God language', then God is the reality of which you are a part. Conceptualise that, and it becomes trivial and false. Attempt to describe it, and you become a fool.

But how best to resist the danger of being misunderstood, or even of misunderstanding yourself? You take your pick – either you opt for atheism, recognising that reality is never adequately described by God language, or you opt to be theist and say that God is that within which you live, move and have your being. Tell people that you live in God, if you dare, but it may raise a few eyebrows.

But in the end it really doesn't matter; you choose whichever form of language you find most helpful.

In his wonderfully clear introduction to atheism, Julian Baggini sets out the logical arguments that might persuade someone to be atheist rather than theist. If you are at a moment of existential crisis, uncertain whether you should be a fundamentalist believer or a rabid atheist, then you might find his work of great value. However, you might also find yourself in a minority, and some may regard you as weird or obsessed. The fact is, most people do not make a rational choice when it comes to fundamental beliefs, they inherit beliefs from their family, friends and culture, and they either continue with them if they find them helpful, or reject them if they conflict with their own experience of life and the many other things that they believe. In spite of Kierkegaard, life's seldom really a matter of *Either/Or*.

The debate between theists and atheists should not be about whether there is something objectively 'out there' that has a label 'God' attached – that is just too simplistic – but about how we choose to see the world and our place within it. That's not a subjective cop out, since our 'view' corresponds to how we actually experience the world. One thing is for certain; there's no claiming a majority view here. The number of believers of various sorts and the number of non-theists, or atheists, or agnostics, or followers of religions that do not require belief in gods of God, are both so huge that, whatever you believe, you are in good company.

WHERE NOW?

So far we've looked briefly at the phenomenon of the world's religions and at non-theistic beliefs. Unless you are prepared to claim that half the world is deluded, the division between theist and atheist cannot be a simple binary one between right and wrong. In spite of the evangelical zeal displayed on both sides, both atheism and theism are likely to remain with us for the indefinite future.

My argument, as advertised by the title of this book, is that atheism and theism may be able to rescue one another from a naïve literalism that does justice to neither. What are the implications of this?

In order to keep the scope of this question manageable, we shall be looking primarily at Western thought, and specifically at the development of Christian ideas, since that is where the theism/atheism polarity is seen at its most stark.

So how has the balance between atheism and theism played out within the developing Christian culture of Western Europe and North America? This, I'm afraid, is a cautionary tale and a rather sad one but, to appreciate it, we need to go back to Greece in the 6th century BCE.

Chapter 3

Ancient Thoughts

Concerning the gods, I have no means of knowing either that they exist or that they do not exist

Protagoras

Something remarkable took place around the town of Miletus, on the west coast of modern Turkey, in the middle of the 6th century BCE: Western philosophy was born. Why it should have happened exactly there and then we shall never know, but likely the Persian rulers, an increase in foreign trade and the first stirrings of democracy had something to do with it.

Nor do we know for certain where the ideas behind this new philosophy came from; possibly from Persia or Egypt. They formed part of a global re-awakening in the 6th century, which included the ideas of Mahavira and the Buddha in India and K'ung Fu-Tsu and Lao Tzu in the Far East.

That part of Asia Minor, known as Ionia, had been settled by Greeks from the mainland some 400 years earlier, and was best known as the home of the poet Homer, author of the epic tales of gods, goddesses with all the wonder, tragedy and misbehaviour of those divine and human characters. Previously ruled by the Babylonians, by the mid 6th century it was on the edge of the Persian Empire. Miletus flourished and traded widely across the Eastern Mediterranean. Clearly, it had become something of a melting pot for new ideas, for there emerged a group of thinkers who developed ideas about evidence, argument and the nature of reality. They made observations and attempted to use them to deduce general principles. In doing so, they initiated two new disciplines: philosophy and science.

THE NEW QUESTIONS

What is the most fundamental substance of which the world is made? Is everything fixed and permanent, or is it in a constant state of flux? Can we know objective truths about the world and how it came about, or is knowledge limited to human experience? If the body has a mind, does the whole universe have a mind? How does everything work together? Is there a single mind (*nous*) or deep reason (*logos*) behind everything we encounter? How do we understand the origins of life? How does one thing grow out of another?

Thales, Anaximander and Anaximenes, the first of what we now call the 'pre-Socratic' philosophers, along with those who followed them, including Heraclitus, Anaxagoras, and Protagoras, threw out questions and theories at a rate unimaginable in modern academic circles.

The first of these, Thales (b. c.624 BCE), attempted to give a rational account of the physical world. He did not evoke the gods as creators, but developed what might be considered today a version of the 'intelligent design' argument, seeing all life as interconnected and displaying a natural design. He thought that the most fundamental substance was water. Anaximander (b. c.610) and Anaximanes (b. c.586) also produced natural explanations of the world, with the latter arguing that the seasons were caused by the position of the sun in the sky, and earthquakes by the drying out of the land. Most of their theories were wrong, but that's not the point; they were trying to give an explanation of things that did not depend upon supernatural beings, and as such were the forerunners of modern scientists and atheists.

From the 6th to the 4th centuries, philosophers asked questions that are still being explored two and a half thousand years later. In particular, they produced arguments about the origins of the universe and the nature of reality that moved in two very different directions.

On the one hand, the sense of a single rational universe gave rise to ideas about 'God' in a sense utterly different from the gods and goddesses of the culture of their day. It is important to recognise that these ideas, which were to become fundamental to theism, did not emerge from religion, but from philosophical questions about the nature of reality.

But the same questioning, as we shall see, led other thinkers to the idea that the whole universe was composed of atoms in a void. For these early atomists, there was no need to posit a conscious or intelligent power in order to account for the universe, consciousness itself developed out of matter and was utterly dependent upon it, and if any gods existed they would be material and perishable like everything else. Atheistic materialism was thus born out of the same set of questions as was theism.

Let's pause to reflect on this for a moment. Today, it is assumed that religious people are generally theists and non-religious may tend to be atheists or agnostics. But – as we shall see later in this chapter and in the next – that is not how either idea originated. Both ideas emerged from philosophical enquiry about the nature of reality. Both were quite separate from religion in Ancient Greece, and we have already seen that religion and morality are quite capable of flourishing without requiring belief in God. The unfortunate truth is that, even in the 21st century, the battle lines between belief and atheism are largely bogus.

From this early philosophy we have the idea that the universe depends on a conscious and intelligent reality, which Parmenides (born c.515) called 'that which is'. However, that didn't stop him from expressing his thoughts through poetry, including the idea of gods and goddesses. It was not an either/or between the gods of religion and the idea of a single personal force. However, he makes it clear that ultimate reality is not to be found in human experience – it is beyond the world of space and time, expressed by the Greek term *to apeiron* (the unbounded). In a similar vein, Empedocles saw the forces that held everything together as the 'sphere of love', in contrast to the disruptive forces that pulled things apart.

From an utterly different point of view, Protagoras saw the universe as essentially meaningless, leading him to describe man as 'the measure of all things' and human experience as the key to what we can or cannot know. Philosophers started to ask for the grounds (*techmerion*) on which one might believe anything, since ideas needed rational justification rather than being simply the expression of intuition or traditional stories. Speaking about gods became problematic. Protagoras said:

> Concerning the gods, I have no means of knowing either that they exist or that they do not exist, nor what sort of form they may have; there are many reasons why knowledge on this subject is not possible, owing to the lack of evidence and the shortness of human life. (quoted by Edward Hussey in *The Pre-Socratics*, p109)

These early thinkers explored issues that were to bedevil Western thought about God and the gods for the next two and a half thousand years.

NATURALIST EXPLANATIONS

Atheists tend to argue for a naturalistic view of the world; in other words, their view is based on empirical evidence, assessed by human reason. This, of course, is what most people take to be the norm in the 21st century, at least for their understanding of the physical world – how they deal with their relationships, emotional life and cultural creations are quite another matter.

The 5th century atomists, Democritus and Leucippus, argued that the world was composed of physical bodies, which could be divided and subdivided until there came a point where they could be divided no more, and hence they called the tiny portions of matter 'atoms', meaning 'indivisible'. What existed between such atoms? It could not be any other entity, because that too would be divisible. So it had to be a void, an absolute nothingness. Anticipating later views, they saw all material things as composed of atoms in a void, and everything as having a natural cause.

They thought that atoms moved in predictable ways, hence the orderly movements of the universe; an idea that was to develop into the 'laws of nature' by the time we get to Newtonian physics. But why should the universe be so well arranged that life became possible? This is the heart of the 'anthropic' argument, used in modern times to argue for a creator God who has organized the world with human life in mind. However, according to Tim Whitmarsh (*Battling the Gods* p66), Democritus had a remarkably modern answer to this. He suggested that there could be an infinite number of worlds, but in some of them life would not be possible. Hence, the fact that life is possible in our universe is down to chance rather than a supernatural agent. For Democritus, the evidence simply did not require a universal designer. His naturalist explanations extended to religion, which he believed to originate either from the sense of wonder at nature, or the dreams of those who had a bad conscience!

What then of the gods? Democritus argued that they were the product of earlier times (speaking from the perspective of a 'modern' 6th century BCE), when people mistook natural phenomena for the work of gods. Yet they could also appear to people in dreams, since they were images that exist in the air and penetrate our bodies. This last idea sounds bizarre today, but it was his attempt to be absolutely consistent in his atomism. His world, of course, was unaware of depth psychology or the origin of dreams.

Xenophanes (b. c.570), born in the Ionian city-state of Colophon, opposed these anthropomorphic images of god. He suggested that if horses could draw, they would depict gods as horses. Man has made god in his own image. He also commented that the gods were badly behaved and showed all the worst of human traits. Better, he thought, to have a single god. He suggested that such a god would not being located, and would be unchanging while causing motion in all other things. In this he anticipated the theism of later centuries, Aristotle's 'unmoved mover' and the theological use of Heidegger's philosophy to describe God as 'Being Itself'. Xenophanes clearly thought that the image of god was a human creation and insisted that there should always remain an element of doubt in dealing with the highest questions.

This is crucial to our story, in that is shows a division, more than two and half millennia ago, between the gods as human-like supernatural entities, and the idea that the world is based on a single divine principle.

Another naturalistic explanation of gods and goddesses was offered by Prodicus of Keos (465-395), who argued that men called 'gods' the elements of nature – sun, moon, rivers, seas and so on – and also those things that that sustained them, such a bread and wine. The gods were thus expressions of the natural world upon which life depended. This, of course, is simply a reflection upon the *Theogony* of Hesiod, who wrote in the early part of the 7th century BCE, giving a catalogue of gods and goddesses, and surrounding the best known by others who reflected corresponding aspects of nature. They are linked logically, so 'sleep' is the offspring of 'night' and so on. This is a polytheistic celebration of all of life, with gods and goddesses linked to one another and to the overall pattern of life. But whereas Hesiod, shaping his literary narrative, considers the forces of nature and names them as gods, Prodicus – coming two centuries later – considers those same gods and declares them to be simply names for the forces of nature. The same process is here viewed from a cultural and creative side by Hesiod, or the pre-scientific and reductive side by Prodicus.

And all this comes before we arrive at the period of classical Greek philosophy, represented by Plato and Aristotle.

PLATO AND ARISTOTLE

In *Beyond Good and Evil*, Nietzsche mischievously refers to Christianity as 'Platonism for the people'. Like many of his best quotes, it is misleading and provocative but has a kernel of truth.

With no ability or inclination to add to the huge body of scholarship on Plato (428 – 348 BCE), I want to explore just one feature of his work that has shaped much of the debate between theism and atheism.

Plato was able a produce memorable images to explain his ideas. One of these, 'The Cave' in his book *Republic*, has often been taken to represent the whole of his work, with unfortunate consequences.

In it, Plato describes prisoners in a cave, chained so that they can only face its back wall. Behind them is a fire, and between them and the fire a succession of objects are carried to and fro, so that their shadows fall on that wall. To the prisoners, those shadows are all they know, and they therefore take them to be the whole of reality. In the story, one of the prisoners gets free and turns round, so that he can see the paraded objects and the fire. It hurts his eyes, and only with difficulty does he drag himself past it and out of the cave, seeing daylight for the first time, and eventually the sun. He now understands that the sun is the origin of light, and that what he previously took for reality is merely the passing of shadows. However, when he returns to the cave to point this out to his fellow prisoners they mock him and continue to be fascinated by predicting what will next appear on their wall. Which is more real, the world in the cave or the world above?

An over-simplified interpretation of this is that reason, and the world of general Ideas (usually translated as 'Forms'), is more real than the particular things we observe around us, and that the highest of the Forms (the equivalent of the sun in the story) is the 'Form of the Good', which gives value and meaning to all else. From this we are meant to learn that reason takes priority over the senses, and that reality is a hierarchy with the 'Form of the Good' at its pinnacle.

Today, we consider 'ideas' to exist within our minds. An idea of a tree, for example, is a general concept that allows us to recognize what is and what it not a tree. But the Greeks did not think like that. For them an 'idea' was external, it was what enabled different things to be called 'trees' rather than anything else. All the things with trunks, branches and roots were 'trees' because they shared in the basic 'idea' of a Tree. That makes sense, because you learn what trees have in common – qualities that existed before your mind (or any other human mind) was there to contemplate them. So Plato's 'Forms' are not debatable extras to life, but abstract and general ways of describing whole classes of things. Hence Plato wants his rulers to understand and appreciate the general principles of justice and so on, and the highest of these is the idea of goodness because that is what gives value to everything else.

With hindsight, theists of later centuries have been all too willing to get the support of Plato by claiming that 'God' is the equivalent of his 'Form of the Good'. But there is a problem here. The main thrust of *Republic* is political. It asks who is fit to rule and how rulers should be trained. The central point of the cave story, therefore, is that an idea ruler should be able to get beyond the day-to-day particulars of life (whatever appears on the ancient Greek equivalent of their social media feeds) and take a broader, rational view about the values by which society should be ordered. Plato's point is that such a broad, reasoned view is not easily achieved, and is mocked by those who continue to be immersed in day-to-day issues.

The story is about the struggle to understand fundamental and eternal principles, as opposed to the ever-changing events and values of everyday life. It is not about a separate, supernatural world above this one. Nor is it about a creator God, because Plato considers that in another dialogue – the *Timaeus* – in which he speaks about the creator being like a craftsman, shaping and making sense of his random materials. This craftsman, whom he called the *Demiurge*, was quite different from the 'God' of later Christian thought, but has a remarkable resemblance to the 'Deism' of the 18th century, as we shall see later.

In *Laws,* a late dialogue by Plato, he opposes those who say that gods to do not exist, or are not interested in what humans do, or swayed by prayers and sacrifices, and offers what amounts to a cosmological proof of the existence of God and an argument for the existence of the human soul. Plato is clearly in favour of conventional religion, but the presupposition of his argument is that there were indeed atheists in Athens who did not believe such things. By arguing that gods were not swayed by prayers, they had struck at a key purpose of religion: that sacrifices to the gods brought results for the good operating of society and human welfare.

On the one hand, Plato is in favour of religion and its social benefits, on the other, he promotes the idea of an an elite of philosopher-rulers who are able to understand and apply the most general principles of justice and goodness. The problem is that, if you try to fuse these two very different things, you end up with a form of religion that requires 'believers' to understand and agree to a set of metaphysical ideas that – on his own admission – are only accessible to an intellectual elite.

Platonism for the people? Nietzsche did indeed put his finger on a key problem.

Although taught by Plato, Aristotle (384-322 BCE) makes a very different contribution. His ideas about God, which combine argument with observation, tend to get boiled down to a single concept: the prime mover, or uncaused cause.

Aristotle explored the idea that everything was produced by four causes – the material cause (what it was made out of), the formal cause (its shape or design), its efficient cause (what actually produced it – our modern sense of cause) and its final cause (what it is *for*, its purpose). This last one led to the assumption that everything had a part to play in some overall scheme of things. It had meaning.

But in examining these causes, Aristotle suggests that you cannot have an infinite regress. The chain of causes simply cannot go back forever, or there would be nothing to have caused it in the first place. Hence he posits the idea of a 'prime mover' or 'uncaused cause' that must somehow lie behind the whole of existence. But, for Aristotle, causality and purpose are found *within* the natural order, rather than being imposed on the natural order by some external designer or craftsman. However, when (in the 13th century) the Christian theologian Aquinas, came to study Aristotle, he thought that this 'uncaused cause' was exactly what people understood by 'God', and promptly appropriated Aristotle for his cosmological demonstration of the existence of God.

Aristotle used the term *theologia* – from which we have 'theology' – for the study of the most general or highest causes and principles. It is found particularly in book *Lambda* (book

12) of his *Metaphysics*, in which he tries to understand the fundamental principles of existence.

But notice that Aristotle's *theologia* is concerned with the highest form of being, an idea that remains impersonal and far removed from the gods of Olympia. It is the product of careful thought, not popular worship. He introduced the idea of 'first philosophy' as a way of understanding the principles that underpin our experienced world:

> ... if there is no substance other than those which are formed by nature, natural science will be the first science; but if there is a changeless substance, the science of this must be prior and must be first philosophy, and universal in this way, because it is first. And it will belong to this to consider being *qua* being – both what it is and the attributes that belong to it *qua* being.
>
> *Metaphysics* (VI, 1, 1026a 23-32)

In other words, quite separate from the cultural world of the gods and their worship, Aristotle proposes a study of reality in its most abstract and general form.

In terms which echo Plato's forms, he points out that abstract descriptions apply to a range of things, so, for example, there are a great variety of things that could be called 'health' (presumably from people and animals, to diets and environments), but the concept of 'health' is the 'first healthy thing'. In the same way, when dealing with being (*ousia*) he is exploring what is understood by 'being' in the most general way. He refers to the hand as the 'first tool' since it is because of the hand that other things become tools.

By the time we get to book XII of *Metaphysics*, Aristotle is describing three different types of substance: transitory, eternal and 'unmoving and immaterial'. He sees this last as making the first two possible. In other words, to use a modern term, Aristotle is proposing a kind of *foundationalism*. We can only understand general terms or the changing world of individual things if we see them against some unchanging background. This is his theology; this is what his 'God' is about. It is the quest for coherence in our understanding of the world. His 'first mover' underlies all movement; his 'first cause' establishes causality in our perception of the world. Aristotle's 'God', the object of his first philosophy or universal ontology is impersonal, a feature of our understanding of the world, unlike the personal, limited gods of religion.

However, there is another element in this. For Aristotle, like Plato, philosophy itself is a spiritual activity, a commitment to serious thought that – particularly later with the Stoics – becomes something of a religion in itself, but one that it open to only the few serious thinkers, rather than the general population. As we shall see later, there is something of the religious about atheism today – a view of life that claims personal integrity, honest analysis of experience and the recognition of moral responsibility. So, while Plato and Aristotle are used to give rational credence to the idea of God, their intention and approach also underpins this view of modern atheism.

Aristotle's quest is for meaning and coherence in our experience of the world. It is most definitely not about supernatural beings, nor is it related to the practice of religion as he would have experienced it. His philosophy becomes 'theology' when dealing with fundamental questions, but it is effectively agnostic with respect to individual gods. He does not deny them, but they are irrelevant to what he is trying to understand.

The impact of Aristotle's philosophy on Western thought has been immense. During the Mediaeval period, he was *the* philosopher, used by Thomas Aquinas (1225-74) in an attempt to give a philosophical grounding for Christian belief. Whether he was right to do so, and whether belief is helped or hindered by such philosophical support is a matter we will be examining later. But for students of theology today, Aquinas demonstrations of the existence of God are still basic for their study of the idea of God.

Aristotle's work has sometimes been seen as a philosophical contemplation of the divine – a delightfully misleading idea, since it assumes a fully-fledged and defined notion of the divine, which is far from the case. The more appropriate question is to ask whether what a believer means by 'the divine' really corresponds to the object of Aristotle's first philosophy.

Aquinas was not the only thinker to appropriate Aristotle in this way. Both Maimonides (1138-1204), from a Jewish perspective, and Ibn Rushd (1126-98) – also known as Averroes – from Islamic one, incorporated Aristotle's ideas into their work, trying to show their compatibility with their respective religions.

One feature of Aristotle's thinking had a particular influence on mediaeval scholasticism – the idea that the world displays meaning and purpose. This had a profound impact on the development of theism, rather than atheism. Indeed, it is key to the division between the two. It is referred to as the 'teleological' perspective (from *telos*, the Greek word for end).

But, although Aristotle's 'prime mover' appears to endorse theism, it is far removed from the Trinitarian idea of God – as three persons, Father, Son and Spirit – that was developed during the fourth and fifth centuries by the Early Christian Fathers. Instead, you have in Aristotle the foundation of an overall metaphysic, or way of looking at the world. However, seeing the world as fundamentally rational and purposeful is often presented as a first step towards theistic belief.

As we shall see later, some forms of atheism, in arguing against any supernatural beliefs, may also claim that the world is, in itself, ordered and purposeful. Indeed, ideas about evolution and the future of humanity often assume just the sort of purposeful outlook that Aristotle presented in traditional metaphysical terms. However, the assumptions about our world have changed dramatically since Aristotle's day and, in spite of Catholic theologians' attempts to do so, *via* Aquinas, his thought does not offer any decisive contribution to resolving the opposition of theist and atheist ideas within modern culture.

The early philosophers were not universally respected. Anaxagoras, who argued that everything was controlled by *nous* (mind) as the supreme power with a plan for the universe, was forced to withdraw from Athens. Protagoras had his books burned publicly, and Socrates – refusing the offer of exile – chose instead to drink hemlock.

However, these ancient thoughts, from the pre-Socratics to Plato and Aristotle, set the agenda for the range of ideas that existed within the Hellenistic world and therefore formed the background to the rise of the three great monotheistic religions, Judaism, Christianity and Islam. Some people may therefore be tempted to look at the ideas of Plato and Aristotle and find in them a rational scheme just waiting to underpin later Christian ideas about God. In fact, by the time Christians were arguing about the nature God, other philosophies had come into play, including particularly those of the Stoics and Plotinus. When Paul came to speak in Athens, or the bishops of the 4th century Christian Church came to debate their beliefs and formulate creeds, they could draw on a whole body of serious intellectual expertise that addressed questions that we would now consider to be the province of both philosophy and science.

But before we enter that world, we need to stay within the culture of Ancient Greece for a moment, to look at three ideas that gave shape to our subsequent understanding of God and religion.

Chapter 4

Mythos, Logos
and Therapy

I walked down to Piraeus yesterday, with Glaucon,
the son of Ariston, to make my prayers to the goddess.
The opening of *Republic* by Plato

In the last chapter we looked at the way in which philosophy emerged in Ancient Greece and addressed the idea of God. But life is more than philosophy. It is also literature and culture, stories and images, religion, theatre and the quest for the good life. The Greek world can therefore illustrate two very different ways of engaging with life – *mythos* (story, narrative, culture) and *logos* (science and reason).

But, as it developed and spread within the later Hellenistic world, philosophy also started to change from a narrowly rational enquiry into a broader set of ideas about what it means to live the good life. Philosophy in the West was catching up with the Eastern thought of 500 years earlier by becoming a vehicle for a thoughtful engagement with life, but one that did not require the trappings of popular religion.

SOCRATES' NIGHT OUT

If you read Plato's *Republic* from the beginning, rather than just the section on the Cave, you find that it opens with Socrates going down to Piraeus – then, as now, the harbour of

Athens – to make his prayers to the goddess Bendis and to see how her festival is to be conducted. He is persuaded to stay for a meal with friends and later to see a horserace with torches. He is told that the festival that will last all night and is assured that there will be plenty of young men to talk to.

He meets his old friend Cephalus, who is wearing a garland, having just come indoors after carrying out a sacrifice. Their conversation starts with issues of old age, living with one's conscience and on to questions of justice, who is fit to become a ruler, and all the material that will be familiar to students required to study Plato. Taken out of context, it is a book about the contrast between eternal realities, and the changing events of life, with extreme views about the training of rulers and the dismissal of artists from the ideal city-state. Its literary form, however, presents a more rounded view of Greek culture.

Plato presents a carefully crafted dialogue about justice, led by his mentor Socrates, but it is set against the background of a festival in honour of the goddess Bendis, whose cult had recently been imported from Thrace with a temple set up in her honour in Piraeus. Bendis was associated with hunting and with the moon – which is perhaps why her festival carried on right through the night. She is depicted as a huntress, often accompanied by satyrs – male nature spirits who dance naked displaying exaggerated erections, lovers of wine, music and women – and maenads – female followers of Dionysus, known for their frenzied dancing and intoxication.

The serious discussion takes place against the background of a wild, all-night celebration of the goddess. You might have thought, reading only the analogy of the cave, that Socrates would have nothing to do with the festival of Bendis. But no, the spectacular celebration goes on all around them, as they discuss how train leaders and grasp eternal reality.

This is fiction, of course, not the factual reporting of an actual discussion between Socrates and his company that night. But that makes the contrast between the discussion and its rowdy context even more significant. This is where Plato chooses to set the discussion, and particularly his hero, Socrates, who had been forced to drink hemlock, in part because he was accused of atheism and corrupting the youth of Athens.

Is it really possible that this – arguably the best known of all Plato's dialogues, and the one that has been used most directly to support the idea of God dwelling within an eternal realm, separate from the world of our everyday experience – is set in the context of the festival of a goddess best known for her wild, erotic, frenzied and drunken followers?

In his dialogue *Phaedrus*, there are two kinds of madness: that produced by infirmity, and the divine release of the soul from convention, produced by inspiration. Plato saw the divine madness of poets, inspired by the muses, as second only to the madness of philosophers, inspired by Eros (*Phaedrus* 244a). At the end of the dialogue, Plato describes Homer – the great teller of tales of gods and men – as a philosopher. How does that square with the conventional division between the gods and goddesses of Homer and Hesiod and the later development of philosophy? The answer may lie in the way in which *mythos* and *logos* blended within Greek culture.

At the opening of Chapter 9 of *Republic*, Plato speaks of education as a matter of telling the best of stories. He approves of Homer, and argues that children should be taught stories of the gods, in order to give a positive view of life promoting goodness rather than bad behaviour. So the gods and goddesses are characters in literature; their stories told for a purpose. Yet often it is the humans in the stories that are wise and morally good, while the gods are mischievous, jealous and vengeful. So, within literature, their legacy is mixed to say the least. But at least their function is clear: it is to provoke and to inspire.

THE ANCIENT GREEKS AND THEIR GODS

During the 5th century BCE, Athens was at its most vibrant and powerful. Its culture included philosophers, playwrights and poets, and its wealth was displayed in its temples, most notably that dedicated to Athene Parthanon, completed in 438BCE, the iconic image of Athens, now simply referred to as 'the Parthanon.'

In Homer's narratives, the gods shape and direct human lives, whether it is to go to war or to fall in love. By the time of the historian Herodotus, however, that is starting to change. He sees the causes of events as human and natural, while using the gods (or 'the divine') as representing some general principles of his view of the world. This trend continues with Thucydides, whose *History of the Peloponnesian War* explains everything without reference to divine intervention and has therefore been described as 'the earliest surviving atheist narrative of human history' (Whitmarsh, *Battling the Gods*, p86). In law, one could no longer argue that a god had commanded the offending action, and any attempt to do so came to be seen as a cynical avoidance of responsibility.

So we find three very different ways of using the idea of 'god'. The older view of the gods as intervening to direct things on earth is in decline, often mocked as an excuse for immorality at a time when personal responsibility was becoming the norm. Secondly, the religious celebration of the gods, through festivals, and temple offerings, was seen as a mark of social identity and an essential part of Greek culture. And thirdly, the term 'god' was sometimes being used in a philosophical context for the underlying reality of the world: infinite and impersonal – 'Being Itself' as opposed to an individual being; a divine principle that would regulate the workings of the world and keep everything in balance.

Within the philosophical sphere, however, there remained an element of agnosticism. Protagoras' *On the Gods* started with the clear statement that he does not, and cannot, know their nature or whether or not they exist. This is remarkable, coming from someone whose intellectual ability was such that his return to Athens excited Socrates, according to Plato's dialogue *Protagoras*.

It is difficult for us to know how most Ancient Greeks thought about their gods, but as cultural phenomena they were alive and well, with temples built in their honour, offerings made, statues carved and stories narrated. However, the 20th century philosopher Martin Heidegger offers an interesting insight. In Benjamin Crow's *Heidegger's Phenomenology of Religion*, 2008, page 45, he comments:

> According to Heidegger, the Greeks experienced their own cultural creations not as products of human creativity, but as a response to the 'nature' of things.

This suggests that we should not necessarily use modern ideas of subjectivity and objectivity to interpret the nature of the Greek *mythoi*. Their stories, if Heidegger is correct, were not so much created as discovered. They are as much a way of understanding the world as their more analytic and empirical philosophy. But they remained part of culture, with a social and political dimension, as opposed to the logical conclusions of abstract thought. They were the background celebration, while Socrates pondered the eternal realities with his friends.

Above all, the religion of Ancient Greece was polytheistic; and people appeared to be free to decide which gods or goddesses they would worship. This led to a flexibility that is utterly unlike societies where a single deity and worship is permitted and all others proscribed; the obvious exception being the need to establish localized gods, whose worship would be taken as a sign of social and political loyalty.

Overall, however, it led to a culturally liberal society, albeit within the limits of freedom imposed by all ancient cultures, and limited to those who were free rather than enslaved.

THE IMPACT OF SOCIAL MEDIA

Philosophy was as much a minority interest in Ancient Greece as it is today, and just as it can be caricatured and mocked in modern social media, so it found its way into the Greek equivalent – the theatre. Greek playwrights were willing and able both to mock the gods and to parody the philosophers.

In Aristophanes' *The Clouds* there is a dialogue between Socrates and Strepsiades. Socrates says "Zeus indeed! There's no Zeus: don't you be so obtuse" and when Strepsiades objects "No Zeus up above in the sky? Then who sends the rain?" Socrates replies that it comes from the clouds. In the play, the clouds – represented by the chorus – are goddesses, worshipped by Socrates and his followers as deities. A naturalistic explanation of phenomena, blended with popular religion, forms the basis of good humour and theatre.

Aristophanes was not above using philosophical terminology in order to mock. In his comedy *Knights*, performed in 424BCE, he has an intellectually gifted slave mockingly ask 'Do you really believe in the gods? On what *tekmerion* do you rely? The term *tekmerion* was used in philosophy, much as modern philosophers would use 'epistemology', to denote the grounds for holding a belief. So, for example, those who, following the ideas of Protagoras, saw sense experience as the basis of knowledge, held that as their *tekmerion*. Aristophanes is poking fun – barbed because it comes from a slave – at both religion and philosophy, and he links them, because the slave sees clearly that the one is going to rely on the other for its justification. The point of his joke, of course, is not religion itself, but the idea that the gods can exist within the sensible world, as objects about which philosophy and science can provide evidence.

The uppity slave in *Knights* thus anticipates the dilemmas of the Enlightenment. The cultural forms of religion and the philosophical quest are here set on a collision course.

In his play *Bellerophon* (of which, unfortunately, we only have fragments), Euripides has a character argue that to speak of gods in heaven was antiquated reasoning, invented to deter bad behaviour, and that they obviously had no power, since the irreligious are seen to prosper. Euripides was ahead of his time in introducing what is now termed 'the problem of evil' – if the gods are powerful and good, how is it that the wicked prosper? On the other hand, the play suggests that denial of the gods was a sign of disenchantment with the world, a negative view of atheism that has persisted to this day.

It seems likely that the theatre both reflected and shaped the attitude of many Greeks to both religion and philosophy, and there is no doubt that both could become a ready target for cultural mockery.

THE MISMATCH

In Ancient Greece we therefore find two very different activities running alongside one another: culture and philosophy. The first leads to an exploration of life through myths, stories, drama and intuition. It is expressed through images, temples and rituals. It appeals to the emotions and celebrates heroes and heroines, gods and goddesses. It is about celebrating and valuing aspects of life, and each person could pick and choose which of the gods to worship, depending on his or her desires and station in life.

The second seeks to understand the world in terms of what is permanent and what changes, about its meaning and value and about the nature of reality itself, but the conclusions of this philosophical activity were not initially used as the basis of religion. The Form of the Good or the Prime Mover, were intellectual attempts to understand and describe reality.

But there is a fundamental mismatch. Neither the world of the ancient Greek gods, not that of the philosophical abstractions fit easily with the idea of God that came to be developed in the early centuries of Christianity.

With the passing of the centuries, the analytic and logical side of philosophy and science has grown in importance, and is now established as the primary way of understanding the world. Yet that should not denigrate the mythological or cultural approach to life. You do not reject a novel because it does not contain sufficient factually correct statements. The point of reading novel is not to understand facts, but to enter into the author's intuitions about life. It may be interesting for a specialist to analyse a work of art, literature or music, but that does not replace the impact such a work can have. If anything, too much analysis can kill cultural enjoyment. If we seek wisdom, a balance is needed between *mythos* of *logos*, allowing them to complement one another.

So science exists alongside culture, and however essential its function, it does not displace the arts, stories, plays, decorations, jewellery, a taste for fine wine, an appreciation of antiques, graffiti, fashions, hairstyles, or the cultural and financial messages given by wearing the right trainers. We all live in a world that is described by science and informed by culture. Plato describes Socrates as happy to take part in a lively religious festival. Then, as now, you did not have to choose between *mythos* and *logos*, you can appreciate and enjoy both. I may read of book of philosophy and then pick up a novel; both will teach me something about the reality of life in this world, but they will do it in very different ways. The difference is that, while everyone can enjoy culture, philosophy and science require training to appreciate and discuss their more abstract ideas.

But notice one crucial thing: 'the Form of the Good' or the 'Uncaused Cause' are not supernatural entities. They are the result of asking rational questions about the world. Whether you accept or reject them depends on the way you think rather than your religious inclinations.

In *The Birth of Tragedy*, Nietzsche introduced two very different approaches to life or caste of mind: the Dionysian and the Apollonian. For him, they represented the spontaneous and the structured. I sense that, in the broadest of contexts, they also represent the impetus to culture and philosophy. We are pulled by the emotional attraction of cultural myths, as well as by the clean precision of analysis and argument, we need to be inspired as well as to understand

CYNICS AND SCEPTICS

Some ancient Greeks challenged supernatural religion in ways that are strikingly modern. Diogenes of Sinope (412 or 404 – 323 BCE) was the original cynic, wit and social rebel. When it was suggested to him that the many temple dedications put up by those who had survived storms at sea were evidence for divine aid, Diogenes objected that there would be many more if those who had not survived had also been able to add their dedications! (see Whitmarsh, *Battling the Gods*). That argument against miracles would have been worthy of David Hume and also happens to anticipate the modern use (or manipulation) of statistics!

As their name implies, the sceptics regarded all claims as suspect, suspended judgement on them, and thus becoming the forerunners of modern agnostics. Carneades (214 – 129 BCE) devised a particularly useful argument against taking the gods too literally. It is a version of the Sorites Paradox, one of the famous paradoxes devised by Zeno. In its original form, the Sorites paradox is about how many grains of sand make a 'heap'. A thousand certainly would be, but what about ten? Might a single grain constitute a heap? Carneades applied the same logic to the gods. If the Olympians are gods, what about Pan? If Poseidon is god of the ocean, what about the gods and spirits of rivers and streams? His argument shows that, if you are going to use the divine to describe some things, you end up using it to describe *everything*; and once that happens, its meaning evaporates.

Although the manuscript has not survived, Clitomachus, a follower of Carneades wrote *On Atheism*, and Sextus Empiricus, a Roman philosopher of the same vintage, was prepared to argue that we cannot know whether gods exist or not. He mocks the idea by asking if gods have lungs, since they are said to speak to us, and about what language they might speak. Here is atheist mockery worthy of the 21st century 'New Atheists'.

By the time you get to Pliny the Elder (d. 79CE) you have a set of arguments about religion that sound remarkably modern. In his *Natural History*, he considers it madness to try to discover the shape and form of a god, and mocks their number, with some always old and others always young. His view it that religion originated in the celebration of human achievements (almost as Feuerbach, 1800 years later), but points out that it encourages us to think that the future as predetermined, or at the chance whim of a deity. He also considered the idea of divinity to have come from the human need to justify rewards and punishments and thus to back up morality. His work provided a serious attempt to explain the worship of gods without resorting to the supernatural.

Clearly, the attempt to take the cultural aspects of religion literally was open to criticism and mockery, but it might be useful to follow the ancestral and social practices of religion, without necessarily committing to any particular philosophical ideas about the existence of the gods. You could be a philosophical theist or atheist in the worlds of Greece and Rome, but it was always advisable to take part in formal religion as a sign of loyalty.

If only all subsequent discussion about God had taken that approach, much damage could have been avoided!

A century earlier, Titus Lucretius Catus, known as both a philosopher and a poet, wrote the epic poem *On the Nature of Things*. In it, he is critical of state religion. Piety, he argues, does not consist in worship and sacrifice, but 'to survey the universe with an untroubled mind.'

But to appreciate the significance of that, we need to step back from these Latin writers and look at an earlier development in Greek philosophy – the attempt of philosophy itself to engender a way of life, based on reason and aimed at happiness and morality. We enter the world of the Epicureans and Stoics, whose therapeutic approach to philosophy in their troubled times continues to find favour in the equally hectic 21st century.

THERAPY, LIFESTYLE AND ETHICS

By the third century BCE, particularly with the development of Epicureanism (initiated by Epicurus 341-270) and Stoicism (by Zeno 342-270) we have philosophical movements that addressed issues of ethics and spirituality, and were concerned to promote the benefits of a disciplined and frugal way of living, offering inner peace and simplicity. They were not the first, however, for the mathematician and philosopher Pythagoras (570-500BCE) had promoted a life of purity and vegetarianism.

However, there was a fundamental difference between those philosophies: the Epicureans were basically materialist and atheist, while the Stoics argued for a single rational principle giving coherence to the universe.

Epicurus – whom Nietzsche (in *Daybreak*) called 'the great soul-soother of late antiquity' – was against superstition, criticised Hesiod's idea of the origin of the gods, and thought that religion was motivated by fear. He argued that the universe had no boundary, so there could be nothing beyond it, and that we are simply made of atoms and will dissolve when we die, with no possibility of an afterlife. Death posed no threat because, for Epicurus, 'death is nothing'. He recommended a life of tranquillity and simplicity, avoiding stress, nurturing happiness and taking responsibility. Asked what he would most enjoy, he opted for a piece of cheese to share with his friends!

The question that divided Stoics and Epicureans was this: Is the universe governed by a single rational principle (*logos*) that gives meaning and coherence, or does everything exist by chance and without purpose. The Stoics opted for the first, the Epicureans the second.

This, in a modern context, is the choice between theism and atheism. Historically, however, both Stoics and Epicureans took a serious and principled approach to life. Both recognised the benefits of simplicity and honesty; both saw reason as the basis for living the good life. Yet neither of them is wedded to the supernatural aspects of religion.

To appreciate Stoic thought in a later (Roman) context, read the *Meditations* of Emperor Marcus Aurelius. It is full of practical wisdom from one who has the responsibility of running the Roman Empire – and therefore who, in modern times, would be desperately in need of the wisdom to establish a work-life balance! The quote from *Meditations* that heads the Introduction to this book has Marcus Aurelius commenting that, before his gods, his father was never superstitious. Today, that sounds like a contradiction in terms. How can you have gods and not be superstitious? The answer is that you see them as cultural phenomena. Both Stoics and Epicureans, like Socrates before them, could acknowledge the social benefits of religion, with its festivals, its celebration of features of life, and its expression of local loyalty. People were not required to set aside their philosophy when they took part, because the social religion of that time was not based on believing a set of propositions to be true, but sharing a commitment to values and to local loyalty.

What we might nowadays think of as 'faith' – commitment to a view of the nature of the world and our place within it – arose primarily within the *philosophical* community, not the religious. For Stoics like Marcus Aurelius, human satisfaction and fulfilment lay in aligning oneself to the fundamental reason that directed the universe. For Epicureans, it lay is cultivating happiness through simplicity and friendship.

The issue that divided them continues to this day. How can life have meaning unless the universe has some purpose and direction? Can such a question have any objective answer? Without getting outside the universe, or being able to compare our universe with others, it seems impossible to give one. But, if so, humankind has to choose the direction and the values by which it will live. Meaning and purpose become matters of choice or intuition, and for human flourishing they need to be established *in spite of* the apparently impersonal nature of the universe.

Notice, however, that the purpose of philosophy in the ancient world is shifting. Whereas it started by exploring the world around us, asking questions about causality and the nature of material things, by the time we get to the Hellenistic world within which Christian thought developed, philosophy was also becoming a matter of personal therapy, seeking to understand and put into practice the good life.

I suggest that this therapeutic quest, which in modern times has been taken to be a major feature of religion, did not originate in conventional religious observances at all, but in philosophy. That quest was moral and purposeful and was undertaken by both theists and atheists. Yet, generally speaking, it took place alongside, rather than within, the conventional, social and cultic religion of that time.

BEFORE HIS EXECUTION

While the Roman world was being rocked by external threats and internal chaos, and the soon-to-be-assassinated Julius Caesar, was dictator in Rome, the great orator, statesman and philosopher Cicero (106-43BCE) was settling into what he hoped would be his retirement in a villa just outside the city.

He was bereaved and feeling his age. Now, more than anything else, he wanted to set down the principles of civilised life and moral values, based on his lifetime's study of philosophy. The result was his book *On the Gods*.

In arguments that have been re-used over subsequent centuries, he outlined the reasons for the emergence of religion and the idea of gods. Anticipating Kant by almost 2000 years, he admits to the sense of the wonder of nature, the starry heavens above and the universal impulse for morality. He summarised the views of Plato and Aristotle, the Stoics and Epicureans, and acknowledged that not everyone believed in the existence of gods.

Reading his work today, the most impressive thing is that, at a time when brute force dominated life, he was sensitive both to human emotions and needs and to the variety and subtlety of arguments. He fully recognised that people will differ radically in their views of religion, morality and the possible existence of divine beings, but also that civilised society needs inspiration and guidance. Although a philosopher, his work spans *logos* and *mythos*, and draws them together in an appreciation of what it is to be human.

In the end, on the insistence of Mark Antony, he was executed – a pawn in the twisted game of power politics.

Cicero achieved an open examination of these issues in a way that was rendered impossible when politics took control of religion, using it as a means of establishing unity across a disparate Roman Empire. For him, philosophy provided a moment of peaceful reflection in a politically troubled world but, within 300 years of his death, religion was to become a tool of Roman rule and Christian beliefs were being negotiated for political ends.

Chapter 5

Doctrine, Destruction
and Schism

*Whoever will be saved, before all things it is necessary
that he hold the Catholic faith. Which faith
unless every one do keep whole and undefiled,
without doubt he shall perish everlastingly.*
Athanasian Creed

What happens when political authority takes charge of the idea of God?

As those in business will tell you, the success of any product depends on identifying a need, finding a gap in the market and demonstrating that your product will satisfy it. The Roman authorities of the 4th and 5th centuries CE provide a fine example of this. Recognising its potential, they transformed what had been a modest and unorthodox Jewish sect into a religious vehicle for maintaining cohesion and loyalty across their fragmented empire.

The transformation was astonishing. A sect that had been persecuted as atheist because its members refused to give an oath of loyalty to the imperial gods, became the official religion of the Empire. Its modest collection of writings had become – under the skilful editing of Church leaders with a good knowledge of philosophy – the basis for a set of creeds to which people could be required to give their assent. By the fourth century, the Nicene Creed, repeated in churches to this day, affirmed the doctrines of a religion that would have been largely unrecognisable to the earliest Christians.

In the first millennium of its existence, Christianity borrowed from the Greeks, gave itself to the Romans, tried to destroy classical culture and finally split between East and West over issues of authority and doctrine.

DEBATES AND CREEDS

As Christianity emerged from its Jewish roots and accepted gentiles into its community, it was forced to explain itself to and engage with the Roman Empire. Its beliefs had seemed to defy both Jewish and Hellenistic expectations, but it still came to be accepted as a legal religion. As a result, however, it came under political pressure from the Roman authorities to define its beliefs, and thereby to show who was a true Christian and who was not.

But here's the problem. Ideas about God that were developed in the early centuries of Christianity did not fit in with the world of the Greek and Roman gods, not that of philosophical abstractions. Neither did they fit with the ideas and literature of Judaism. The Jewish people had moved on from their earlier henotheism – the idea that you should worship only one god, although other gods existed – towards the monotheism of a single creator God, uniquely powerful and omnipresent. Nevertheless, being focused on scripture, they had retained the idea of a god who was personal and intimately involved with the life of his people. They believed that the God they worshipped was related to them in a special way, although universal in his reach and power. According to the Gospels, Jesus spoke of God as his Father, as every Jew could. He was not a philosopher; but a Galilean rabbi. His language, even when critical of religion, was steeped in the tradition of the Jewish scriptures.

However, by the time St Paul came to speak about God in Athens, the author of John's Gospel picked up his pen, or the bishops of the 4th century Christian Church came to debate their beliefs and formulate creeds, they were able to draw on a range of Greek ideas addressing questions that we would now consider to be the province of philosophy: ideas that mirrored features of Plato and Aristotle in the broad and varied intellectual climate of the Hellenistic world.

The Bishops who were engaged in the task of writing the creeds of the Church were well educated, with a good grasp of philosophy. In explaining their beliefs they were able to use terms that had been developed in a secular context, with Stoicism and the Neoplatonism of Plotinus providing a respectable and intellectual backing for their debates.

The Stoics argued that the universe was fundamentally reasonable, based on the Logos, or Word. If you want to see how Stoic language could be imported into Christianity, just take a look at the opening of St John's Gospel: 'In the Beginning was the Word, and the Word was with God, and the Word was God'.

For Plotinus (c204/5 - 270) there was a perfect, eternal realm, beyond that of space and time. He saw the divine Word as embodying imperishable archetypes – the 'Forms' in Plato. More than a century later, Augustine of Hippo (354 – 430) followed this tradition as a Christian Platonist. Just as Plato's philosophical ruler had to leave the cave in order to go up into the light, so the Christian had to leave behind worldly concerns, escape from the prison of the body, and seek the transcendent, eternal realm. For Augustine, the Church was a spiritual 'City of God' to be contrasted with the earthly city.

Plotinus considered God, which he referred to as 'the One', to be incomprehensible, without beginning, and containing the full power of being. This influenced all three of the great monotheistic religions and contributes the intellectual basis of the later Christian concept of God. This was no god of popular culture, but the most absolute and abstract of ideas.

However, for Plotinus, 'the One' does not itself exist, rather it is the explanation of all existence. Neither can it be a 'thing' alongside other things. Hence it is certainly not part of the universe, nor can it be known or proven. With Plotinus, we take an absolutely crucial step away from the gods of popular culture – gods who interfere with human activities on a selective basis – and move into the realm of metaphysics, although it retained one key feature of the personal: mind. For Plotinus the One has also the quality of being the universal mind, animating everything, just as our own minds are associated with and animate our bodies.

Inspired by the metaphysics of Plotinus and the rationality and ethical seriousness of the Stoics, the bishops of the Church were prodded by the Emperor Constantine to define the Christian faith that he had newly embraced.

They addressed the fundamental problem of believing that Jesus was fully divine (the Greeks had no problem with stories of gods begetting children, but the idea that they would themselves be divine was certainly more problematic), that the Father was the creator of the world (Greeks would have thought 'demiurge', a craftsman) and that the sense of an indwelling spirit among believers, the Holy Spirit, was also God. But in spite of appearing in those three contexts, there was only one God, although seen in those three persons, faces or masks (*prosopa*). In the end, after excluding and those with minority views, the bishops defined their triune God.

However, the idea of the Holy Trinity was presented as a mystery, rather than a definition. It insisted that the divine could be experienced through the created order, through the person of Jesus as the Christ, living within the Church, and as the Spirit that inspired and motivated the Christian community. All of these things were fully 'God', yet there were not three gods but only one. Rather like a Buddhist *koan*, it served to challenge and shatter simplistic answers to the question of what we mean by 'God'.

Concerned that 'God' should not be misunderstood, Basil of Caesarea (c330-79) argued that God was not a mere being, and that he was unknowable, because all our knowledge is limited to our experience of the physical world. He developed an idea of the Trinity that was (and in the Eastern tradition of Christianity continued to be), a way of preventing people from thinking of God in literal or logical terms. In Christ, God and humanity were becoming inseparable, and rather than being 'saved' (presumably from future punishment, as became the norm in Western Christianity), the significant feature of becoming Christian was to become deified. In other words, God becomes flesh in order that flesh might become divine. The key word that Basil and others used for this was *theopoesis* – literally 'becoming God'.

Notice the implication of this. The Early Fathers were trying to explain, using the best philosophy of their day, their experience of the divine – in the world around them, within themselves and in what they experienced as the indwelling Spirit. This was not metaphysics, nor pure philosophy, and it was often far from rational, but it was *the description of an experience* that they believed to be fundamental to Christianity.

The rejection of an external God was made clear by events that disrupted the Church in Alexandria. Just as Christianity was being adopted as the official religion of the Roman Empire, there was a dispute between two leaders of the Church in Alexandria: Arius and his bishop, Athanasius. Arius claimed that God was the creator, and therefore beyond the world he had created. His view – which I guess would be assumed to be the norm by many professing Christians today – was regarded as heresy, because it separated the idea of 'God' from reality itself, making him something 'out there' rather than a reality within people and their experience.

I remain astonished by the implications of the Arian heresy for modern belief. Regarded at the time as the greatest threat to orthodox Christianity. The rejection of an external God, which today would be seen as atheism, was the defining feature of the Trinitarian doctrine. What most atheists today reject is actually the Arian heresy!

However, the claim that God had created the world *ex nihilo* (out of nothing) became orthodox belief but created its own problems. On the one hand, it removed the idea of God as being a craftsman, like Plato's demiurge, shaping existing material; but on the other, it put a great chasm between God and his creation. Everything in this world was seen as ultimately dependent upon God: an attempt to express the inexpressible – reality itself – after the external craftsmen had been disposed of.

The various wriggles conducted by the bishops of the 4th and 5th centuries as they battled to get an acceptable statement of belief for their creeds, ending with the triune nature of God – as Father, Son and Spirit – was a major feat of intellectual debate and political compromise. But it was based on a tradition, maintained in the East after the division of the Church, called the *apophatic* (unknowable) way – God is not an object and hence cannot be located, named or described.

This idea of God as Trinity was radical, secular and unlike any previous philosophical or religious concept. It attempted to shatter naïve conceptions and secularise abstract ideas. Can there be any scientific evidence for the existence of God? The orthodox view of the early Church, like that of modern atheists, is that there is not and cannot be any such evidence. God is not that sort of 'thing'.

But, to make matters worse, between then and now, it seems that something has been lost in translation…

THE LINGUISTIC SHIFT THAT RUINED BELIEF

The Greek word *pistis* means 'trust', 'loyalty' or 'good faith', but when St Jerome came to translate it into Latin at the end of the 4th century CE, he used the word *fides*. That was entirely appropriate, since Fides was the Roman goddess of faithfulness – exactly what the Greek word had stood for. His problem was that there was no verbal form of *fides*, so he used the term *credo*, meaning 'to give one's heart'.

So far; so sensible. Those who originally recited the Christian creeds were 'giving their hearts' to what followed the opening word: *Credo*. However, in the 17th century, *credo* was translated into English as 'I believe', which was also quite appropriate, since 'believe' comes from the Middle English *bileven*, meaning 'to prize, value or hold dear' and is related to the German *belieben*, 'to love'.

Towards the end of the 17th century, however, at least in scientific circles, the word 'believe' changed its meaning from love and commitment to intellectual assent. To believe something now meant to agree that it was true. And so the damage was done. Thirteen hundred years after the creeds were set out as statements of commitment and trust, they became lists of items to which one was expected to give intellectual assent.

Through until the 19th century, the term 'belief' retained its original meaning, and even today it lives on in the phrase 'believe in' rather than 'believe that'. To say 'I believe in you' means you are giving someone your love and trust; you are not claiming to know that he or she actually exists!

So it was that 'belief' in God, as well as being a matter of the heart, also became an answer to a question that originally belonged to philosophy rather than religion: 'Does God exist?' Believing in God is not, was not, and certainly was never intended to be the same as asserting that God exists. In my view, that mistake has had the most terrible consequences.

DOCTRINE TO 451.

One of the papers for a theological degree at King's London in the 1960s was called 'Doctrine to 451'. It traced the process of negotiation and definition that led to the creeds. I found it fascinating, because it was clear that the popular concept of God, as presented in the churches I had encountered, was nowhere near as sophisticated as that debated by the Early Fathers.

How did this subtle attempt to explore the meaning of spirituality end up with arguments about what appeared to be a supernatural and external creator? How did we move from such sophistication to the barbarism of conflict in the name of religion, or the persecution and torture of those considered heretics? How was it possible to move from a culture that allowed philosophical thought to embrace both theism and atheism to one in which the latter would be condemned?

If anything, it was the study of early Christian doctrine that led me to describe myself as an atheist; not because those Early Fathers were in any way lacking in human insight and intuition, but because of the damaging legacy of their work over the following centuries.

The Athanasian Creed, from the early 6th century (in other words, after Christianity gained is position of strength in the Empire) gets off to a bad start…

> Whoever will be saved, before all things it is necessary that he hold the Catholic faith. Which faith unless every one do keep whole and undefiled, without doubt he shall perish everlastingly.

This is a blunt, political instrument for ensuring conformity: believe this or perish!

The content of this creed is fully Trinitarian – the Father, Son and Spirit are all equal; three persons, not be confounded nor divided. All are uncreated, all unlimited, all eternal, all infinite and almighty, and all are *incomprehensible*. All three are God, but there are not three Gods by one. It then focuses specifically on the person of Christ, who is to come to judge the living and the dead. When he comes, every one who is dead will rise again with their bodies (no disembodied souls here, but a renewed body) to give an account of their own works. Those who have done good will go into life everlasting, those who have done evil into everlasting fire.

Why do I mention this antiquated formula, other than the fact that it is still used on solemn occasions to define the Christian faith? Simply because it is very different from the idea of God that appeared in later (post Enlightenment) discussions and in the arguments studied in the Philosophy of Religion. It is the official definition, and yet it has been quietly set aside in discussions between atheists and believers. Such discussions might well be the successors of those between Stoics and Epicureans in ancient Greece, but it was not even vaguely on the agenda of those who defined Christianity in the 4th to 6th centuries.

Its saddest feature is the threat of damnation for those who do not believe incomprehensible and illogical claims. Whether produced by fear, or extracted by torture, forced correction became a method of saving souls. As such, it did not follow the theological musings of the early bishops, nor the flexibility of the gods of Greece and Rome, nor yet the philosophical debates of those times. No; it became an instrument of political power.

The problem with creeds is that they create a self-perpetuating deception. By reciting the creed, others assume that you are affirming it to be factually correct. The assumption (which I have made of others) is that, if a person whose views I respect appears to believe that stuff, then my own doubts must arise from my own misunderstanding. Many years ago, when I was still clinging to the Church by my fingertips, I was advised to recite the creeds simply as an affirmation of belonging to a community of Christians who would once have expressed their faith in that way, not because I thought them to be factually correct. My problem with that approach was that it would involve both self-deception and the potential of deceiving others about my true beliefs – and that, as the ordination service when I became a priest had pointed out, would make me liable for a 'horrible punishment' from God. My choice was between refusing to recite the creeds, leading me to 'perish everlastingly' and reciting them in a way that might harm others, leading to the 'horrible punishment'. Given that choice, the only sensible option was atheism.

After I left, some who remained in the Church said I should not have taken it all so seriously or literally. Were they right?

As has been said in another context, power corrupts and absolute power corrupts absolutely. That is as true of formal religion as of rulers. Once you start to define 'God' for political purposes, you may also feel the need to destroy all whose idea of God or the gods differs from your own.

CHRISTIANS ON THE RAMPAGE

Having become accepted as the official religion of the Empire, Christianity sought to destroy all opposition. In the 4th century, Christian zealots went on the rampage in an attempt to wipe out classical culture. Henotheistic rivalry came to the fore, with Greek and Roman religion and literature branded as idolatry. Images of gods and goddesses were defaced or hacked apart, books burned and temples pulled down. What we prize now as the culture of a golden age, is simply the residue that Christianity failed to destroy.

This sad episode has been well documented and need not delay us, except to reflect that it was the liberal polytheistic culture that allowed for new gods to be accepted, and therefore enabled Christianity, once it emerged from Judaism, to gain traction and eventually to become accepted as a legitimate religion. It was to be another thousand years before, at the Renaissance, classical imagery was again to be appreciated and celebrated, gradually taking its place within the culture of Christendom.

The same sad fate befell philosophy. In 529, under the Emperor Justinian, Plato's academy was closed, and the teaching of philosophy banned. Preserved by Islamic and Jewish thinkers, it was not until the 12th century, that Aquinas and others were to rediscover Aristotle and other Greek thinkers and start to use them to underpin Christian ideas.

Overall, from the 4th century, political and religious authorities sought to move away from the freedom and moral dubiousness associated with polytheism, towards a situation where a single religious hierarchy could dictate what should be believed and how one should worship. For a thousand years, the teachings of Christianity and the authority of political rulers were fused into a single authoritarian structure, within which it is difficult now to discern whether particular teachings and events are religious or political. Were the confrontations between Christianity and Islam religious or political? How should we view the crusades? Political power may justify its actions by cloaking itself in religious garb.

In itself, this does not invalidate religious ideas, but sets them in a context in which they may become fossilized and imposed by an authority that refuses the luxury of free discussion.

By the late 4th century, the Emperor Theodosius outlawed atheists, a term that included everyone who did not accept the orthodox teachings of the Church, so heretics and those belonging to other religions were also regarded as 'atheists'. Just as, in Ancient Greece and Rome, anyone who did not acknowledge the gods of the city could be seen as a dangerous outsider, so now anyone who did not accept Christian dogma was branded 'atheist' and seen as a political threat.

MYSTICS AND SCHISM

If the tendency of political religion is towards creedal formula and the enforcement of belief, there is a whole tradition that looks in an entirely different direction: mysticism.

There is no scope here to start to explore the mysical tradition that runs through all three of the world's great monotheistic religions and cultures. It is above all based on the *experience* of what may be called God, and sits alongside the broader *apophatic* approach of Eastern Christianity, with its rejection of a literal description of the deity. It serves to remind us that defining what we mean by 'God', proving his existence, and branding as heretics or atheists those who do not agree, is only one aspect of religion, and a rather sad one at that.

Dionysius the Areopagite, a first century Athenian judge, considered the godhead to be above name, thought or imagination – although exactly how much may be ascribed to Dionysus himself and how much to the 6th century mystical writings of an author now referred to as Pseudo-Dionysius, is problematic. Similarly, but almost 1300 years later, the German mystic and theologian Meister Eckhart saw God as 'incomprehensible light' and, among the Early Fathers of the Church, Gregory of Nyssa was certainly a mystic, Origen considered 'that the real world is within' and Clement of Alexandria spoke of 'gnosis' (or secret knowledge) in a way that suggests that he may have been aware of the Hindu and Buddhist monks who may have been in Alexandria in the 1st and 2nd centuries CE.

Mystics experience the divine in many, often physical ways – the most blatant example depicted in the white marble sculpture 'The Ecstasy of Saint Theresa' by Bernini, a masterpiece of High Roman Baroque, where the saint has her head thrown back in a state of orgasmic rapture. Hildegaard of Bingen experienced herself as a 'feather on the breath of God', and Lady Julian of Norwich saw the whole creation as no bigger than a hazelnut in the palm of her hand. No attempt at definition here, but only an array of images, experiences and a sense of wonder and ecstasy. Eckhart even suggested that, to approach 'God', one needs to get rid of the idea of God.

Sadly, however, it was politics rather than mysticism that shaped the Church. With the Empire itself divided, and the Christian centres at Antioch and Alexandria, taken over by Muslims, the rival cities of Constantinople and Rome came to represent the Eastern and Western branches of Christianity. The Eastern Orthodox churches continued the idea of God as 'being itself', a mystery about which nothing literal could be said (the *apophatic* way) and the idea of salvation through *theopoesis* – literally 'being made into God', while in Rome and the Catholic West – perhaps more influenced by the views of Arius – the approach was more legalistic and God tended to be described as a separate being about whose existence there could be debate. The final schism came in 1054, over a theological debate but reflecting political rivalry between the two great centres of power.

From now on, the West would be dominated by argument, definition, persecution of heretics and a grudging toleration of mysticism as an exceptional approach. Ossified in words and creeds, 'God' became a political and cultural concept imposed by the authority of Rome.

WHAT NOW?

From the first millennium of this era we have two very different approaches to the idea of God. On the one hand, from the Early Fathers and the mystics, there is the idea of a God who is beyond description, experienced as the Trinity, omnipresent and inspiring, while on the other there remained the idea of a God who acts selectively in this world, endorsing some and condemning others – an omnipotent version of the capricious gods of Greece and Rome. These two different ideas of 'God' are incompatible; that is our problem. It is visible today in the contrast between the intellectual, liberal wings of all three major monotheistic religions and their radical and political counterparts.

In the early years of the Christian Church its ideas were confused, and have long since been set aside. In spite of the best efforts of Paul to write letters of advice and correction, or of the author of Luke-Acts to give coherence, the range of actual views and beliefs was astonishing. Some groups had not even heard of the 'Holy Spirit' and others were uncertain about whether Jewish food laws had to be obeyed. Quite apart from the outlandish apocryphal gospels, only two of the canonical gospels had any reference to Jesus' resurrection. Ask most Christians whether they believe that the world is literally going to come to an end, the dead raised up in judgement, or whether illness is caused by demon possession, and they will immediately start to explain that these things are images and symbols, but not to be taken literally. Most of those early ideas have quietly evaporated.

According to the Athanasian Creed, most believers today are in line for eternal punishment. The fact that this does not cause universal panic within the Church is due to the background assumptions of atheism – namely that human reason and the rational applications of the values we hold dear are the standard by which the doctrines of religion are judged. Extremism is rejected by a majority, even if justified by scriptures, because it goes against fundamental values that are shared across the divide between theism and atheism.

Hopefully, the positive effect of atheism on religious beliefs is to moderate them by common sense.

Chapter 6

Culture and Murderous Enthusiasm

Observe the forms and beauties of sensible things
and comprehend the Word of God in them.
John Scotus Eriugena

Kill them all; God will know his own.
Ascribed to the Pope's representative
before the massacre at Bezier in 1209

I was still at school when my parents took my brother and I on holiday to Tenby, on the coast of South Wales. They never resisted the opportunity for a boat trip, so we set out to spend a couple of hours on Caldey Island, less than a mile off shore. On the way over, we learned that the island was owned by the Trappist monks of Caldey Abbey.

That glimpse of monastic life astonished me: the simplicity, the sense of purpose, the discipline and devotion to spiritual values. The monks seemed to be living a life unlike any I had seen: authentic, almost graceful, a life nourished by centuries of tradition within the world of mediaeval Christianity.

Was it for me? Attending retreats with the Benedictines at Nashdom Abbey, I immersed myself in a routine that was both productive and sublime. It spoke of deep peacefulness and purpose, of an ordered life in contrast with routine human chaos. But this was the 1960s. Living in London, as the world seemed to be on the brink of social revolution, I was torn between monastic life and the heady days of radical theology. London won.

But there is no denying the cultural legacy of Mediaeval Christendom – Gothic cathedrals and churches throughout Europe; polyphony; art; illustrated manuscripts created with infinite patience and devotion. Its richness is astonishing.

Nourished by such spiritual energy and creativity, it seemed a world in which atheism would be impossible. Actually, it was a world controlled by the power of royal and religious authority, in which atheism was illegal. Alongside the sublime there was much crude superstition, exploitation of the gullible and extreme cruelty. My original view of the mediaeval life was about as realistic as that painted by the Pre-Raphaelites of the 19th century.

During the centuries leading up to the Reformation and the 17th century wars of religion, the idea of God had become entwined with the power of absolutely monarchies and the prestige of Popes, bishops and the monastic orders. But serious theology and philosophy were not entirely lost. It is tempting to think of Eastern Christianity as being the more theologically subtle, with the West dominated by the authority of Rome and Latin legalism, but that was far from the whole story. Here are two famous exceptions:

Boethius (480-524) was a Roman senator, philosopher and Christian. His *Consolations of Philosophy*, written while in prison awaiting execution on a charge of treason, became an influential work through the Early Middle Ages. Using dialogue form, it argued that, in spite of the inequalities and sufferings of this world, there is a higher power, the maker of everything, ruling according to reason and the highest good – *omnium summum bonorum*. He interpreted Christian teachings in the light of Greek thinking and did much to promote philosophy before it was banned in 529.

Another extraordinary exception is John Scotus Eriugena (c800-877), an Irish monk who explored both physics and metaphysics in this book *De Devisione Naturae*, and became head of the palace school in *Aachen*, then the capital of the Carolingian Empire. In all probability he did not have direct access to secular Greek philosophy, but was able to study it via the works of the Early Fathers and Augustine. Generally described as a neo-Platonist, he effectively extracted the philosophy of Plotinus from those early Christian writings, learning Greek in order to do so. He saw the structure of reality as parallel to that of the human mind, and as produced by the *logos* of God, established as a graded hierarchy. He considered God to be simple, unchanging and eternal, and therefore impossible to depict or describe, since he considered language to be limited to the things known through the senses. He would easily have dismissed any crude notions of God.

One of the astonishing things about a book entitled *The Supernatural*, by the Jesuit theologian J P Kenny, is its claim that, from the Early Fathers through to the period between the 10th and 14th centuries, the main concern of theology was not whether God existed (that was not a sensible question to ask) but about how people could become divine – how they could share in the life of God. Since the Early Fathers' idea of *theopoesis*, theology was not about the possible existence of God, but about how human life could be elevated above its material form.

That puts a fundamental question mark over much modern Philosophy of Religion. While, at a practical level, the church was politically and economically compromised, the best theology presented the idea that, through belonging to the Church, people could share in the life of God.

When the 'death of God' theologians of the 1960s, rejecting what they described as the 'traditional' image of God in favour of something more secular, they were actually doing no more than *returning* to a tradition that would have been familiar to the educated minority from the early centuries of Christianity through until the Middle Ages.

THE RETURN OF PHILOSOPHY

Once Emperor Theodosius banned secular philosophy, Plato and Aristotle vanished from the debate. However, their ideas had already been absorbed into the writings of Christian bishops, and were later preserved within Islamic culture, emerging again in the 13th century, when translations of Aristotle circulated in the newly established universities.

The Persian philosopher Avicenna, also known as Ibn Sina (980 – 1037), was an astonishing thinker, physician and polymath. He translated Aristotle into Arabic and was instrumental in re-introducing Greek thought in the West. His work spans poetry, philosophy and medicine, with a subtlety far beyond the rivalries that were dividing the Christian West at the time. He studied and expounded Aristotle, without being uncritical. That might sound obvious from an academic point of view, but in theological debates it was relatively rare. Avicenna saw philosophy as the discipline by which we may purge the mind of superstition and anthropomorphism with respect to God, with the aim of preventing idolatry.

In the battles between atheism and theism, subtlety and truth are early casualties. And that is as true today – including among philosophers who should know better – as it was when the early Christians were branded atheists for not sacrificing to the traditional gods of Empire. As we shall see later, an Enlightenment caricature that sets reason and science against obsolete religious superstition is not only wrong, but fails to do justice to the subtlety of many earlier arguments. Atheists have been as guilty as believers when it comes to historical distortion.

But returning to the revival of philosophy...

Archbishop Anselm of Canterbury, imported from Normandy by William the Conqueror in the 11th century, was totally unlike the caricature of mediaeval believers as unthinking and superstitious. He produced what came to be known as the Ontological Argument for the existence of God, an argument that haunts examination papers in the Philosophy of Religion to this day. But actually, far from being an argument for the existence of a supernatural god, it introduces a new level of subtlety into the idea of what the word 'God' might mean.

He starts with the idea that God is 'that than which no greater can be thought', and proceeds to argue that such a concept must refer to something that exists, for if it *didn't* exist, it would be possible to imagine something greater that *did*. The logic is sound, but irrelevant. What he has actually done is to shift the idea of God away from the realm of the supernatural to locate it as the ultimate of our thought or imagination. In effect he is suggesting that 'God' is the name we give to the ultimate in our intellectual quest or our sense of value.

So here we are back with the *logos* idea from the Ancient Greeks. We are not dealing with the various gods of culture, but with the intellectual quest for Plato's Form of the Good, or the Stoics principle of reason. We are also pitched into the human experience of transcendence: being in a state of awe, and sensing a wonder in the world beyond the mundane. God becomes part of the human intellectual and emotional quest for meaning and significance, not a supernatural entity that might or might not exist.

At that time, few would have had Anselm's level of sophistication and most would probably have been superstitious, credulous, and always looking for a magical way to improve their lot in life. But that does not entitle us to assume that his argument was aimed to catch people into being superstitious, as some modern cynics assume.

Even in the 11th and 12th centuries, with the disruption and brutality of the Norman takeover of England, there was a resurgence of culture, with the building of places of worship in parishes up and down the country. Amid superstition it was still possible for thinkers like Anselm to take a nuanced and intellectually sophisticated view of God.

Thomas Aquinas (1225 – 1274), discovering the newly available philosophy of the Greeks, sought to show that it was not only compatible with Christian thought but able to give it support. So, for example, he presented Aristotle's idea of an 'uncaused cause' as that 'which all understand to be God'. His five demonstrations – now wrongly regarded as 'proofs' – of God, tend to be seen as the bedrock for belief in God's existence, and have become a necessary part of the Philosophy of Religion. Yet their function is ambiguous.

The problem – here as with Anselm – may be summarised by the latter's phrase *credo ut intelligam*. Mistakenly taking *credo* to mean factual assent, this has sometimes been weaponised by secular thinkers to suggest that the arguments were never open-ended, but loaded in favour of God. Correctly interpreted, it means that these things can only be appreciated by those who give their heart and loyalty to them. In other words, they are *the intellectualisation of an experience*. But notice the historical context. It was a time when Christianity was mandatory and philosophy was only just becoming re-accepted as legitimate. Hence these 'proofs' are more a way of validating philosophy than religion; they show that Christian ideas were in line with the best of earlier Greek thinking, and that the faithful therefore have no need to fear secular reason.

NOT THE BEST PATRON

Aristotle was hardly the best person for medieval theology to pick as its patron thinker, because there remains a fundamental mismatch between his philosophy and early Christian thought. This boils down to two issues:

First of all, Aristotle is presenting a metaphysical postulate. In other words, having examined the nature of causality, he comes to the conclusion that the world requires there to be an 'uncaused cause'. However, to call this 'God', makes him a physical theory about the universe. A postulate is something required by, but not part of, what is being examined; so God cannot be active within the world and at the same time used as its possible explanation. This is indeed the 'God of the philosophers' but it is a million miles away from the image of God used in worship, or the personal agent of rewards or punishments seen in both the Jewish and Christian scriptures.

Secondly, Aristotle held that the world was eternal. This was at odds with the idea that the world was created at a moment in the past, and that it would one day come to a fiery end, with judgement for the living and the dead. Hence, there may or may not be an uncaused cause – that's a matter of logic – but either way, it is not what 'God' was assumed by most people to be about.

The background to the New Testament, with the end of the world expected soon, demonstrated vividly in the Book of Revelation, has more in common with a computer game than a philosophical postulate. Destruction of the earth, the rising of the dead from their graves, the heavenly descent of Christ as judge, the separating out of the blessed from the damned, and the eternal blessings or torments awaiting each is – whether on the walls of medieval churches or in the mouths of modern hellfire preachers – a world apart from the philosophy of Aristotle.

Both philosophy and computer game imagery are part of human culture, but they engage us in very different ways, one stimulates the cerebral analysis of experience, the other works on adrenalin, promoting a quest to succeed in a dangerous world. So while medieval prelates and scholars could contemplate metaphysical possibilities with all the subtlety of modern academics, most people experienced the terror and the damnation of the wicked under the hand of a god of wrath and judgement.

Images depicting the Biblical stories decorated church walls, with the creator God presented as an elderly man, 'Christ in glory' as a divine ruler, and the Spirit as a dove descending to indwell and inspire believers. The whole narrative from creation to the end of the world, with Christ as the bringer of salvation to a damned world, became the inspiration for artists and musicians – it was a rich narrative within which people could find their place. The wealthy patrons of the arts found themselves lurking with the shepherds in a nativity scene, now lifted from a historical Bethlehem stable and set in a fantasy world with contemporary architecture.

In the medieval West, the world of religious thought had become utterly schizophrenic. Its convulsions at the Reformation, and its transformation following the rise of science, were made almost inevitable by its own internal contradictions.

THE SWITCH THAT TURNED ATHEISM ON

As we shall see later, something was seriously wrong with the general conception of God that emerged in the 17th and 18th centuries, effectively setting a very negative agenda for the relationship of theology and philosophy. But the origins of that error lay back in the 14th century, in a disagreement between Aquinas and Duns Scotus (1265/6 – 1308).

Aquinas did not consider God to be 'within the order of existing things.' In other words, God should never be seen as something that exists in the same way that objects within the world exist. So, if we say 'God exists' we need to recognise that it is not a literal, objective statement, but only an analogy, since ordinary language cannot be applied to that which is eternal, infinite, or omnipresent. In *The Cambridge Companion to Atheism* (p41), Gavin Hyman explains this very clearly, and the implications are devastating for what passes today for belief in God:

> If both God and humanity shared the same quality of 'being,' then God and creatures would both be members of a common genus, which Aquinas explicitly rejects.

However, Duns Scotus argued that human reason *can* understand 'being' and apply it literally, both to creatures and to God. In other words, the claim that 'God exists' becomes the same as claiming that anything else exists.

Take a deep breath and consider the implication of this. In the 20th and 21st centuries people are still discussing whether or not there is evidence for the existence of God, but that question assumes that God's existence is like the existence of everything else – a matter of evidence. To ask 'Is there a God?' becomes the equivalent of 'Is there a unicorn?' Any evidence? No. Case dismissed! If it is claimed that God exists in a literal sense, the word 'God' is no longer a word used to describe reality itself, but the name of *part* of that reality, and clearly a very optional part.

In any debate about whether God exists or not, *both* sides implicitly support atheism; indeed, the very *context* of the debate is atheist! Once you change 'God', from being a word describing 'being-itself' to the name of *a* being whose existence can be debated, the theist case is already lost.

I'm not claiming that Duns Scotus pushed things that far, since he was, a Catholic priest and Franciscan friar, as well as a university professor. But, if there is one word (apparently coined by Duns Scotus himself) that sums up this debate it is the Latin word *haecceitas*, which is generally translated as 'thisness'. It is the quality of being a particular thing, not some general term. So, for example, 'person' would not have 'thisness' but 'Betty Smith' would. The question for the theist therefore changes: not 'Does God exist?' but 'Does "God" have 'thisness'? If you think he does, then Aquinas is going to dismiss your claim, on the grounds that God does not belong to the order of existing beings. If you think he does not, just shake hands with the atheist and agree to regard 'God' as an optional word for describing reality itself.

Nothing frustrates me more than listening to debates between a New Atheists and Christian fundamentalists and concluding that there has been almost no progress over the last 700 plus years. If anything, the best 13th century thinkers argued with greater clarity and precision!

For Duns Scotus, and later William of Ockham (1287-1347), you could not prove God's existence by means of reason alone. Like Immanuel Kant in the 18th century, they saw no means of bridging the divide between our experience of the natural world and reality itself. God, for them, was to be a matter of faith, not a rational hypothesis. But, by making God a specific thing with 'thisness', the supernatural collapsed into the natural, and it therefore became liable to be eroded by lack of evidence.

THE ENCHANTED AND BARBARIC WORLD

The mediaeval world was both enchanted and grossly superstitious. A largely illiterate population relied on church officials to interpret documents, and religious doctrines were mainly promoted by the design and decoration of churches. Images of angels, heaven and hell, vividly presented, may have intimidated the 'faithful', or may have been largely ignored by a population for whom obedience to authority was necessary for survival. We have no means of knowing.

But alongside that, you have mystics, producing ideas that were at odds with popular beliefs, and thinkers who are able to use the best of classical philosophy in the service of religious interpretation yet, for most people, ideas were controlled in a way that became impossible after the spread of literacy. It was certainly a world of miracles, saints and devils; one in which events were given spiritual interpretation. Yet it was also a world of sophisticated argument and subtlety of interpretation

It was a world in which meaning and significance were assumed for everything that happened, but yet remained hidden. Illness, flood, famine and good fortune were seen as caused by God or the devil. The idea that the world might be exclusively material, directionless and without inherent value had been considered in Ancient Greece, but not – so we are led to believe – by the mediaeval peasant. But we simply do not have sufficient evidence to make that claim. We see what happens, but we do not see the patterns of thought that lie behind it, except in the case of the small minority of academics and clerics.

If the king is anointed by God, any form of atheism becomes political rebellion, so atheist thoughts are best kept private. Creeds were a matter of loyalty: infidels, heretics and Jews were frequently expelled or punished. Eastern religions were largely unknown.

Alongside the sophistication of some pre-Reformation thinkers there was a whole other world of superstition, crudely magical beliefs, and also of the most terrible actions carried out in the name of religion. One only has to think of the burning of heretics, the suppression of whole religious cultures, or the Crusades, to recognise the damage that can be done in the name of religion.

In my view, the worst example and the most blatantly cynical occurred when the Catholic bishops sought to exterminate the Cathars of south-west France in the Albigensian Crusade of the 13th century. When the population of Béziers took shelter in the Cathedral in 1209, they were surrounded by Catholic troops. The papal legate, Arnaud Amalric, gave the order to massacre the heretics, but was asked how the soldiers were to distinguish heretics from Catholics. The legate's view was straightforward: "Kill them all, God will know his own." That is crude power, with hardly a veneer of religion. It would be nice to think that, with the passing of over 800 years such barbarity would no longer be possible. Sadly, however, that is a view that can only be maintained by being selectively blind to much of the history of the 20th and early 21st centuries. The killing of the innocent in the name of religious and cultural differences continues, to the despair of the liberal majority within each religion. When it comes to power politics, social manipulation, or the ability to whip up opposition to minority groups, we live in a world that is still remarkable like that of the Middle Ages.

Considering the legacy of religion in our secular age, we tend to be selective – wanting to retain the culture and the sense of wonder, but jettisoning the crude and the cruel. And that selection is not usually made on religious grounds but on secular ones. We have a notion of value that is independent of religion, and one shared by theists and atheists alike.

REFORMATION AND WAR

Beliefs can be undermined as much by the actions of those who hold them as by their logical incoherence. That has to be the case with the traumas following the Reformation, and particularly the 30 Years War, which brought inconclusive slaughter throughout Europe in the name of religion.

We should not simply dismiss this as political rather than religious, but take an honest look at what has happened in the name of religion. Religious ideas need to be considered in their historical context to see how important this debate is.

The Black Death may have carried off about a third of the population of Europe in the mid 14th century, but the wars of religion killed off a similar percentage three centuries later. Why is that relevant? Because if you believe that God exists, is engaged with human beings and is in charge of what happens, then you need to take note of what has actually happened. The problem of evil has long been presented as the most serious challenge to Christian faith. How is belief in a loving God compatible with acts of brutality carried out in the name of religion? The theist may argue that God is like a father, giving his children freedom in order that they may gradually learn from their mistakes and grow into good human beings. But at what point does the waywardness of children suggest bad parenting, or even an absence of parental control of any sort?

From 1618 until the Peace of Westphalia in 1648, Europe was torn apart by adversaries who defined themselves in terms of being Protestant or Catholic. Millions died, both directly as a result of the fighting, but also from the resulting famine and disease, most of them civilians.

Of course, it would be naïve to pin responsibility for the tragedy of those years exclusively on religion; it was indeed a political struggle, and atheist societies have been no less brutal. However, between religious and atheist societies there is a fundamental difference: atheist ones have no excuse for their atrocities, while religious ones may excuse themselves by claiming that they were obeying God's orders.

This leads to a further question. What kind of God becomes vulnerable to being used as an excuse for divisive behaviour? And here the finger points to henotheism, the commitment to a single god, whose loyalty is partisan. If God is seen as 'being itself' – whether in a mystical or in a philosophical sense – it is impossible to use him to justify partisan rivalry.

But we need to step back to consider the Reformation itself…

In *A Secular Age*, Charles Taylor sees the Reformation as the point at which the disenchantment of the world and the growth of secularization take root, at least in the European context. The reformers opposed spiritual hierarchy, made all believers equal, criticised the crudely superstitious use of sacraments, relics, and indulgences, and insisted that salvation came directly God on the basis of an individual's faith.

Prior to the Reformation, the world was seen as 'enchanted', in the sense that spiritual forces were thought of as operative, through gods, spirits, demons and so on. Following the Reformation, there was more emphasis on reason, and the interpretation of biblical texts. And alongside that, particularly within Calvinism, you have the attempt to give moral direction to the whole of society, to say how one should dress, and behave, and how one should be governed. Reason and a rational interpretation of scriptures, rather than the capricious benefits of particularly spiritual objects, places or forms of words, were to direct the path to salvation.

With the Reformation, there is a double shift. On the one hand, justification by faith – along with Calvin's doctrine of predestination – cut away the whole religious world of spirits and rituals; nothing that a person can do, in the sense of religious activity, can justify them, for that comes only through God's grace. Hence the trappings of religion slip away. Equally, if all are equal in the sight of God, then so is ordinary secular life. Through family life, rather than ascetic celibacy, and through ordinary work and business, rather than renunciation of worldly pursuits, people were able to see their own fulfillment as a blessing from God.

There is far more the explore here, but the key point for my argument is that a step is taken away from other-worldly religion, towards a appreciation of the meaning and significance of the secular world. That does not, in itself, promote atheism, but it integrates religious ideas into secular culture. The Reformers, of course, had life tightly defined in terms of the grace of God – but it was a God who was everywhere and worked through everything.

The problem with this shift to the secular was that ordinary events were then seen as in some way an indication of God's approval or disapproval. Hence, for example, business success and wealth could be taken as a sign of God's blessing – the Calvinist view of predestination seems to be a continuation of natural cause and effect into the spiritual realm. The danger was an increased emphasis on internalized religion and guilt, with natural events taken as a sign of punishment. 'What have I done to deserve this?' is a complaint that assumes natural events to be part of God's plan. God then becomes and optional and problematic way of interpreting events.

Broadly speaking, the European settlement was that each country should follow the religion of its ruler, and later in Britain the Act of Toleration, allowing all forms of religion to be practices alongside one another. Notice the dramatic change that has taken place here. The nature of religion, and the form that belief in God takes, are now to be determined either by political conformity or by the democratic right of individuals to choose what they will believe and how they will worship. God has become a feature of human society, not an absolute entity controlling the world. With the criticism of each side at the Reformation effectively cancelling each other out, it might have been hoped that people would therefore be free to believe, or not, as they saw fit. But – and it is a major 'but' – that did not preclude the persecution of those whose views differ from the political norm; both Catholics and Protestants had their martyrs.

As a result of the Reformation, the concept of God's activity was partly collapsed into the natural. Instead of considering the miraculous primarily as associated with saints and their relics, there was a new emphasis on God as being active and known through the natural world – a view that had always been there in theology, but less so in popular religion. This had the effect of giving spiritual approval to the rise of science, and explains why so many scientists of those centuries continued to hold religious beliefs, albeit in what they would have considered a more 'modern' form.

But there is something more. It was possible in the pre-Reformation era to think of the world as a mere prelude to heaven, and that has certainly continued to be a feature of theism in some quarters. But the Lutherans and Calvinists brought a new energy to the business of living here on earth. With an emphasis on being morally grounded and energetic in doing good and prospering in God's world, they introduced a spiritual atmosphere focused on the secular. I don't claim this as a prelude to atheist spirituality, but they had in common with it a sense of personal responsibility and practical engagement.

However, this new secular emphasis, along with the success of the scientific method, led some to see an effective expulsion of God from the natural order, and hence to a distortion of the best theological thinking of earlier centuries. This unfortunate shift in the idea of God made the rise of atheism inevitable.

This shift, with the adoption of a new 'hybrid' God, with practical atheism as its alternative, will be explored the next two chapters.

Chapter 7

Science and Enlightenment?

The greatest invention of the West was that of an immanent world in Nature, whose workings could be systematically understood and explained on its own terms, tearing open the question whether this whole order had a deeper significance, and whether, if it did, we should infer a transcendent Creator beyond it.

Charles Taylor, *A Secular Age*

…it must be the same to you, when you do perceive it, whether we say, God has wisely willed it so, or nature has wisely arranged it so.

Immanuel Kant, *The Critique of Pure Reason*

When in eighteenth century Europe religion began to be replaced by secular creeds, the Christian myth of redemption was not abandoned but renewed in another guise. A story of redemption through divine providence was replaced by one of progress through the collective efforts of humanity.

John Gray, *Seven Types of Atheism*

We now arrive at a pivotal moment in the story that leads to today's confused ideas about God and the possibility that atheism might be able to rescue the situation.

It is sometimes said that, with the rise of science in the 17th century and the European Enlightenment of the 18th, superstition gave way to rationalism. But that's only half true. In fact, during earlier centuries, accounts of miraculous happenings were examined critically and many of the most extreme – such as those in the apocryphal gospels – were rejected. Even in mediaeval times, claims about miracles were investigated properly rather than taken at face value. That was always the official approach of the Catholic Church, and it continues to this day. Common credulity and superstition, of course, are quite another matter.

In an era when divine agency was taken as a serious option, claims could be examined without assuming that any account lacking an obvious physical explanation should be regarded as bogus. By the 18th century, however, the parameters of acceptable explanation were shifting. With the rise of science the world was increasingly understood in terms of cause and effect and the laws of nature, such that God could effectively be discounted as the direct cause of particular events.

That shift seemed to have only three logical outcomes: either God could be identified with nature, or he could be an external designer, or atheism. When none of these seemed satisfactory to the religious, some opted for the worst of all possible outcomes and created a 'hybrid' God, with which the world has been saddled ever since – but more of that later.

In short, the Enlightenment may have sought to enlighten, but with respect to the idea of God it only served to confuse.

THE BACKGROUND IN REASON AND SCIENCE

There is no need to go through the amazing changes to our knowledge of the world brought about by the likes of Galileo (1564 – 1642), Francis Bacon (1561 – 1626) and particularly Isaac Newton (1642 – 1727), endorsed by the founding of the Royal Society in England and the Academie des Sciences in France in the 17th century and followed by the developments in technology during the 18th. For a basic introduction to the issues there is *Religion and Science* in the *Access for Students* series.

However, their implication was an increased confidence in the ability of humankind to understand and improve the world.

Science became almost a religious vocation. It did not replace existing beliefs – many of the leading scientists also professed belief in God – but it was undertaken with a sense of wonder and moral seriousness.

Isaac Newton saw the universe as pointing beyond itself to God as the cause of its regularity. Some might argue that his scientific rationalism was essentially religious. Others might argue that, in pointing to a god who was effectively beyond the universe, he distanced God from the immediate experience of reality, which had been the god of Eastern Orthodox spirituality, the apophatic way and the best of mediaeval theology. A god who exists 'out there' as a final cause or universal designer is hardly going to satisfy the religious believer as an object of devotion, but equally, a universe entirely understood in terms of empirical cause and effect can easily lead to an impoverished atheism that cannot address the full emotional and cultural experience of humankind.   Newton's approach might easily lead to a universe for nerds, with a god for fantasists tacked on!

Sadly, the rise of science in the first half of the 17th century took place against a backdrop of the wars of religion on continental Europe, and the challenge to the religious authority of monarchy in England, leading to the execution of Charles I, the establishment of the Commonwealth and the growing impact of Puritanism. Those tumultuous years re-framed the context in which people saw their relationship to God, as it emerged in the 18th century.

With the European Enlightenment, the supernaturalism of earlier centuries gave way to what became liberal humanism. The scientific examination of the world, based on reason and evidence, became a norm that appeared to exclude the supernatural, with atheism again a rational option.

This shift in thought was, of course, mainly limited to an intellectual minority, for although we may like to think of the

Enlightenment as a time when people gathered in coffee houses for serious debate, a large part of the population probably continued with beliefs that were not so different from those of earlier centuries.

The shift away from taking God into consideration in worldly matters can be illustrated from early in the 17th century in the views of the Dutch jurist Hugo Grotius. He argued that the principles of international law should be seen as valid *etsi Deus non daretur* – as though God did not exist. This did not suggest that Grotius was atheist, but that human reason and evidence should be sufficient to validate legal claims. The law did not require God in order to be valid and effective.

Just as an old-established political party can sometimes transform itself and become populist, so ideas of God that had been marinating in spiritual experience for centuries started to give way to images of the divine that caught the popular imagination. If the world was a finely-tuned mechanism, everything within it explicable in terms of Newton's laws of nature, many saw God's role (if any) to be that of an external creator and designer. This view, known as deism, became widespread, popular and hugely influential.

Much has been written about the place of reason in the European Enlightenment so they need not delay us. For our purpose, in order to see the balance of theism and atheism, we will look at just one idea each from three monumental figures of that time: Descartes, Hume and Kant.

But first, a word of warning...

FROM NOOSE TO GUILLOTINE

The Enlightenment is generally seen as a time of rising intellectual freedom. Exemplified by the appearance of pamphlets and coffee houses, people felt empowered to challenge, question and express their personal convictions. Hence the claim to be atheist, which existed from earliest

112

times, was less likely to result in persecution and death, although atheists were still in a minority and were distrusted on the grounds that – without some sort of belief in God – self-interest might be their only remaining value.

However, the danger of openly challenging orthodoxy remained. On the afternoon of January 8th 1697, Thomas Aikenhead, a 20-year-old Edinburgh student, was hanged for blasphemy, having questioned Christian doctrines, claiming that morality was created by people and their governments, rather than revealed in scripture, and that theology was 'a rapsodie of feigned and ill-invented nonsense'. To go public with such views was ill-advised, since they contravened the Blasphemy Acts of 1661 and 1695. It is therefore hardly surprising that, although some pamphlets warned of the growing number of atheists in England at that time, we have little written evidence of their views.

Sixty year later, in the same city, the Ecclesiastical Assembly tried to excommunicate the philosopher David Hume for claiming much the same thing, but the trial failed. Hume was a prominent writer, historian and philosopher. Along with Adam Smith, James Boswell and Francis Hutchinson, who held the chair of moral philosophy at the University of Glasgow, he was part of the vibrant Scottish Enlightenment. In the decades between Aikenhead's trial and Hume's, the world had changed, not just in terms of freedom of thought and speech, or the seriously secular attitude to life, but in the relative power of Church authority. By the late 18th century, serious questions in philosophy and theology could be debated without the fear of being condemned to death for doing so. Hume's commitment to empirical evidence challenged traditional religious ideas and led him to be described as an atheist. If so, atheism was starting to rescue the idea of God from the clutches of religious authority and open it up to intellectual scrutiny.

By the end of the 18th century, particularly in France, reason seemed to have prevailed over religion. But with the French Revolution, there came a concerted effort to destroy the Christian cultural legacy, carried out with a determination probably not seen since the destruction of the Classical Civilisation by Christians in the 4th century, or the expansion of Islam in the 7th. It presented an image of humankind striding forward, dominating the world by the application of reason, along with the destruction of religion's power base in the aristocracy and the church.

In 1793, an atheist Cult of Reason was set up to replace Christianity as a state religion of France, with Churches re-dedicated as temples to reason. 'To Philosophy' was inscribed over the cathedral doors at Notre Dame in Paris, now re-purposed as a shrine to the Goddess Reason. That cult was short lived, replaced by Robespierre the following year by the deist Cult of the Supreme Being (with both banned in 1802) but at the time it was seen as a great step forward. Today, the only notable legacy of the Cult of Reason is its motto: Liberty, Equality, Fraternity!

Reason and efficiency may replace superstition but do not guarantee freedom from cruelty. It seems illogical that a movement based on reason should be maintained by the terror of bloodshed, inflicted not only on the aristocracy but on many other sections of society. Its symbol became the guillotine, devised as a way to carry out executions quickly, efficiently and humanely, replacing hanging or crushing.

It presented terror with greater immediacy than the threat of punishment at the Last Judgment. The guillotine does not in itself count for or against belief in the existence of God, but it does sweep aside simplistic notions that religion lies at the root of all cruelty and bloodshed, with atheism inevitably promoting liberty, equality and fraternity. Secular and atheist regimes can arguably match religious ones for intolerance and cruelty.

But back to our three Enlightenment thinkers…

DESCARTES' DUBIOUS DILEMMA

Descartes was a good Catholic. Fearing that the Christian faith was vulnerable to fashionable scepticism, he sought to provide it with an indubitable foundation. Playing the devil's game, as he saw it, he doubted everything that it was possible to doubt. Experience, engagement, intuition, emotion; it could all be a dream, as could his physical body. His famous conclusion was that he could not doubt himself as a thinking being, for the very act of doubting involved thinking. Hence 'I think, therefore I am' – the famous declaration from which the world has suffered ever since.

He claimed to be questing for certainty in a world where scepticism was an easy option, but his conclusion was an almost complete capitulation to the very thing he feared. Only once certainty is reduced to his own act of thinking can he start again, building up a world on the basis of his trust that God would not actually deceive him. Thus the real world is dismissed and replaced by a world based on nothing but an act of (wishful) thinking.

In coming to that conclusion he divided the world between matter on one hand and thought on the other – a dualism that was exactly what the world did not need at a time of the rise of science. He re-introduced the radical dualism of Plato's Forms, but this time limited to the mind, set within an impersonal, physical universe.

Not only did this introduce a gulf between the physical and the mental, it also encouraged a diminished and naïve idea of God. Most educated people are not superstitious, they ask rational questions about the world around them, but accept that there are some things we don't understand. But their thinking, like their experience, comes *within* the physical world, not from a realm of pure thought. For a philosophy that engages with reality, Descartes should have argued for 'I am, therefore I think', but that's another story.

Having established his mind/matter dualism, Descartes had the problem of how mind might initiate actions, but thought he had solved it by positing a single point of interaction between them – the pineal gland, located within the brain. Eventually, of course, that particular gland was shown to be nothing of the sort, so the problem remained. If mind and matter are radically different, how do I act within a physical world? Equally, if God is not part of the physical world, how can he act within it? An argument that well illustrates both this problem and the impact on religious ideas of the rise of Newtonian science comes from David Hume.

HUME ON MIRACLES

Hume's argument is very straightforward: since the laws of nature are founded upon observed regularities, and since miracles are seen as the exception to what is normally expected, it is always going to be more likely that the account of a miracle is mistaken than that it has actually occurred. In other words, if you believe that every account of events should be justified by reason and evidence, then you will automatically reject as improbably any claims that are unique, unreasonable and miraculous.

Those opposing Hume generally avoid trying to counter his argument head on, simply because they too wish to place reason centre-stage. Instead they tend to re-define 'miracle' in various ways, allowing it to be compatible with happy coincidence, or rational explanation. Biblical miracles were to suffer from this attempt to wriggle away from Hume. Rather than have God open up the Red Sea to allow the Israelites to pass through on dry land while drowning the pursuing Egyptians, new explanations attempt to get round the miraculous nature of such good or bad fortune (depending on whether you are on the Israelite of Egyptian side). It's not the

Red Sea at all, but the 'Sea of Reeds' – marshy land across the light-footed could walk but sufficiently boggy to trap the chariots of the Egyptians. Or perhaps that it was indeed a strong wind that dried out the sea at that point, only unfortunately for the Egyptians it happened to stop blowing when they were about to cross. The former is simply a physical explanation, while the latter appears a fortuitous miracle of timing. Some argue that 'miracle' is an interpretation of an event, rather than an account of its relevant rarity.

But then you have the weird interpretation of the 'miracle' when a sole survivor of some disaster is pulled out alive, without seeing how the same 'miracle' would be viewed by the relatives of those who did not. And we are back to the ancient Greeks, with Diogenes commenting that there would be far more plaques around the temple of Poseidon if those who had drowned had also been able to place them.

The adoption of reason and evidence at the Enlightenment was not new at all; it simply reinstated arguments of the ancient rationalist and materialist philosophers. Atheism and common sense suggest that supernatural language should be modified or abandoned. Without detracting from wonder or moral significance, it would prevent its trivialisation.

KANT'S ATTEMPT TO SORT IT OUT

Immanuel Kant is a pivotal figure for the philosophy of the 18th and 19th centuries and is generally regarded as the archetypal Enlightenment thinker.

In the preface to the second edition of his *Critique of Pure Reason*, published in 1787, Kant takes a hard swipe at metaphysics which he mocks it as 'a completely isolated and speculative science of reason' which so fails to make progress that 'it has rather become an arena, specifically destined, it would seem, for those who wish to exercise themselves in mock fights', where the method used is no more than 'groping among mere concepts' (translation by Max Muller, p xxxii).

He goes on to make the much-misunderstood claim that what he is doing is clearing away reason to make way for faith. That is only partly true. What he is actually claiming is that speculative metaphysics, such as the arguments for or against the existence of God, cannot work because they attempt to get beyond reason's grasp of our experienced world to something that exists in itself, beyond experience. It simply can't be done, he thinks, because all our practical thinking is based on sorting out our experience. Speculative reason, he suggests, offers 'groundless groping' and 'uncritical vagaries'. He is determined to deprive metaphysics of its 'pernicious influence.'

He then makes the most obvious of claims that really should have silenced most of the subsequent debate between theists and atheists. Who loses if we get rid of speculative metaphysics? Not humanity, he argues, but only the 'schools' (of philosophy). The ideas of the immortality of the soul, human freedom and the existence of God, put forward as philosophical ideas, had never penetrated the public mind or had the slightest influence of people's convictions. What is it, he asks, that leads people to believe that the world has a great and wise author? A sense of the wonderful ordering of things is all that is needed for the practical reason and morality. Speculating and arguing about it achieves nothing.

Kant therefore sees the idea of the immortality of the soul, human freedom and God as postulates of the Pure Practical Reason. People use them as ideas to give their lives direction and purpose. Although about to crush the traditional arguments for the existence of God, he does not deny that the idea of 'God' may be useful, because people have always sought an *ens realissimum*, a sense of that which is most fundamental and real.

118

So how might we apply Kant's approach to our present question about the relationship between atheism and God? Clearly, in an intellectual discussion, one person might end up claiming to be a theist and another an atheist, but that, from Kant's point of view, is irrelevant to ordinary life. Within culture, the idea of God acts as an inspiration, giving a sense of wonder and purpose. Does this gothic nave inspire? Fine. Does this music give you a tingle of wonder? No problem. Does this act of kindness strike you as fundamentally right, or that cruelty fundamentally wrong? Fine; they are your intuitions of what is real. Do you want to give the name 'God' to the source of those intuitions? No problem, 'God' becomes, for you, a postulate (or presupposition) of your pure practical reason - a feature of how you see the world.

On the other hand, if you see the attempt to argue for the existence of God beyond human experience, or to pontificate on what he or she demands, as fatuous nonsense, you can indeed take an atheist position in such arguments. But that does not preclude you from enjoying a deep sense of what the word 'God' has pointed to in human culture. You are not cheating if, as an atheist, you enjoy visiting cathedrals, or standing in silence before the sublime calmness of a Buddha image. These things touch reality, and you do not add anything to that reality by adding the term 'God' – unless, of course, you find it helpful. And whether you do so or not may say more about your background, upbringing and experience of religion, than about your intellectual conviction.

At the very time when the rise of science was pushing the idea of God out of the experienced mechanistic world, leading some to speculate about the existence of an external 'deity', Kant puts his finger on the simple fact that we cannot reason and argue about reality itself, only about our experience. The metaphysical nonsense that motivates fundamentalist believers and militant atheists, is a form of intellectual sport that has no relevance to real life.

Kant is notoriously difficult to digest, because his language can be dense and his arguments protracted, but he clearly had a wicked sense of humour and certainly did not suffer fools gladly. Famous for the regularity of his working life, we are also told that Kant was good company and fond of social gatherings. Re-reading the preface to his second edition of the *Critique of Pure Reason*, I can fully believe it. His incisive arguments happily swipe away pretension and nonsense. I imagine he would have been happy to raise a glass or two in celebration of having done so.

At the opening of 'The Elements of Transcendentalism' in his *Critique of Pure Reason*, his theory of knowledge is set out with absolute clarity:

> Whatever the process and the means may be by which knowledge reaches its objects, there is one that reaches them directly, and forms the ultimate material of all thought, viz intuition (*Anscauung*). (p21, translation: Muller)

In other words, through what he calls 'sensibility', our minds are able to receive intuitions from our direct contact with reality.

This has immediate implications for what we may call God. Intuition is about a direct relationship, an engagement. It is not something about which we may have a debate, or subject to rational analysis. It is about a reality that lies behind our concepts, and which theologians have suggested can only be described using symbols. It is also the reality that the Eastern churches were reluctant to describe literally. If 'God' refers to a fundamental intuition, it is quite different from the use of 'God' to describe a dubious supernatural entity. You do not have to 'believe' an intuition, you simply allow it to emerge from within your experience. Atheists also have intuitions without the need to frame them in terms of 'God'.

Here's Kant on ideas and ideals (p386):

These ideals, though they cannot claim objective reality (existence), are not therefore to be considered as mere chimeras, but supply reason with an indispensable standard, because it requires the concept of that which is perfect of its kind, in order to estimate and measure by it the degree and the number of the defects in the imperfect.

In other words, the ideas do not exist as entities, but are necessary to provide a standard by which we judge and understand the limited features of our world. Take away any sense of the ideal and we will be at a loss.

Here is another crucial feature of the balance between atheism and God. The complaint that atheism leads to nihilism assumes that God needs to exist as an entity in order to provide the guidelines that people seek. But exactly the opposite is the case – it is because ideals *cannot* claim objective reality that they can become the measure of objects. 'God' only works as a productive idea if he does not exist in any conventional sense.

Here, we return to Thomas Aquinas in the 13th century. He too argued that God could not be 'of the order of existing beings', and that is exactly the point Kant is making. Having shown the logical impossibility of the traditional arguments for God, he can now show the importance of God as a regulative concept. In effect, God becomes a feature of looking, rather than something at which one looks.

Hence Kant is able to say that the idea of a highest Being, original Being, or the 'Being of all beings' nevertheless 'leaves us in perfect ignorance as to the existence of a being of such superlative excellence.' (p391)

Here atheism provides a necessary counterbalance to any tendency within theism to make the mistake of thinking of God as a separate entity. Even if there were such an entity, we could know absolutely nothing about him.

Once again, we have a moment within the history of ideas, where a major thinker comes down to the same fundamental position: if the idea of 'God' is going to work for us, then God cannot exist in any normal sense of that word.

At the end of a very long and carefully explained argument, Kant sets out what can or cannot be claimed about the existence of a Supreme Being. Having admitted that the sense of natural wonder and purpose, and the way in which nature contrives ends and means, suggests to some that there exists a Supreme Being as its creator, he comes back with the established limitations of philosophy and argues that:

> …it must be the same to you, when you do perceive it, whether we say, God has wisely willed it so, or nature has wisely arranged it so. (p454)

This is exactly the sort of argument used in modern debates between theists and new atheists. Both sides acknowledge the wonder of the world, but one side uses it to argue for God, while the other simply stays with the experience itself.

Kant's regulative principles are valuable in themselves but…

> … if they are misunderstood and mistaken for constitutive principles of transcendent knowledge, they produce, by a brilliant but deceptive illusion, some kind of persuasion and imaginary knowledge, but, at the same time, constant contradictions and disputes. (p456)

> We knew beforehand with perfect certainty that all these pretensions, though perhaps honestly meant, were absolutely untenable, because they relate to a kind of knowledge to which man can never attain. (p456)

Here then, is one reason why the dispute about whether or not God exists has continued down into the 21st century. Mistaking a valuable *regulative* concept (we see nature as exhibiting creative design) for a *constitutive* one (there exists, beyond the empirical world, a creator and designer) ventures beyond the realm of possible human knowledge.

THE CULTURE OF PROGRESSIVE IDEAS

In looking at the world of Ancient Greece, we followed Karen Armstrong and others in making the distinction between *mythos* and *logos*, the cultural and the philosophical. We can make a similar distinction in the 18th century between the new world of science and reason and the cultural continuity in religion, literature art and music. A progressive intellectual of the time would still enjoy music and literature. Literacy was increasing and the 17th and 18th centuries saw the rise of the novel. In houses and gardens, the classical and rectangular expressing a sense of order and purpose, and in music we have the exquisite regularity and phraseology of Mozart. The 18th century was a time of elegance and style, for those who could afford it. Science and technology may have been transforming the world, but culture was also thriving.

John Locke saw society as the free association of individuals, and Kant argued that all individuals should be treated as free and autonomous, a sentiment that reinforced the Protestant conviction that individuals had the right and responsibility to interpret the scriptures for themselves, rather than accept the authority of religious leaders.

Some took a wry view of religion, summed up by the cynical comment for Edward Gibbon, in his *The History of the Decline and Fall of the Roman Empire* about Roman religion:

> The various modes of worship, which prevailed in the Roman world, were all considered by the people, as equally true; by the philosophers, as equally false; and by the magistrates, as equally useful.

Gibbon's assumption is that, even in the ancient world of Rome, intellectuals didn't believe in the gods of popular religion, but were prudent enough to comply with it, hoping that the common people would be kept in their place and perhaps even civilised by it. Its first volume being published in 1776, it also reflected the assumption of his time that intellectual questioning of religion was fine, but not something to be shared with the servants.

By the end of the 18th century in Europe, leaving behind the rich superstition of the medieval world, religion had been simplified down to a set of very general propositions about God, propositions that might be intellectually dubious but could give comfort and even hope to the common people.

As the philosophical world turned its attention to questions of *how* we know, rather than *what* we know, John Locke – committed to evidence-based knowledge – believed that the human mind starts as a blank sheet (a *tabula rasa*) upon which experience can write. The world lies open to reason and experience, while God becomes a background concept, a guarantor of morality and source of ultimate value.

Gone, in this new, enlightened perspective, is the supernatural world of miracles, divine interventions, superstitious practices, the expectation of the irrational and the miraculous. The world has become secular; if God has any role to play, it is as part of our understanding of that world, a (perhaps) necessary part of the human mental apparatus, a guarantor of our highest aspirations or moral intuitions. Locke only feared that atheists could not be trusted to keep their word because they appeared to lacked a sense of ultimate authority.

During this time, there arose a new idea of God – Deism – that became hugely popular both in Europe and in the American colonies. Intellectually satisfying for those with a mechanistic view of the world, it lacked the emotional and personal dimension of theism. However, rather than acknowledging those limitations, it became fashionable to accept the deist god, but to project onto him a rich confection of emotions and personal qualities, giving rise to a 'hybrid' form of God, with which the world has remained cursed.

Chapter 8

The Birth of a Hybrid God

*The God of Christians is not a God who is merely the author
of mathematical truths and the order of the elements: that is the
point of view of heathens and Epicureans.*

Pensées, Pascal

*There's a friend for little children
Above the bright blue sky*

Albert Midlane, hymnwriter

The God that most people claim to believe in today was born towards the end of the 18th century – a hybrid of deism and theism, supplemented by a whiff of nostalgia and much wishful thinking. Although the worst of all possible options, it took root in the popular imagination and somehow survived.

The hybrid was an attempt to retain the idea of a personal God, while holding to the new parameters of science. It has dominated Philosophy of Religion ever since, and is probably responsible for the rise of both atheism and indifference towards religious beliefs.

DEISM AS THE POPULAR OPTION

Deism is the belief that there is a Supreme Being, the creator and designer of the world. In its purest form, it is based on reason alone, and tends to reject the supernatural, revelation and the authority of scripture. It argues – in what is known as the 'design' argument – that a rational understanding and appreciation of the world, with its complexity and appearance of intentional design, leads to the idea of God.

Probably the best-known deist was John Toland (1670 – 1722), who wrote *Christianity Not Mysterious* (1696). Brought up an Irish Catholic, Toland argued for rationalism and the idea of God as designer. However, his religion was shorn of the supernatural and was regarded as incompatible with biblical revelation and traditional beliefs. A year after its publication the book was banned and publicly burned.

Another deist, Matthew Tindal, argued – as the title of his book *Christianity as Old as the Creation* (1730) suggests – that a rational view of creation is basic to and supportive of Christianity. This, of course, glosses over the whole history and development of that religion, but finds its 20th century equivalent in the assumption that creation as described in Genesis is to be upheld at all costs in the face of scientific evidence for evolution.

Thomas Paine (1737-1809) was an English-born political thinker who first emigrated to America and inspired independence from Britain and then become involved with the French revolution. Back in England, but finding that his political ideas put him in danger, he fled to France and wrote *The Age of Reason* (1793), arguing for freedom of thought and against institutional religion. Also in America, both Benjamin Franklin and Thomas Jefferson were deists (although Franklin called himself a Unitarian) and the constitution of the United States gave freedom of worship, while insisting that the political establishment was not based on Christianity. Jefferson, although separating church and state, was nevertheless of the opinion that religious people made the best citizens.

In France, Voltaire, Robespierre and Rousseau were deist, and the Cult of the Supreme Being became the state religion of

France for three months, seen as more moderate than the atheist Cult of Reason that had been established the previous year. Anticipating the 19th century views of Feuerbach, d'Holbach (1732 – 89) argued that religion arose either from fear and superstition, as a projection, or as a way to fill the gaps in our knowledge.

A major feature of the appeal of deism was that it continued the sense that the world had a purposeful creator, but at the same time it removed God from the particular actions in human history – understandable, perhaps, following the Reformation chaos and the wars of religion.

Traditional ideas of God did not sit well alongside the overall *culture* of the 18th century. The prevailing sense of human achievement went against the idea of humankind as fundamentally fallen and in need of redemption. The idea of the future coming of Christ as sweeping aside the wickedness of the world and establishing the Kingdom of God, did not fit with the idea of moral progress and, thanks to Newtonian physics, the world that appeared rational, purposeful and well-designed. Hence, the traditional God became a casualty of the European Enlightenment.

However, it was always clear that the deist approach did not match up well with the more personal elements of religion. Although considered a deist, Voltaire (1694-1778) spotted the mismatch immediately, contrasting 'the God of the philosophers' with 'the God of Abraham, Isaac and Jacob'.

Pure deism itself was not enough for most Christians. Among Protestants, Bible-based religion supplemented deism's general claims about God as creator by using the scriptures as a handbook for all practical decisions and as a means of interpreting God's doings in the world. In the 17th and 18th centuries, the struggle to discern 'God's will', a key feature of spirituality, was heavily reliant on the scriptures. Deism was also challenged by the rise of Pietism and Methodism, which emphasized the need for a personal relationship with God.

Apart from anything else, deism ignored the second and third persons of the Triune God of Christianity. Deists would only accept 'revealed' truths if they could also be validated by reason, and therefore accepted God the Father as creator on the basis of a rational view of the world as a product of design. Their rejection of the Trinity led to the establishment of the Unitarian Church, which continues to welcome and accommodate those whose views are agnostic. But it struck a deep chord with the times, and the influential philosopher John Locke, who contributed both to the theory of knowledge and political philosophy, rejected the supernatural, arguing that everything should be based on reason and experience.

Although deism became less fashionable by the 19th century, a shadow of deism continues into the present. Considering the range of views outlined in the Introduction, a significant number of people today say that they believe there is some kind of God or spiritual power, although not as in the Bible or conventional religious teachings. Thus it lurks in the 21st century among those who 'sort of' believe but do not practice one of the major religions.

Religion needs personal engagement, not abstract arguments, and deism was always in danger of becoming a dead end unless it could find some way of enriching its basic tenets without resorting to the superstitions from which it claimed to free the world. The deist God is a possibility, not an experienced reality, and is located behind – rather than within – our encounter with life. But somehow it has managed to wriggle its way into academic discussions of the Philosophy of Religion, and has often blocked a more radical and nuanced approach to understanding ultimate reality.

The religious inadequacy of its beliefs is endorsed from a most unlikely quarter – the 17th century Catholic, scientist, mathematician and philosopher, Blaise Pascal, who wrote:

> The God of Christians is not a God who is merely the author of mathematical truths and the order of the elements: that is the point of view of heathens and Epicureans.   *Pensées* (translated Turnell, 1962)

He considered deism to be as far removed from Christianity as atheism:

> they assume that [the Christian religion] consists simply in the worship of a God who is considered great and powerful and eternal; this properly speaking is deism, which is almost as far removed from the Christian religion as atheism, which is the exact opposite of it.

This – almost unbelievably – from the author of the infamous wager! But it makes sense, coming from Pascal, because the deist god was not one to reward or punish, which is the assumption of his wager, but is a feature of secular philosophy, closer to philosophical atheism than engaged religion.

So, following Pascal's logic, what has continued into the 21st century as an argument between believers and atheists, is actually utterly irrelevant, because neither touches on what religion is about. For spirituality, the deist option is far more problematic than the atheist.

The survival of deism into the present has been possible because it morphed from its pure form into a 'hybrid', combining its naïve concept of God with sufficient emotional and personal elements to enable it to function. Even if emotionally satisfying, this hybrid disaster is not intellectually defensible and has come to confuse the debates between theists and atheists.

THE PROBLEMS WITH A HYBRID GOD

If deism was off the scale, the hybrid god was just close enough to the genuine article to corner the market in cheap alternatives to serious metaphysical thought.

The god whose existence is still debated in on-line discussions, and which inspired 'death of God' thinking from Nietzsche onwards, was not theism at all, but this hybrid god – born during the 18th century, almost killed off in the 19th and 20th, dead but still staggering forward in the early 21st and just possibly gaining traction among the young today.

So what is this 'hybrid' god? Basically, it is deism with a personal face and emotions attached.

The problem, which developed over the earlier centuries but came to a head from the 17th century with the rise of modern science and the Enlightenment, was to reconcile two very different uses for the word 'God':

a) 'God' was described as infinite, omnipotent and omnipresent, a word standing for Being Itself rather than an individual being. Such a God does not exist, in the ordinary meaning of that word. It may be that 'within which we live, move and have our being' (to use St Paul's words), but it is not a 'thing' whether natural or supernatural. It is the ultimate philosophical abstraction, the mystery in life that our mind cannot fully understand, but which we may appreciate intuitively.

b) 'God' was also described as personal, loving, having a will, able to intervene in the world to perform miracles, or answer prayers. That god was part of the ancient literary world of 'mythos' and was celebrated in ritual. Without that personal aspect, religion appeared to be reduced to philosophy.

The problem is that these two very different ideas of God do not mix well. If kept separate, as with the *mythos* and *logos* distinction of ancient Greece, they each function well enough

– with conventional religion becoming an expression of social commitment and personal growth, while philosophy explores what can and cannot be said about Being Itself. However, forcing them together into a single concept, creates a mass of internal contradictions, encouraging some people who value the cultural and spiritual contribution of religion to identify as humanists, agnostics or atheists, rather than compromise their integrity.

There are three particular problems with the hybrid God:

The first is language. Literature and popular devotion requires that words mean something, but literal language cannot apply to an infinite God, so you have to explore analogy (where you only know one of the things to be compared, since you do not have direct knowledge of God) and symbolism. Language is stretched to breaking point if God is said to be infinite and omnipotent, but also personal and engaged.

The second is miracles. If God is infinite, he does *everything* and is in every situation, good or bad, but such a God cannot logically intervene by producing miracles for those who ask nicely. The various attempts to wriggle out of the problem of miracles only shows the fundamental problem that the literal hybrid view of God has caused.

The third, and most significant, is the problem of evil and suffering. Any attempt to suggest that God is all-loving, as well as all-powerful, leads some to suggest that God has some hidden purpose in allowing suffering and evil. That is, at best, the sort of language that might be applied to the ancient gods of Greece and Rome, now long appreciated as myths rather than literal descriptions of the world we live in. At worst, it seems to suggest a God who is partisan or vindictive.

I want to look at the challenge of dealing with this hybrid from both a personal and an intellectual standpoint, so I'll start with a personal anecdote…

CANCER AND THE GOD OF LOVE

Many years ago I worked for some years as chaplain in a hospital specializing in the treatment of cancer. What took place on a daily basis there was inspiring: the devotion and kindness of the medical and nursing professionals, the support given by friends and relatives, the positive appreciation shown by so many patients. It was a place of joy and of tears, of struggle and of love.

At the end of my time there, I wrote a book entitled *Cancer and the God of Love*. Its title deliberately followed John Hick's famous *Evil and the God of Love*, with which I took issue. Hick had outlined arguments to justify God in the face of evil – for example, that he might use it for some higher purpose. His outline of the thought of Saints Augustine and Irenaeus failed to convince me, not because they were illogical, but because they did not address what was actually happening all around me in that hospital. I was convinced that whatever 'God' meant, it was about the reality of life and the love that was being shared. It was nothing to do with an external deity.

Here is part of my conclusion to that book:

> The Christian faith proclaims that the ultimate truth about human life is shown in humility, love and service and comes to the fore *within* human fragility and suffering, and not in spite of it. We may therefore expect to see symbols of transcendent love in a situation of suffering, rather than one of superficial success.

> In the case history of a person suffering from cancer there will be many important things that never show up in the medical notes. These are the moments of human insight and truth, pointing to what life is really about. They are moments that proclaim that the most real thing is not suffering and disease, but *the person who is going through them*. Our concern for the cure of disease is at all points secondary to our concern for the person who is sick; and if

it is *not*, then we are not practising medicine, but only playing with medical possibilities.

The symbols of transcendence that appear within our situation may be resymbolized in terms of God. 'God' will be the name we give to the ultimate truths and depths of life that are revealed. It is an optional resymbolization, but a valuable one.... *To believe in a God of love is to declare that love is at the heart of true human living, and should be the ultimate motivation for all human activity.*

Anyone who gives himself to the task of helping others, reveals his valuation of human life. It may never be resymbolized in terms of God, but is no less real for that.

In that hospital, few seemed to want to speak of God, let alone discuss the problem of evil. Any discussion of the difference between theism and atheism was utterly irrelevant. What counted was the ultimate reality of that place, and the values that made life worthwhile, however fragile.

The omnipotent, omniscient but personal hybrid God, with his secret intentions behind all that happened, evaporated for me on the wards of that hospital. I became convinced, not just that no such god existed, but that the very idea was an obstacle to dealing with life.

Religious stories deal with hopes, fears and the struggles of fragile human beings to make sense of life. They are richly symbolic, exploring life in a way that is both thought-provoking and emotionally satisfying. They may also find expression in rituals and ceremonies that give a sense of purpose to life. But they should not be taken literally and they were never intended to be. There is also the philosophical quest to understand 'Being Itself' the reality within which we find ourselves. Both are important aspects of human life and experience, neither should be denied, but neither is properly compatible with the 'hybrid' God.

A WAY OUT OF THIS MESS?

On an intellectual front, the problem of the hybrid god is still with us. Take the following comments by Richard Swinburne, Emeritus Professor of Philosophy at the University of Oxford in *Faith and Reason*. He claims that religious beliefs are beliefs about

> ... transcendent reality, including beliefs about whether or not there is a God or an after-life, beliefs about what properties God has (what God is like), and what actions He has performed

and that we want

> ... to have beliefs on these matters as probably true as we can get

Swinburne argues that

> ... there is no point in worshipping a non-existent creator, or asking him to do something on earth, or take us to heaven if he does not exist; or trying to live our lives in accord with his will if he has no will. (*op cit* p83)

Pause for a moment and consider what lies behind this assertion. If, as has been believed by centuries of religious thinkers, 'God' refers to being-itself, the reality within which we all live, then any reference to a creator who might or might not exist is, at best, an example of the Arian heresy, and at worst self-contradictory nonsense.

John Hick, in commenting on Swinburne's approach, says 'My point here is that, for me, it is not a *truth* but a *reality* that is eternal and ultimate.'

And there, in a nutshell is the problem with the hybrid God: it is based on a proposition, something that might or might not be true, something that might or might not exist. But – as we have seen from Plato, through the early centuries of the Christian church to modern theologians such as Paul Tillich – that is a very particular and inadequate use of the word 'God'. It claims to name 'a reality' of which Swinburne can then go on to discuss its possible existence. And that, of course, is to totally miss the point of that word.

To claim that 'God exists' is a form of atheism. It is the claim that some individual thing – distinct from the reality within which we all live – is ultimate and absolute. It is why the ideas of Arius were rejected by a majority of the Christian bishops in the 4th century. The old name for it was idolatry – treating some idol, physical or mental, as though it were reality itself.

Why is this dangerous? Because in the name of such idols people have persecuted one another. A wrong description has led to death by being burnt alive. It has generated crusades and divisions. To explore an us/them division – between 'believers' and 'non-believers', theists and atheists – is to utterly miss the point of what lay behind the idea of God.

It also drives a wedge between those who see a sense of wonder in the way complex life has evolved, and those who insist that life cannot evolve by itself but needs some external creator. From the ancient Greeks to the best theologians of the Christian era, the idea of an external creator has been a distraction from a full appreciation of the wonder of being, a wonder that can be shared by everyone, whether of not they practice a religion.

To escape religious fantasies and focus on reality, the hybrid god needs to be set aside, but if you want to know what many Christian people believe just listen to a few hymns…

THE GOD OF HYMNS?

While revising this chapter, I went to the Service of the Passion at King's College London. In the semi-darkness of its Victorian chapel, lit by rows of candles in the windows and along the choir stalls, the story of the final days of Jesus' life was told through readings, beautiful pieces of choral music by the likes of Orlando de Lassus and William Byrd, and hymns.

Having read the book thus far, you might assume that I'd be the last person to appreciate such an event, but no. It is profoundly moving to enter into the events of Passiontide, not just because it deals with the sufferings of Jesus, but because it becomes emblematic of the innocent in every age caught up in political and religious oppression. But what attracted my attention most were the hymns…

There were three. The first was 'My song is love unknown' to words by Samuel Crossman (1642 – 83), the second, 'O sacred head, sore wounded' by Paul Gerhardt (1607 – 69) and the third, 'When I survey the wondrous Cross' by Isaac Watts (1674 – 1748). All are hugely popular Passiontide hymns, intense and emotionally engaging. They focus on undeserved, deliberately inflicted suffering, love and a personal response such that, in the words of Isaac Watts, 'My richest gain I count but loss, / And pour contempt on all my pride.' But notice, if you are familiar with those hymns, that the word 'God' hardly gets a mention – none in Crossman or Gerhardt's hymns, and only a single reference to Christ as 'my God' in Watts' (which itself suggests that the location of 'God' is in Christ, not in some metaphysical postulate). The whole focus of the hymns is on our response to innocent suffering. They probe life at its most harrowing, and the issues they address are as relevant to an atheist as to a theist.

Notice, however, the dates of their authors. They come from the period of the rise of science and the early development of Enlightenment philosophy, yet they express a religious devotion that is utterly alien to the intellectual world of Hume and Kant. They avoid the hybrid god by ignoring metaphysics, and heading straight for real-life experience.

Hymns – like the chorales in the Bach Passions – express personal responses to what is being presented, and this can provoke all sorts of reactions: the blood is stirred with 'Onward Christian soldiers, marching as to war', or determination strengthened by 'A safe stronghold our God is still, a trusty shield and weapon' or, as the Titanic goes down, the resignation to fate in 'nearer my God to Thee'.

The best – like the three at the Passiontide service at Kings – manage to avoid the hybrid of popular belief. Others mix emotionally engaging ideas with concepts of God that are, at best, Arian and at worst idolatrous. However beautiful the melody by Orlando Gibbons, to which it is normally set, there's no escaping the hybrid in J. W. Chadwick (1840 - 1904) 'Eternal ruler of the ceaseless round / Of circling planets singing on their way', although – to be fair to Chadwick – he does get a Trinitarian balance before succumbing to the questionable 'to follow truth, and thus to follow thee.' The worst of all examples, in my view, is given in the terrible lines 'There's a friend for little children / Above the bright blue sky', with which no friend on earth can compare, according to A. Midlane (1825 - 1909). Here, God and heaven are located elsewhere, above that bright blue sky, giving supposed compensation for the high infant mortality rate in Victorian England. That is the hybrid god at its most destructive, even as it attempts to offer comfort; it is remote, dubious, and clearly a projection of human wishes.

Some hymns to the hybrid god have an on-going appeal. Take the ever-popular 'All things bright and beautiful', written by Cecil Frances Alexander (1818 - 1895) in 1848, published just eleven years before Darwin's Origin of Species. It celebrates nature, from 'each little flower that opens' to 'the ripe fruits in the garden' in true Panglossian style. Everything is provided by a loving creator, for which people are bidden to give thanks. Even social divisions are ordered by god, since…

The rich man in his castle,
The poor man at his gate,
God made them, high or lowly,
And ordered their estate.

Gone is the New Testament reference to poor Lazarus begging at the gate of the rich man, where post-mortem the roles are reversed and the injustice of the situation is revealed. For a hybrid deity that makes all things 'bright and beautiful' the moral dimension of the original Christian message is swamped by a happy deist gloss. As with the equally popular harvest hymn 'We plough the fields and scatter' by Matthias Claudius (1740 - 1815), everything is providentially organised, the weather is always good and harvests fruitful. Unlike the earlier Christian tradition, where suffering and inequality were addressed, the deist hybrid simply provides a personal and loving face for a selective interpretation of a universe provided for the sake of humankind. That's pure deism.

Why have I chosen to use hymns to illustrate the hybrid god? Simply because, for many believers, this is the image of God they ingest from childhood. Shorn of the gritty reality of the teachings of Jesus, or the intensity of reflections at Passiontide, it presents a deity that is equally simplistic and incredible. It has provided a suitable target for atheism and skepticism during the last two hundred years, and is the god from which 'God' needs to be rescued.

Chapter 9

Romance, Reason
and the Killing of God

I had no need for that hypothesis.
Pierre-Simon Laplace

...And I have felt
A presence that disturbs me with the joy
Of elevated thoughts: a sense sublime
Of something far more deeply interfused,

William Wordsworth

If only I had the courage to think all that I know.

Nietzsche

There's nothing like a whiff of romance to set an agenda, but it can take many forms. In 1791, Constantin Francois Chasseboeuf de La Giraudais (later known as the Comte de Volney) published *Ruins: Meditations on the Revolutions of Empires*. He claimed that, during his travels in the Near East in 1784, he fell asleep in the ruins of Palmyra and received a revelation from a genie! His reason was inspired by the exotic. But, whatever the source of inspiration, he set about giving a radical critique of the politics and religion of his day. He viewed all religions as being the product of their particular time and place, and sought to find the core principles that might unite them. His fundamental question amounted to this: Given the diversity of beliefs, what is there that anyone could believe? Predictably, of course, given that this is the end of the 18th century, he comes down in favour of deism – belief requiring no supernatural trappings.

But deism was not to remain the only fashionable option for, in the 19th century, its reasoned arguments were to become enriched by intuition, the romantic movement, and the emerging sciences of psychology, sociology and evolutionary theory, blowing apart any simplistic answers to the relationship between theism, atheism and religion.

WHAT A CENTURY!

The 19th century had it all! From the intellectual idealism of Hegel, who saw *Geist*, or spirit, as 'the inner being of the world', through the period of romanticism – with emotionally charged poetry that both celebrated and despaired of God – and from the social impact of the industrial revolution and rural poverty through to the flourishing of emotionally charged religion and a religious establishment that often ignored the zeitgeist and retreated into hypocrisy. It was the century that gave us Darwin, statistics, psychology and Marx, and hence new perspectives on the human situation. It was a century of dramatic changes, in industry, culture and personal piety, with nostalgia for the mediaeval set alongside the emergence of new ideas.

The quotations that open this chapter, as the 18th century was about to tip into the 19th, hint at the range of views that the latter century would explore…

Pierre-Simon Laplace (1749 – 1827), an extraordinary French scientist and cosmologist, claimed that he had no need to include the hypothesis of a creator God in his five-volume *Celestial Mechanics* (the first volume published in 1799), when asked about this lack by Napoleon. Yet, in the previous year,

William Wordsworth had penned his romantic, spiritual, almost mystical *Lines composed a few miles above Tintern Abbey, on revisiting the Banks of the Wye during a tour: July 13th, 1798*.

Their views could not have been more different. The one, modern, scientific and intellectual, has no need of supernatural explanations; the other, oppressed by urban life and returning to the beauty of the River Wye for inspiration, intuits a sense of meaning in nature.

By the 19th century, we see religion presented more as a personal, internal cultivation of faith than a theory about the nature of the world, and the attempt to describe ultimate reality can now be presented as a 'sense and taste for the infinite' (Schleiermacher) with its god as a projection of the highest human qualities (Feuerbach), or as an analgesic against hardship (Marx).

It was understandable in the 19th century, burdened with the economic reality of industrialism and capitalism, to yearn for simpler, more spiritual and romantic times, as we see in the art of the Pre-Raphaelites and the neo-Gothic revival in architecture. To take a domestic illustration that continues to shape our dwellings: while Georgian houses tended to be classic in design, with rooms fitted into a perfectly rectangular box, with the domestic architecture of Augustus Pugin, homes became irregular, shaping themselves to fit the needs of their occupiers – bay windows, conservatories and porches burst from the constraining lines of the previous century. So it's not surprising to find that, in the 19th century, we have both a different approach to the idea of God and a sense of his absence from daily life.

ESCAPING KANT

Kant had created a difficult legacy for the philosophy of religion by insisting on the absolute distinction between reality itself (noumena) and our experience (phenomena), thereby denying knowledge of anything beyond immediate experience. What then can religion know?

Hegel (1770 – 1831) responded to this by exploring the idea of 'God' in a way that links back to earlier Christian thought, but is utterly different from the Deism of popular religion. In his 'Lectures on the Philosophy of Religion' (1824) he claimed that 'Religion is consciousness of the absolute universal object.' He argued that, if God is infinite, he certainly cannot be 'a being' – since beings are only known because they can be identified within the world of experience. Rather, he explores the idea of self-transcendence: that we could be more true to ourselves, more 'real' than we are in our actual lives. He presents God as that higher degree of reality that we intuitively know within ourselves.

Hegel combines this experience of personal transcendence, with a philosophy of being and saw philosophy itself as a pure form of religion, dealing with fundamental ideas, whereas religious practices were a simplified, cultural approach to the same human quest to know the ultimate.

I have a feeling that you can almost sink into Hegel and drown. His work is erudite, rational and deep; it explores the process of being and change, and yet it is all rather too much. At the end of the day, what he offers is a step further along the road already taken in the 3rd century by Plotinus, categorised as metaphysical monism: the quest to find a single principle of consciousness and rationality sustaining the world.

However, Hegel can form a bridge between thinkers such as Aquinas, and the 20th century thinker Paul Tillich – neither of whom see God as 'a being', because that would be self-contradictory; God is exactly *not* that. But all three strive to express what Being-Itself might be, if it is not simply another experienced being.

The significance of Kant's division of experience from reality was not lost on the poet Goethe (1749 – 1832), who reckoned that, although one could not speak directly about the Absolute, one might experience and derive great benefit from it. But *how* might one experience it? Clearly, this is not experience as sensation, but experience as intuition and insight. The same could be said of Samuel Taylor Coleridge, for whom the poet's awareness of the Absolute leads to a sense of divine harmony. Poets boldly go where post-Kantian philosophers not only fear to tread, but assume they will never be able to tread.

Philosophers and theologians still tried to explore the nature of religious experience. Friedrich Schleiermacher (1768 – 1834) presented the essence of religion to the skeptical and secular society of his day. In his *Speeches on Religion to its Cultural Despisers*, he suggested that religion was concerned with 'a sense and taste for the infinite'. Notice the context. Schleiermacher saw that crude deism (with or without the personal qualities offered by the 'hybrid') was rejected by an increasingly agnostic society, and therefore sought to counter it by exploring ways in which religion can offer a more profound view of reality – looking to 'being itself' rather than deism's external god. Coming from the starting point in religious experience, he effectively parallels what Hegel was doing from a standpoint of pure philosophy. His claim: you may despise religion but, if you value culture, you will appreciate the taste for things eternal.

Later, and the very opposite of this, Kierkegaard argued that religion was not rational at all, but a subjective truth. Faith addressed the chasm between the infinite passion of individuals to find the truth, and a precarious world. Hence it was a subjective conviction – something that you accept, even if it seems absurd, as opposed to something you know. Faith is not about facts, for Kierkegaard, nor reducible to scientific propositions in any way, but is a matter of personal conviction and commitment in the face of life's radical uncertainty. His *The Sickness unto Death* is subtitled 'A Christian Psychological

Exposition for Upbuilding and Awakening', showing how much his theology is about internal experience and a sense of quest. No place here for impersonal facts; everything is about the inwardness of a spiritual journey.

But if religion is about an inner sense and quest, what is the statue of its language, including the idea of 'God'?

GOD AS PROJECTION OR COMPENSATION

Ludwig Feuerbach (1804 – 1872) considered God to be a projection of all that is best in humankind, having a function in the world, but not being *part* of the world:

> The divine being is nothing else than the human being, or, rather, the human nature purified, freed from the limits of the individual man, made objective – i.e. contemplated and revered as another, a distinct being.
>
> (*The Essence of Christianity*, 1841)

Feuerbach's broad intention is to retain the essence of Christianity as a religion and belief system, but at the same time to free it from its supernatural trappings. But, in doing this, he also links back to an earlier Christian tradition:

> … if man is to find contentment in God, he must find himself in God.

Here we are back with the Early Fathers, for whom the spiritual path is that of becoming God (*theopoesis*), rather than believing in a god who exists externally. This implies that the proofs for the existence of God must automatically fail:

> The proofs of the existence of God have for their aim to make the internal external, to separate it from man.

In other words, for Feuerbach, God is not to be confused with anything that can be known or experienced outside the self. Rather, belief is an internal experience

> … if I do not believe in a God, there is no God for me.

And that follows from Anselm's point – *credo ut intelligam* – understanding God only happens in the context of giving one's heart and of commitment. Feuerbach's argument that God is a projection is just another way of exploring the idea that God is something intuited and experienced. Far from an atheist attack on religion, his view turns out to be a positive resource – denying the external deist God, and returning faith to an internal experience.

But Feuerbach does not hold back in his criticism of religion:

> The essence of religion is the immediate, involuntary, unconscious contemplation of human nature as another, a distinct nature. But when this projected image of human nature is made an object of reflection, of theology, it becomes an inexhaustible mine of falsehoods, illusions, contradictions, and sophisms.
>
> (*The Essence of Christianity*)

He seeks 'the identity of the divine being with the human' and suggests that the hidden essence of religion is love, for 'Love identifies man with God':

> Love is not holy because it is a predicate of God, but it is a predicate of God because it is itself divine.

The atheist Feuerbach, far from being presented as an enemy of religion, should be numbered among its supporters!

His views were echoed at the end of the 20th century by the anthropologist Sir Raymond Firth, who argued in *Religion: a humanist interpretation* that:

> ...concepts of the divine, of 'ultimate reality', and of the extremes of knowledge, wisdom, morality and power associated with the divine, are just a summation of the absolutes of human imagination.

> ... It may seem harsh to say that God is an example of the fallacy of misplaced concreteness. But while at an abstract, figurative level the ideas of God, Yahweh, Allah, Brahma can provide spectacular symbolic expressions and penetrating thoughts upon the human condition, at bottom they are just essentially human constructs.

Concluding that:

> ... I would argue that there is truth in every religion. But it is a human, not a divine truth.

> ... Many of the values of these religious faiths are true values, in the sense that if honestly adopted, they make for a more viable social life – self-sacrificing thought for others, avoidance of deceit, care for more vulnerable members of society, integrative meaning of rituals, strength in cooperation. (p204)

Coming from a 20th century humanist, this sums up the best of the 19th century religious thought – that there are truths that need to be put into practice for the benefit of society, even though they are expressed through projection and myth.

Of all people, it was Karl Marx who puts his finger on the popular function of religious belief. In his famous quote (from the *Introduction to the Critique of the Hegelian Philosophy of Right*), he describes religion as 'the heart of a heatless world' and 'the opium of the people'. But that heartlessness was not just the result of a narrow view of reason and science in the previous centuries, but of the inhuman conditions that led people to long for another world as compensation for present woes. Marx argued that the comfort religion offered was an illusion, distracting people from taking practical steps to improve their lot in this present life. He therefore saw the abandoning of religion – and of the belief in God that sustained it – as offering profound political and social benefits.

Hence, Marx thought that religion would diminish once people found satisfaction in their lives here and now – engaging positively and creatively with life. But such engagement could well be seen (by Schleiermacher and others) as a direct experience of Being Itself, or 'God'. Marx may thus be saying, indirectly, that a direct experience of reality renders religion superfluous.

And here we have a new possibility – that atheism, as a rejection of religious ideas, may find a positive contribution by engaging with Life directly. And this, of course, was what many older philosophies would have thought of when they used the term 'God'. The Christian doctrine of the Trinity aimed at locating divinity within Christ and the community sharing in his Spirit, in addition to finding it within the order of creation. It was about the here and now, not about an external and impersonal creator – that was the view branded as heretical from Arias onwards, revived as deism, and mistakenly identified with 'God' by many in the 21st century. Marx therefore points to atheism rescuing God from an external and illusory projection.

EVOLUTION

Charles Darwin's *On the Origin of Spec*ies marks a pivotal moment in the development of the sciences. He is used to justify atheism on the basis that his theory of evolution provided an option to the traditional religious argument from design. In fact, however, his situation was quite different from the assumed caricature presented by the New Atheists of the 21st century. As a true scientist, Darwin was interested in all phenomena, including the phenomenon of religion, and particularly how religion engaged with society. His local contacts in the village of Down saw him supporting religious initiatives, especially those where religion was spearheading help for the poor. His active support for the local Friendly Society was a sign of active social interest, but he was also supporting of religious movements where they made a positive contribution to the life of those touched by them. For a serious and balanced exploration of Darwin's view, see particularly *The Evolving God* by J. David Pleins.

Beliefs in the 19th century were changing, and Darwin's scientific views certain proved controversial in the eyes of the conservatively religious. But the option was never an either /

or of evolution or religion. The great service to religious belief rendered by Darwin was the shift from looking at religious ideas as hypotheses, to seeing them as functional. If there was any one thing that forced Darwin to challenge a glib and superficial claim for the existence of a benign deity, it was the death of his daughter. The problem of evil, revealed in such an immediate and personal way, forced him to look again at religious beliefs, but did not prevent him from taking a lifelong interest in the place of religion within society.

His achievement, for our purposes, was to deal a blow to the earlier forms of deism, since they required belief in a designer-God, whereas Darwin presented design as a result of natural selection. His theory rendered the deist God redundant, while endorsing a sense of wonder at the evolving majesty of life.

Hence, Darwin's supposedly 'atheist' contribution was in fact entirely positive, relocating a sense of wonder in the world, rather than in the deist illusion of an external creator.

THE KILLING OF GOD

In his dramatic story (in *The Joyful Science*, 1882) Nietzsche has a madman enter a square in broad daylight carrying a lamp, and claiming that he seeks God. He is mocked by the cynical crowd. The people clearly have no use for God anyway, laughing that perhaps God had gone off or become lost. The madman is horrified by this, and declares that God is dead, that we have killed him, and that 'The holiest and the mightiest thing the world has ever possessed has bled to death under our knives: who will wipe this blood from us?'

For the madman, the death has come as an aching sense of loss, not a triumph of emancipatory murder. Nietzsche saw that what was happening around him amounted to the death of God, that the moral framework had been removed, and that the world was unchained from its sun, and drifting towards the cold and dark.

The killing of God was, for Nietzsche, the observation of a fundamental shift in popular thinking, in which the transcendent was no longer taken into account. Hence the mockery of the crowd who hear of the madman's desperate search for God, and fearful declaration that he has been killed. The madman is distressed, but the people in the market place do not see that there is a problem.

In a way, Nietzsche is not the spokesman for atheism as such, but the voice pointing out that atheism is now the default view. With morality and values threatened, Nietzsche attempts to find direction in a directionless universe.

For Nietzsche, the death of God was a tragedy – a crime that humankind had committed:

> Who gave us the sponge to wipe away the horizon? What did we do when we unchained the earth from its sun? Where is it moving now? Where are we moving?... Is there still an 'above' and 'below'? Are we not wandering through an endless nothingness? Does not the emptiness of space breath at us? (*The Joyful Science*, book 3, section 125)

Nietzsche recognises the terrible emptiness of a world without a foundational concept. It is cold and without direction, its scale of values has gone.

In killing God, people had also taken a sponge to wipe away the horizon of meaning and culture. Without some form of God figure, something to which to aspire, he feared that the world would simply drift, as though a void. He saw that the threat of atheism was that it would lead to nihilism. So, in place of God, he sets up the *übermensch* (superman) – the next step along the path of evolution, a higher form of life.

Whatever else Nietzsche contributes to our discussion, the key point is that, if God is removed, an alternative is needed, and since his day there have been plenty of alternatives on offer, from the capitalist dream of everlasting growth, to the dictatorship of the proletariat, to the Nazi vision of the Reich that would last for a thousand years.

In *Twilight of the Idols*, Nietzsche lays the blame squarely on Plato, accusing him of creating a world of abstracts that he then claimed as the 'real' world. Nietzsche argues that the opposite is true. The 'real' world is the one in which we live, while 'God' is an abstract idea, presented in human form in order to appear as part of the real world. His challenge is to replace God with a future for humankind that builds on its life now; humans are on a rope between the ape and the superman, a work in progress, a species with a self-transcending ambition.

He contrasts the *Übermensch*, who strive to surpass themselves, with the 'last man', where humanity aims at nothing but itself, seeking contentment rather than transcendence. It is this contrast that enables Nietzsche's 'atheism' to come to the rescue of ideas of God. For Feuerbach, God was a projection of all that is best in humanity, but this tends to make humanity a goal in itself. Nietzsche adds another dimension: that man is something to be surpassed. Here he comes to the rescue of a God who is reduced to a kindly smile. God is not a kindly old man of any sort, but a challenge to find direction and purpose within an impersonal world. In early Christianity, the human challenge was *theopoesis* – becoming divine – while the idea of God against which Nietzsche campaigns is a pathetic image that limits and, for him, 'castrates'.

Notice the difference between Nietzsche and Darwin. Darwin's 'natural selection' provided the mechanism by which species, including the human species, had reached its present state, but did not, in itself, provide a future goal. For Darwin, the chance variations that enable evolution are 'reactive', in that they respond to changes in the environment. For Nietzsche, the will to power is 'proactive', seeking to develop itself within its environment. Darwin offers objective observation; Nietzsche personal challenge.

Clearly, if God is seen as a possible being, external to the experienced world, then discussion about his possible existence is, at best, a distraction, more likely a hindrance. For Nietzsche, the reality of 'God' is to be found in the impulse to live, to grow, to develop. God is embedded within the world – that may be theist or atheist, but it is certainly not deist!

Nietzsche may be contrasted with the Buddha, for whom the starting point of the spiritual quest is the recognition that everything is in a constant process of change, does not have a permanent essence, and never lives up to our dreams. For the Buddha, you need to recognise the nature of change and accept your place within it. It is exactly the conceiving of existential ambitions that are a hindrance to real progress, and Nietzsche's *übermensch* may be a distraction from the recognition of the value of life as it is here and now. In this sense, the Buddha is closer to Marx than to Nietzsche.

FROM BEACH TO FUNERAL

A hotel room in Dover is not everyone's dream honeymoon destination, neither is the invitation to a newlywed to feel the cool night air necessarily going to lead to pessimistic thoughts about the state of religion, but for Matthew Arnold (1822 – 1888) poet, critic and school inspector, it is the moment for which he is best remembered.

His poem 'Dover Beach' introduced the phrase 'the Sea of Faith' which was to live on as the name of a group of radical theologians led by the late Don Cupitt. These key lines on the state of Victorian religion reflect a sense of loss that matches that of Nietzsch's madman:

> The 'Sea of Faith'
> Was once, too, at the full, and round earth's shore
> Lay like the folds of a bright girdle furl'd
> But now I only hear
> Its melancholy, long, withdrawing roar,

Retreating, to the breath
Of the night-wind, down the vast edges drear
And naked shingles of the world.

His response, is to see the world as having nothing to offer –
'no joy, nor love, nor light, nor certitude, nor peace, nor help
for pain', ending with 'Where ignorant armies clash by night.'
Hardly a comforting moment for his new wife!

For Arnold, the loss of faith exposes us to a cruel world: a
vision that brings despair as certainty ebbs away, like the 'slow
withdrawing roar' of the sea on the pebbles. Psychologically, it
sees religious faith as making that world bearable. Here
Arnold touches Marx, for whom religion is the 'heart of a
heartless world'. The difference is that Arnold sees only loss,
while Marx challenges to transform the human situation, to
face up to that which has led people to seek the comfort and
consolation of religion.

However, Matthew Arnold remained concerned that the
moral basis for life, which a majority of people took from the
Bible, would continue to inspire and keep the common people
in order. He was, when not being poetic, the government
inspector of schools, and knew what was needed for people to
conform to moral norms. So, much as he might regret the
'deep withdrawing roar' as the Sea of Faith retreated, he
wanted to retain the positive contribution of religion.
Recognising that most people did not engage in metaphysical
discussions, he sought to promote a view of religion that
might encourage devotion and obedience, with a Jesus who
would inspire kindliness, but without metaphysical claims, or
beliefs that were unsuited to ordinary people.

In effect, the romantic and conservative Arnold was, for
pragmatic reasons, moving towards the situation where
commonplace atheism (or, more likely, indifference or non-
theism) could still provide fertile ground upon which
spirituality and Christian morality might take root.

In many ways, Matthew Arnold, at his most cynical, was to anticipate popular Christianity in the 21st century, continuing to proclaim the inspiring figure and teachings of Jesus, while turning a blind eye to the atheism of everyday life. Why proclaim the necessity of doctrines that most people cannot be expected to take seriously? Modern liberal Christianity may well quietly set aside issues such as demon possession and the coming end of the world on exactly that basis. Accepting a mildly atheist norm of belief allows Christian values to take root without supernatural distractions. The minimal requirements probably come down to the idea of 'God' and some form of life after death, without being too specific about either. A personalised deity, and the idea that those who have passed away are 'still with us', is easier to present than the Athanasian creed and bodily resurrection at the last day. It is as though Arnold accepted that the hybrid god was the most one could expect people to believe in.

Less well known, but desperately serious, is Thomas Hardy's poem 'God's Funeral' published in 1912. In it, with all the skill with which his novels drag their characters through harrowing situations, he sees a bizarre funeral procession, with mourners grieving…

> O man-projected Figure, of late
> Imaged as we, thy knell who shall survive?
> Whence came it we were tempted to create
> One whom we can no longer keep alive?

Nietzsche would have loved that! Like Marx, Hardy presents the God figure as one created to provide comfort, but now mangled by 'rude reality' and he regrets that we can no longer lie down at eventide 'And feel a blest assurance he was there!'

By stanza 13, he describes a crowd of 'sweet women, youths, all incredulous' who follow the funeral procession, but…

> Who chimed as one: 'This figure is of straw
> This requiem mockery! Still he lives to us!

And then the painful truth…
> I could not prop their faith: and yet
> Many I had known: with all I sympathized
> And though struck speechless, I did not forget
> That what was mourned for, I, too, once had prized.

When it was first published, the poem had a subtitle: 'An Allegorical Conception of the Present State of Theology.'

It was also possible to assess religion in utilitarian ways. J. S. Mill argued that is was 'perfectly conceivable that religion may be morally useful without being intellectually sustainable' (*The Nature and Utility of Religion*, 1855). Commitment and moral direction had always been seen as a contribution of religion, at least since the time of the Emperor Constantine, but in the 19th century, these became more significant as the credibility of metaphysical claims went into decline.

POSITIVE THINKING

Not all 19th century thinking was as depressing as Arnold or Hardy. Auguste Comte (1798 – 1857), creator of 'positive philosophy', established his Religion of Humanity, with daily rituals based on the fashionable scientific theories, in effect a practical version of the earlier worship of the goddess Reason. Waking each morning to feel the bumps on one's head, and thus deduce one's mental traits, may have reflected the fashionable theory of phrenology back in the early 19th century, but, like most scientific theories, it did not stand the test of time.

The idea that reason and science can render religion redundant is a curiously 20th and 21st century idea found among the more extreme advocates of simplistic atheism. The rationalists and romantics of the 19th century had already disproved that hypothesis. Left to their own devices, Comte shows that reason and science are in danger of producing a sillier version of conventional religion!

However bizarre its rituals, Comte's 'Religion of Humanity', devised in the middle of the 19th century, led to the establishment of secular, humanist organisations, and his heart was clearly in the right place, since he is often credited with devising the term 'altruism' – his conviction that human beings can genuinely come to be of service to one another – as a key feature of his new religion. Like Matthew Arnold, he saw that most people would not accept the full range of metaphysical doctrines associated with traditional religion, but equally that people needed religion of some sort to be motivated to behave morally.

Equally positive, but more level-headed, was 19th century Liberalism, with its faith in progress, individual rights, and freeing individuals from institutional fetters. So, for example, J. S. Mill was brought up without religion but with a strong conviction in the ability of reason to aid human progress. His only crisis in life came when he started to doubt the validity of the Utilitarian creed in which he had been brought up.

Many others made a positive contribution to an atheist view of life, including T. H. Huxley (1825 – 1895), whose view that one should not believe things without sufficient evidence, led him to coin the term 'agnosicism' and to defend Darwin's theory of evolution by natural selection. There was also George Holyoake (1817 – 1906) who edited a secularist paper 'The Reasoner' from 1846, and Charles Bradlaugh (1833 – 1891), politician and free-thinker, who founded the National Secular Society in 1866. The 19th century was a time when it was possible to be openly atheist, fashionably so in some quarters, and critical of established religious ideas. The problem, of course, was that the ideas they reacted against largely reflected the 'hybrid' god of popular belief, rather than the serious theology of the intellectual minority of earlier centuries.

The sociologist Max Weber (1864 – 1920) took the view that, as science expanded its reach, explaining more and more about the world, so religion would naturally decline. But the error here is the assumption that religion is basically a way of explaining things, a way that belongs to a crude, pre-scientific era. What we find in the 19th century – both from the new sciences and the arts – however, is the recognition that there is more to the mystery of life than can be solved by factual, scientific explanations.

Whether it is Schleiermacher's 'sense and taste for the infinite' as a human experience and longing, or the trauma of Hardy's description of those who follow God's funeral procession, or the loss of direction following the Death of God in Nietzsche, the 19th century explored the depth of human experience – a depth that cannot be satisfied by the superficially scientific offerings of Comte's worship of Reason, or a simplistic acceptance of supernatural entities that are at odds with a modern scientific view of the world.

A LADY PHILOSOPHER...

Before leaving the 19th century, with its pantheon of great thinkers, there is one person who deserves a special mention, as she touched on so much that relates philosophy to religion. Harriet Martineau (1802 – 1876) was a most remarkable woman and a prolific writer on subjects including economics, politics, society, religion and the role of women. She was well connected in intellectual circles, being a close friend of Charles Darwin's brother Erasmus. She exchanged views on atheism with George Holyoake, translated the works of Auguste Comte, and produced articles and fictional tutorials on economics and politics that were hugely popular. By 1832, she was out-selling Dickens!

Martineau, whose beautiful portrait by Richard Evans may be seen at the Royal Academy, was of Huguenot descent, and was brought up as a Unitarian, a religious group with ideas that go back to the Arian controversy in the 4th century, accepting a personal deity but not the Trinity. She studied ancient religions, taking a particular interest in Egyptian ideas. However, when it came to the experience of life and death, she saw little difference between ancient Egyptian ideas and those of Christianity, and suggested that religious beliefs followed a gradual and universal development – a radical idea at that time, which challenged Christianity's claim to be uniquely valid.

She became friendly with the Darwins who, like her, tended to take a Unitarian view of religion and were progressive in their political views. Erasmus gave her a copy of his brother's *On the Origin of Species* and she welcomed it, because it gave an account of creation and evolution that did not depend upon theology, commenting that:

> In the present state of the religious world, secularisation ought to flourish. What an amount of sin and woe might and would then be extinguished.

Her secular views were not based on the rejection of arguments for the existence of God, but simply that she wished to be positive about life, and to avoid what she saw as a sin-dominated religion. She wrote to the secularist George Holyoake, welcoming Darwin's book because it required neither revealed nor natural theology. She held that, if there were a First Cause, it would be unknowable, and saw the tendency of belief to be moving in the direction of 'philosophical atheism', since religion would become increasingly abstract in its ideas.

Hers was an atheism that did not deny God, but simply claimed that, if he existed, he would be unknowable (a view that, as we have seen, has a long history within the church). Philosophically, however, she saw atheism as the logical conclusion to the direction in which metaphysical beliefs were going.

Her concern with religion was not so much philosophical as personal, seeing it as a human phenomenon but one that offered a negative view of human life as sinful, in contrast to her positive view of life in general, including, of course, the role of women.

She was, in many ways, both a representative of her own day, but also way ahead of her time. She saw that philosophical atheism did not necessarily deny everything about religion, but that it offered emotional positivity in place of religion's tendency to focus on human unworthiness and sin, implying that a judicious dose of atheism can be healthy for religion.

She was not alone in taking a positive view of the future. By the end of the 19th century, many religious thinkers saw divine providence as guaranteeing that everything was going according to God's plan, with Christian missionaries dispatched to the ends of the earth to save the unenlightened from the potential vengeance of a loving God towards the unbaptized. In some ways, the global success of Christianity was a religious version of the traditional Whig interpretation of history, in which society is gradually improving, with international trade would promoting peace and economic growth. Western civilisation would become global. It was a century that faced many demons – not least the horrors of the slave trade and the brutality of its wars – and yet retained some sense of hope. Many saw God, Christianity and Western civilization as inseparable.

That vision, secular and religious, was soon to be dashed by the coming of the Great War.

Chapter 10

The Quest for Certainty

Humankind cannot bear very much reality
Four Quartets, T.S. Eliot

Things fall apart
The centre cannot hold
Mere anarchy is loosed upon the world.
from *The Second Coming,* W B Yeats

Whereof one cannot speak, thereof one must be silent.
Tractatus, Wittgenstein

The world experienced too much reality in the years 1914 – 18. The old political, social and religious order was shaken to its core, along with the positive views about progress and the confidence of the 19th century, leaving a devastated landscape strewn with the corpses of men, hopes and ideals.

Conventional religious belief never fully recovered from the Great War: its authority was challenged, free-thinking became more common and philosophy of religion went on the defensive. But, at the same time, there was a resurgence of religious yearning, especially among the millions who were bereaved and who sought – as memorials to the dead were erected in every town and village – comfort in religious ideas. Spiritualism thrived. There were also efforts to start again and find a solid, credible basis for religion: Karl Barth sought to base Christianity entirely on the words of scripture; Paul

Tillich took refuge in philosophy and suggested that religious symbols could answer existential questions; Teilhard de Chardin held on to traditional Catholic teaching, but gave it an evolutionary twist; fundamentalism sought to simplify things by insisting on defending basic beliefs; existentialists – both secular and religious – grappled to find meaning in a world dominated by the experience of loss.

It was a time when things indeed seemed to be falling apart. It was also a time of economic and political chaos, the rise of both Nazi and Soviet ideologies, and brutality on an industrial scale. Above all, two questions hung over religion and philosophy in the first half of the 20th century: 'Of what can I be certain?' and 'How can I find meaning in my life?' The first is the subject of this chapter.

THINKING IN NO-MAN'S-LAND

Ludwig Wittgenstein (1889 – 1951) joined the army and volunteered for an almost-suicidal post, guiding artillery from a dugout in no-man's-land. With shells from both sides flying overhead, he started to make notes for his famous *Tractatus*, which opens with 'The world is all that is the case' and builds up logically as one short, numbered statement follows another. Already well qualified as an engineer, mathematician and philosopher, he wanted to use his considerable powers of logic to establish exactly what could or could not be stated with certainty. His work inspired a philosophical movement known as Logical Positivism. Its key thesis was the 'verification principle', which insisted that all meaningful statements needed to be based on empirical evidence. It therefore dismissed metaphysics, religion and ethics as meaningless, rather than simply wrong. In Britain, its arguments were popularized by A. J. Ayer's *Language, Truth and Logic*, a radical and angry book, brushing aside all that failed to conform to the new criteria of truth. So far, so clearly atheist as far as certainty goes.

However, in his later work, Wittgenstein shifted from seeing meaning in terms of empirical verification to meaning in terms of use. The implication of this is that meaning can be shown, even if it cannot be described directly. This approach was taken up by some theologians to argue that, to understand 'God', you need to see how that word is used in religious discourse, as part of the religious 'language game'. Here the atheism that lies behind Wittgenstein's early work comes to help us appreciate the flexibility of 'God language'. The word 'God' is not used as a hypothesis, but describes an experience, or a conviction about what matters most. The use of the word 'God' in the practice of religion is therefore very different from its use in the Philosophy of Religion.

However, Wittgenstein's major contribution for our purposes comes from that early work in the dugout. He was interested in mysticism, and was fully aware that there are some things that can be experienced but cannot be empirically verified. He therefore ends his *Tractatus* with the remarkable statement 'Whereof one cannot speak, thereof one must remain silent.' What he has effectively done is to eliminate God from the empirical world – God does not exist in the usual sense – but he allows that there is a level of reality that cannot be put into words: exactly the point made by Aquinas and others. The superficial atheism of Logical Positivism did not do justice to the unspoken assumption of Wittgenstein's thought, namely that there is reality beyond the empirical.

EVIDENCE?

Wittgenstein was concerned with what we could or could not know or say, and of what we could claim to be certain. This question – as part of the quest for certainty in a world vulnerable to the horrors of war – also lay behind the growth of religious fundamentalism, but to appreciate the rise of that movement in the early 20th century, we need to reflect for a moment on an older philosophical approach: evidentialism.

This tradition stems from the advice of Hume, among others, that a wise man proportions his belief to the evidence – as used by him against the idea of miracles. It was taken up later by William Clifford (1845 – 79), who was a mathematician as well as a philosopher, famous for his theory of 'mind-stuff', existing at the lowest level as atoms but building up to form consciousness, and for his work in algebra. But, for our purpose, his key claim is that:

> It is wrong, always, everywhere, and for anyone, to believe anything upon insufficient evidence.

The Ethics of Belief (1877)

His views were later opposed by William James, who suggested (in *The Will to Believe*) that we gather and interpret evidence in the light of *what* we believe, rather than *in order to* believe. If that is the case, it would be unwise to suspend all belief until one gets sufficient evidence.

My personal view is that James has the stronger case. After all, nobody falls in love, marries, moves home or takes a job only on the basis of sufficient evidence. If all evidence for the problems of bringing up children were to be presented pre-conception, the human species would die out. But that does not stop the wonder, delight and crazy hopes we have for our children. In most of what makes life worthwhile we need to step beyond proof and give scope for hope, as democracy and the entrepreneurial spirit illustrate. However, Clifford's point is not whether a belief is helpful, or comforting, or pleasant, but whether it is *true*.

More recently, the philosopher Alvin Plantinga has argued for 'basic beliefs'. These are not conclusions from evidence, but form the starting point from which we interpret evidence. He holds that, although these need to be warranted by other beliefs that follow from them, they do not depend upon evidence. The implication of his position is that something may be basic for one person but not for another, depending on their commitments and way of looking at the world.

Although used as a common sense way of judging people's views by most of us, it is unsettling for those who seek a single and unambiguous truth.

Theists and atheists look at the world differently, and will therefore form different 'basic beliefs'. We therefore need to keep in mind the continuum of possibilities between those for whom empirical or logical evidence is absolutely necessary (a view held by many, if not most, philosophical atheists), those who are flexible about how evidence is interpreted (and therefore hold that there is an iterative process between getting evidence and forming beliefs), and at the other end of the scale those (called fideists) for whom everything depends of faith and evidence is a distraction.

Every point of view is coloured by its own history. My first encounter with the rational rejection of religious belief came through reading Bertrand Russell while still at school. But Russell's view of atheism was inspired by that of J. S. Mill, who rejected beliefs that amounted to deism rather than traditional theism. Hence at least some who, in the mid 20th century, were taking atheism as the norm for modern thought, were actually doing no more than rejecting deism, which may well need to be abandoned if God is to be rescued from those who define him in ways that render his existence logically impossible.

THE SHRINKING OF THEOLOGY

The term 'fundamentalism' was coined during the 1920s in the United States, based on a pre-war pamphlet entitled 'The Fundamentals', which argued that the Bible was the inerrant word of God, emphasised the Second Coming of Christ, and called for a separation of the faithful from the secular world, which it regarded with distrust.

As a religious movement, fundamentalism became widely known through its involvement in the Scopes Trial, in 1925, which sought to enforce the ban on the teaching evolution through natural selection in schools in Tennessee. Evolution became one of fundamentalism's pet hates, being contrary to a literal reading of the Book of Genesis, along with opposition to Communism, claiming it to be in league with the Devil.

The dilemma for the radical theologian, in this or any era, is to maintain a balance between exploring religious ideas against a background of contemporary thought and conforming to the expectations of religious believers. On the one hand he or she may attacked from some philosophical quarters for entertaining ideas that cannot be decided by reason and evidence. On the other, he or she may be attacked from the standpoint of the fundamentalist religious believer, for whom any attempt to import subtlety into religious doctrine is seen as a capitulation to philosophical fashion.

Fundamentalism sought to define and defend a limited number of doctrines as the essence of religion, and to interpret them literally. This played directly into the hand of the narrowing philosophical view of religious claims – particularly by the logical positivists – so that both sides of the argument accepted definitions of 'miracle' or 'God' that would have been anathema to a mediaeval theologian. Some thinkers, such as Paul Tillich (in *Biblical Religion and the Search for Ultimate Reality*) continued to explore the nature of 'Being Itself' but were well aware of the apparent conflict between Biblical religion and this philosophical approach, and that their view would be rejected by those who were conservatively religious:

> It is understandable that some reject biblical religion completely because they are called in the depths of their being, or their intellectual and moral conscience, to ask the radical question – the question of being and nonbeing. They become heretics or pagans rather than bow to a religion which prohibits the ontological question. (p56f)

By detaching religion from universal human experience, fundamentalism becomes irrelevant to the secular. But without

164

some serious exploration of basic values and a sense of the meaning of life, secular culture is in danger of becoming rootless, denying that there is any ultimate truth to be explored. Today, in a world of 'fake news', where any view appears to be accepted as equal to any other without reference to factual reality, this is exacerbated. Equally, political and social issues may be discussed without key terms, such as 'growth', 'profit' or 'efficiency', being challenged as to whether they are genuinely foundational.

In this situation, both philosophy and theology miss out on the benefits of mutual exploration. Theology narrows to a set of propositions to be defended, while philosophy devotes itself to logical precision, even when dealing with matters that require a broader conceptual basis.

But here we are jumping ahead of ourselves. Suffice to say that, in the 1920s and 30s, partly as a reaction to the war, Western culture polarized on issues of religion and certainty. On the one hand there was the insistence on the Bible and a rejection of secular thinking; on the other a wide range of philosophies, lifestyles and political views competing with one another.

In pointing to the confrontation between biblical religion and philosophy, Tillich suggests that:

a confrontation would be impossible if philosophy were logical analysis and epistemological enquiry only, however important may be the development of these tools for philosophical thought. Yet philosophy "love of wisdom" means much more than this. It seems to me that the oldest definition given to philosophy is, at the same time, the newest and that which always was and always will be valid: Philosophy is that cognitive endeavour in which the question of being is asked. In accordance with that definition, Aristotle summarized the development of Greek philosophy, anticipating the consequent periods up to the Renaissance and preparing the modern ways of asking the same question. The question of being is not the question of any special being, its existence and nature, but it is the question of what it means to *be*. It is the simplest, most profound, and absolutely inexhaustible question – the question of what it means to say that something *is*. (p5/6a)

Aristotle referred to ontology as 'first philosophy', and it is unfortunate that it has been stuck with the name 'metaphysics' simply because it followed the books on physics in the collection of his writings. The frustration with that term is that it has been taken to refer to realities that are beyond the empirical, in 'a world behind the world, existing only in speculative imagination.' (Tillich *op cit* p7)

In this way, theology and philosophy have been set up against one another, with metaphysics seen as concerned with what is external to the empirical world of solid matter and facts, and therefore consigned to the supernatural and uncertain. What is lost here is the sense that metaphysics is about the reality of solid matter, but including non-physical questions about its meaning and its significance for us.

BARTH'S CHALLENGE

No account of Protestant theology in the 20th century makes sense without reference to Karl Barth (1886 – 1968). He took a stand against the liberal theology of the 19th century but, in doing so, took a view very different from Tillich's.

Tillich was interested in the human quest for meaning and the transcendent dimension, and explored it through both religion and culture – in art, music, literature and so on. He saw Christianity as part of this broader quest. Barth, by contrast, had no interest in broad cultural questions. For him, Christianity starts with the person of Christ. God was not some hypothesis or a general theory of Being Itself, but the reality that confronted him in Christ.

When Nietzsche's madman was mocked, he claimed to have come too soon. Perhaps he had, for in the eyes of Karl Barth, the moment when the liberal theology of the 19th century died was on the 4th of August 1914, the day when 93 German intellectuals signed an open letter approving the war aims of Kaiser Wilhelm II. Not only was Harnack, the leading figure in 19th century theology, a signatory to that letter, but he had been responsible for drafting it. Barth was horrified. Liberal theology had presented God as essentially a projection of human perfection, and it was assumed that civilization would continue to progress, inspired by Christian values. How were the teachings of Jesus in any way compatible with the horrors of war unleashed on Europe in 1914?

Barth wanted to draw a line under the whole liberal approach to theology and get back to the Scriptures. For him, God was the one who speaks through the biblical text, challenging human values through the teaching of Christ. He thought that theology and religion tended to hide God, rather than reveal him. God had disappeared into a human dream of perfection, a humanist ideal. Barth was convinced that the focus of Christianity must be the scriptures, with no need for natural theology or arguments about the nature of God.

For Barth, the First World War demonstrated the failure of 19th century theology. Feuerbach had argued that God was a projection of the human ideal; now Barth saw that it was exactly that – that the whole object of liberal theology had been nothing but projection. It was time to draw a line under all that and start again.

Basing everything on the teaching of Christ, as recorded in scripture, raises all sorts of questions about how one should interpret ancient texts, but they were largely ignored by those who followed a 'Bible-based' approach to religion. The written word, however interpreted, is there in black and white, waiting to be interpreted to fit particular circumstances and inclinations.

Gone is general philosophy and culture; everything is a matter of one's response to a man who lived 2000 years ago, a man whom Christians claim to be God incarnate. Barth goes back to the period before the Fathers of the early Church took to Greek philosophy in order to explain their beliefs and frame the creeds. He bypasses the debates about the nature of God, but concludes that the real enemy is not philosophical atheism, but an atheist attitude to life, even in someone who professes belief. Here (quoted in Joseph McLelland *Prometheus Rebound: the Irony of Atheism*, 1988) is his conclusion in 'The Rationality of Discipleship':

> The atheism that is the real enemy is the 'Christianity' that professes faith in God very much as a matter of course, perhaps with great emphasis, and perhaps with righteous indignation at atheism wild or mild, while in its practical thinking and behaviour it carries on exactly as if there were no God.

Barth states clearly that the real enemy of faith is not philosophical atheism, but a superficial and naïve view of God that is able to co-exist with a practical atheism in ordinary life. I never thought I would agree with Barth, but here I do. The enemy of spirituality, or personal faith, or confidence in life – call it what you will – is not atheism, but superficial belief.

IN THE TRENCHES

There are moments when the sheer scale of horror swamps both rational thought and emotional engagement; the Great War was one of those times.

The war poetry of Wilfred Owen offers a uniquely powerful and poignant cry of anguish about the senseless killing of trench warfare. In 'What passing bells...?' there is a blast against the simplistic formalities of conventional religion, culminating in 'no mockery for them in prayers or bells.' It is an anguished protest against any form of religion that tries to give respectability or even tries to make sense out of the carnage of war. And yet, beneath that cry, which could be taken as a straightforward rejection of God and religion, there is a deeper cry on behalf of those who have been slaughtered 'as cattle.' The anger protests that there is value that has been wasted, a depth of life that has been cut off, a world that has been torn apart. It is not the cry of nihilism, for nihilism cannot create tragedy or anguish. It is the cry of longing for a world of meaning, in the chaos that rips away all conventional formulas.

Whatever else one may say about such poetry, and however much a superficial reading castigates conventional religion, or the nationalistic pride that leads to such carnage, it is utterly profound. It cries out for some sense to be made out of the madness of death on this industrial scale.

In my view, the most biting line from the poem that begins 'Move him, move him, into the sun' poses the ultimate question: 'Was it for this the clay grew tall?' That question hangs over the whole development of modernism in the 20th century. What is the point of life? How do we make sense of it? How does it rise above the tragedy of human folly and physical frailty? Embodied in the culture of the confused 20th century is a yearning for transcendence. By saying this, I'm certainly not trying to smuggle in a comforting image of God, merely pointing out that the lack of an overall sense of meaning is tragic and leads to a further quest for a goal in life – whether personal, political or social. This is not metaphysics in any conventional sense. It is not even the attempt to argue that there is some objective meaning or direction in the universe. It is merely pointing to the questions and longings that modernism displays.

War provoked theological reflections, a radical attempt by Wittgenstein to re-think philosophy in the midst of carnage, and the most poignant poetry from Wilfred Owen and Siegfried Sassoon – poetry that dug deep beneath the foundations of conventional piety to reveal the harsh reality of trench warfare. Above all, the war put an end to 19th century assumptions about the inevitability of human improvement. What had been seen as European society informed by reason and social progress, had collapsed into senseless, brutal carnage, in which life was thrown away for a misplaced sense of patriotism. Staring at the brutal reality of war, glib answers to life's fundamental questions no longer carried weight.

Two of the theologians who were shaped by that war, Paul Tillich and Pierre Teilhard de Chardin, have been the subject of my earlier book *Through Mud and Barbed Wire*. They fought on opposite sides at Verdun, came from very different religious backgrounds (Lutheran and Catholic), and responded to the challenge of a world taken apart in very different ways. Tillich saw the essence of religion in terms of responding to the depths of reality – Being Itself – as opposed to the worship of anything finite. He had been brought up in a comfortable Lutheran environment in which God was seen as underpinning the order of things; now that world was gone, and he felt shattered. After two nervous breakdowns and postwar years teaching secular philosophy, he opposed Hitler, escaped to America, and gradually emerged as a systematic theologian.

By contrast, Teilhard, following the Catholic tradition of metaphysical thinking, but trained in science and committed to the idea of evolution, sought to find God in the equivalent of Aristotle's Prime Mover – but now projected ahead in the form of 'Omega', the end point of the evolution on Earth. He was committed both to science and human progress and also to a spiritual ideal. Torn apart by this 'double love', publication of his religious writings banned by his Jesuit superiors and stifled in the narrow confines of religion, he continued to work as a scientist. His life was both inspirational and tragic.

In the end Tillich went for existential commitment, while Teilhard went for an evolutionary structure. Each picking up on aspects of current culture in order to maintain some semblance of what God had become, or why he was still needed. But both operated against a background in which religion was becoming increasingly problematic, with atheism an option that both wanted to avoid.

EINSTEIN'S GOD

In 1940, Einstein gave a paper at a conference on Science, Philosophy and Religion (see Tillich, *Theology of Culture*, p127). In it he gave four arguments against the personal god accepted by theistic religion:
1. The such a personal god was not essential for religion
2. That it is the creation of primitive superstition
3. That it is self-contradictory
4. That it contradicts the scientific world-view.

Leaving aside his claim that it is the product of primitive superstition, three of his claims are obviously correct. Religion – in the sense of a rule of life that embodies moral principles and also offers meaning and value – is quite possible in a non-theistic environment, as for example in Buddhism or Taoism. But the third and fourth arguments fit well with the criticism of the post-Enlightenment hybrid god. It is self-contradictory to claim that a god is infinite and eternal, and then at the same time describe him as, literally, active and having a distinct personal character. He cannot be both an individual being and also being-itself. But it is also true that the idea of an interventionist god, able to tinker with the normal workings of the world, goes against the scientific assumption that everything had a cause within the empirical world. God cannot simply be imported as one cause among others.

I suggest that neither Tillich nor Richard Dawkins – to take representatives of both theist and atheist views – have a problem with Einstein's god. In fact, what Einstein's view exactly reflects the necessary recognition that the personal god of biblical narratives and popular devotion is a symbol, rather than a literal description.

The quest for certainty in the first half of the 20th century polarized thinking between the Biblical fundamentalists on one extreme and Logical Positivists on the other. Most people adopted neither position, but sat somewhere between them, with a gradual decline in formal religion but continuing levels of claimed belief in God. What that 'God' amounted to was debatable, particularly given the comments from thinkers as different as Barth and Tillich.

However, there was another branch of philosophy that seemed more relevant to questions of life and its meaning, and more compatible with Einstein's view: existentialism.

Chapter 11

Existential Efforts

*The unconditionally atheist is closer to the truly faithful
than is thoughtless mediocrity.*

Karl Jaspers

*By love he can be grasped and held,
but by thought, neither grasped nor held.*

The Cloud of Unknowing (anon)

A few years ago, the editors of the 'Teach Yourself' series decided that every book should start with a very brief summary of what its subject is about, under the heading 'Only got a minute?' This is how Nigel Rodgers and I summarized our *Understand Existentialism*, so – delaying you for no more than about 20 seconds – here's how it started:

What is human life about? What does it mean to be an authentic human individual? Am I trapped by the circumstances of my birth, or can I genuinely transcend them? How do I understand and cope with the hopes, fears and anxieties that shape my life?

These are existential questions. They do not require an overall explanation about the nature of reality. Nor can they be answered in scientific terms. Instead, they start with the basic fact that human individuals live in relation to the world around them. People have projects that they seek to fulfill; their choices are based on hopes for the future. Yet life is finite and we face an inevitable death. What, if anything, is therefore worthwhile?

These questions have long been explored through art, literature and religion, but they are also central to one particularly tradition in philosophy: existentialism.

The question about 'God' is an existential question, not a logical or scientific one; it is essentially about whether one can find meaning and direction in life.

Existentialism itself is a huge subject, from its precursors in St Augustine, Pascal, Kiekegaard, Nietzsche, Dostoyevsky, Kafka, Lao Tzu and the Buddha, through to Heidegger (although he never wanted to be identified as an existentialist, but that's another story), Jaspers, Merleau-Ponty, Buber, Sartre and Camus. It comes in both theist and atheist flavours and is seen in art and literature as well as philosophy. So, in this chapter, we shall address no more than a few existential questions: Do we sometimes need fiction to make sense of life? Can we get beyond the subject-object division and see ourselves as 'in the world'? How might religion respond to existential questions?

KINDLY DECEPTION?

In an example used by Peter L. Berger and quoted by John Bowden in *Voices in the Wilderness*, a child wakes in the night and, finding itself alone in the dark, screams in panic and despair. A moment later, its mother appears, cuddles it, and assures it that all is well. The child relaxes, reassured, and goes back to sleep.

Where is the truth in this? Is the child right to feel panic and despair, because it really is alone in a dark and heartless world, facing nothingness and death? Is the mother right to say that all is well, giving the child the sense that all is under control and loving, when she – if she is radically honest – knows that she cannot always be there for her child?

What sort of truth about the world do we need in order to live and be happy? A purely physical description is bleak; at the cosmic level we are all doomed. At the personal level, we shape our lives around things that we value and which give us a sense of meaning. Such value and meaning are inevitably self-generated, but does that make them any less valuable as tools for living?

In the introduction to *The Oxford Handbook of Atheism*, edited by Stephen Bullivant and Michael Ruse, the existential choice is set out starkly:

> A world with God and a world without God are two very different places, with very different meanings and obligations for us humans who occupy them. Humans created, loved and supported by the deity are humans very different from those who wander alone, without external meaning or purpose, creating their own destinies.

This is the existential crux of the matter: it is hard to challenge the idea that the sincerely held conviction that there is an omnipotent but caring deity is comforting, or that an impersonal world is threatening and heartless. That, of course was how Marx saw things, in calling religion both the opium of the people and the heart of a heartless world.

But that's not really the point. Comfort given on the basis of false assurance is superficial and leaves a person open to nagging doubt. Might it not be better, and less painful in the long run, to face reality with courage?

These questions are not new, of course. They feature in the distinction between the Stoics (who thought that there was a fundamental rationality in the cosmos) and the Epicureans (whose world was impersonal, but who responded by cultivating simple pleasures to make life worthwhile) and were highlighted in the 19th century by the debates between religion and science. Marx probed it as a critique of religion. And when whatever comfort the 19th century had provided in Europe was swept away by the Great War, the immediate result – as we saw in the last chapter – was the quest for certainty.

Yet, while that quest concentrated on factual claims – as typified by the Logical Positivists or the defence of atheism by Bertrand Russell – existentialist thinkers recognised that people do not live by factual bread alone. Hence the mother's need to give reassurance to her frightened child.

The novelist Albert Camus saw the world as 'absurd', in that our longing for order and reason conflicts with our awareness of the irrational and the impersonal nature of the universe. It's not the world itself that is absurd, but our conflicted longing for it to be other than it is. Camus is atheist, because he presents the answer to our absurdity as accepting the world as it is, without the need to long for it to be otherwise. But that only matches what the Buddha was saying two and a half thousand years earlier: that the fundamental cause of suffering is that we want things to be different, pretending to ignore the fact of constant change in everything around us and the inevitable impact that has upon us as individuals.

It leaves us with a question to which I can offer no general answer, since it needs to be based on a personal choice. In a world that inevitably fails to match our hopes, should we opt for a comforting narrative, or face bleak meaninglessness? Also, if we take the comforting option, will it still work for us if we harbour the conviction that it is not based on reality?

There is no doubt that the hybrid god – as seen in some of the hymns we examined earlier – can offer comfort, but can it continue to work in a world where the default approach to most things is non-theistic?

The intellectual challenge of accepting that rather simplistic and deist view of God, may suggest that the idea of God is more useful as an existential guide, rather than a factual proposition. In other words, to return to Kant, God becomes a 'regulative' rather than a 'constitutive' concept – a way of looking, rather than something at which one can look.

The answer to this, explored in the practice of Buddhism, is a personal commitment to see things as they really are, along with the pursuit of wisdom and compassion, leads to both contentment and positive living. Buddhism is not atheist, in a narrow Western sense, but non-theist, in that it avoids requiring concepts and images, including that of God, of those who follow its path. That said, of course, the practice of Buddhism as a religion can also embrace any number of Buddha and Bodhisattva images, and a wealth of traditional stories. The general point, however, is that Buddhism can use them without being committed to them. May this be a suitable way of approaching God?

BEING IN THE WORLD

There are two fundamentally different ways of understanding the world: the engaged and the alienated.

Engagement is the more natural way of living, and humans share it with all other sentient beings. It acknowledges the obvious fact that the world is that within which we live. Alone in a jungle at night, we are unlikely to debate whether or not the world around us is real. Our senses are attuned to what is around us in order to deal with it, to survive, feed and breed. From this perspective, to be disengaged is to be unnatural. It takes nerves of steel and the utmost philosophical detachment to sit in a dugout with Wittgenstein and write 'The world is all that is the case.' There is no logic to the chance falling of shells!

But here's the problem. Human intellect allows allows us to take a detached and analytic view. We can think of ourselves as separate from the 'external' world, and assume that our brains merely analyse our sense data and suggest courses of action. In that scheme, the world is 'out there' and we may well ask whether it is a dream of a reality. Do we live in a simulated environment? Although fun to contemplate in science fiction, and useful in conducting scientific research, this is hardly a normal way to see ourselves. It deliberately brackets out most of what makes life worth living, along with most of the skills that allow that living to continue.

In his monumental work *Being and Time*, Heidegger argued that God is all about our experience of being embedded in the world, rather than being separate from it. Although not identifying as an existentialist, Heidegger's influence on it is immense. One particularly important aspect of his thinking is the attempt to get behind the split between objectivity and subjectivity. Kant divided the world into noumena and phenomena – the former being things as they are in themselves, and the latter the experience we have of them. The former remain unknown and unknowable, because all our knowledge is based on experience. For Heidegger, however, we need to get behind this subject/object split and explore Dasein – literally 'being there', the way we live in the self-world, dealing with it in a way that has meaning and significance for us.

He sees the religious way of 'being in the world' as engaging with life at its most general. This is, in effect, the experience that mystics have always described – that of a self-world, in which the self is 'being-with' experience. It is, in effect, the reason why mindfulness practices are useful, because they help to cultivate a 'mood' (to use Heidegger's term) of direct engagement, of being-in-the-world.

Karl Jaspers (1883 – 1969) made significant contributions to existentialism, psychology and philosophy of religion. In his *Reason and Evidence* (from lectures given in Groningen in 1935) he speaks of 'the Encompassing'; this is not something experienced, but the limits of our experience. We *are* the

Encompassing, for we cannot be described as part of the objective, external world:

> The Encompassing itself, whether it be the Encompassing which we are or Being in itself, escapes from any determinate objectivity. An Encompassing which has become objective is no longer a true Encompassing. (p70)

That objective emcompassing is the same as the failed attempt to see myself as an object. I am more than that. The objective is never more than part of myself. Transcendence is therefore always something unknown, something beyond our concepts. You could almost develop this idea of Jaspers to say 'A God which has become objective is no longer the true God.' When shifted from existential awareness to scientific theory, God evaporates.

This is why all arguments for the existence of God fail, because they attempt to locate him within the world of experience – but the Encompassing, or Transcendence, cannot be located in that way, and all arguments for the existence of God therefore fail – a view endorsed by thinkers as different as Kant and Aquinas.

For Jaspers, Existenz is 'authentic self-awareness' without which any sense of transcendence, which can't be addressed through empirical means, is lost:

> without Existenz everything seems empty, hollowed out, without ground, fake, because everything has turned into endless masks, mere possibilities, or mere empirical existence. (p63)

Jaspers speaks of 'existential guilt' – the feeling that one has not lived up to what one might have done, recognising our limits and relative failure. We encounter existential questions and guilt particular in the context of 'boundary situations', such as facing our own mortality, or struggling with moral dilemmas. But that guilt can only be addressed in engaged living, not by observation. As with Heidegger, reality is not the same thing as objectivity, and it can be discovered only through engagement in life. For Heidegger, it was unthinkable that God should be reduced to the status of a being, for God is *Sein* (Being-itself).

In what Peter Lipton (1954 – 2007), the American-born philosopher of science and Hans Rausing Professor at the University of Cambridge, called the 'immersive approach' (see his article in *Philosophers and God*), he suggests that, without accepting the literal truth of beliefs or stories included in scriptures, it may be possible to discover the value of those beliefs or traditions by critically immersing oneself within them. They offer a perspective, and therefore answer existential questions, without requiring that one should first accept their literal truth.

It is possible, therefore, to see the immersion in religious worldviews as a process not unlike Thomas Kuhn's view of scientific paradigms: one inevitably lives with one paradigm until its internal contradictions reach a level at which one has to abandon it and attach oneself to another.

The issue for atheism, or course, is that it claims to have *no* worldview, but simply to follow the empirical evidence. However, that is not really the case, because many of those who make a very positive claim to atheism are thereby deliberately taking on a worldview that eliminates all elements of the supernatural, along with most metaphysical claims. As such, there is a fundamental difference between the atheism of, say, a Buddhist, whose view simply does not include (or need not include) the existence of a God or gods, and one who claims to be atheist on the basis of a wholesale rejection of a previously held religious view.

One might therefore consider degrees of atheism, based on the way in which its ideas are accepted existentially, as part of the culture within which we find ourselves. And this relates back to the quest for certainty that had such a hold on society, religion and philosophy through the middle decades of the 20th century. In a century of upheaval and threat, certainty looks a valuable tool in establishing the meaning of one's life.

Religion becomes a choice, a preference, a way of life to be adopted. It is optional, and may (or may not) confer benefits. And those benefits could be individual (a sense of belonging, or reconciliation to the facts of life, perhaps also to death) or social (a society held together through rituals, beliefs and celebrations), as had been explored by the sociologist Emile Durkheim back in the 19th century.

Most religious people believe that what they mean by God, and the values that they hold to be paramount for them, are not simply self-generated: they are 'found' rather than simply chosen, and they believe them to be foundational to the world. They are not just 'how I choose to live' but 'what life is about'.

CHOOSING AND RESPONDING

That religious belief should be a matter of personal choice and commitment is far from new. Pascal argued for it in the 17th century, Kierkegaard in the 19th, and it featured in Barth's revolutionary rejection of conventional and idealist thinking. But the rise of existential thinking in the 20th century, in both religious and atheist forms, gave it a new significance.

Modern existentialism appears centred on the experience of self, but that by no means precludes it for being a vehicle for exploring the meaning of God. The classic expression of the mystical quest is given in the 14th century mystical work *The Cloud of Unknowing*, which recommends the task of knowing oneself as a means of coming to know God.

Similarly, Buddhist practice, based on attention to the passing of emotions and awareness as a means of personal liberation, does not depend on rituals, authorities or scripture. Like existentialism, it rejects the idea of a permanent self, to which one is bound to conform, but points to the experience of developing oneself through the process of living – 'existence precedes essence', to use Sartre's phrase.

The challenge of existentialism is to take responsibility for how we live our lives, while recognising – as did the Stoics – that there are some things that are beyond our powers, and others over which we have a measure of control.

In *Existentialism as a Humanism*, 1946, Sartre argued that 'existence precedes essence' in that there is no 'essence' of a human being that is given by a creator; rather, each person creates his or her essence in the process of living. Thus the self is still real and important (perhaps too important, one might think, given the intense preoccupation with it) although self-generated. For Buddhists, exactly the opposite is true; the self is an illusion from which we try to free ourselves, a hindrance to our perception of the truth of how things are.

Supernatural religion had tended to blur that distinction, in that it was assumed that what God brought to our way in life was directly related to whether or not we believed, or prayed, or lived morally. The secular world was blunt in pointing to the realities of life and death, and argued that that science was quite able to offer explanations that did not depend on fate, or the will of the gods. Now, with the effort to see religion in an existential context, the responsibility returns to us. The question is not whether there is a known foundation to life, a successor to Aquinas' and Aristotle's 'uncaused cause', but whether we have a constructive part to play in shaping our own lives.

Existentialism has sometimes been presented as almost exclusively self-referential, and so it can be. But it is not necessarily so, for it can also present the challenge of engagement and effort. The issue, however, is that religion becomes a matter of insight and practice – something that we do and share – rather than a list of things that we are meant to accept as true. And this shifts the whole philosophy of religion in the direction that Wittgenstein took: from language as pointing to language as use. Religion is not a set of metaphysical claims, but a human activity that people engage in to make sense of the process of living.

Following Sartre's 'existence precedes essence', our reality is something that we ourselves create in the process of living. However, that should not be taken to extremes, for we are never going to be totally in charge of life: atomic structures and genetic codes are not within our control. But there is a profound shift with this way of thinking – from a passive acceptance of fate or a designed and providential world, to one where engagement is the only way to forge the future. There is a striving towards transcendence, but that is not the same as believing that there is a fixed transcendent to which we are obliged to strive.

And there is a second issue here. If there is a providential God, he already knows the future and what he has intended for us, so any appearance of freedom and choice on our part is an illusion. Existentialism, like atheism, cannot retreat into any such acceptance of a divinely provided destiny. Perception and reason become the basis for establishing norms and becoming committed to them. If theology has a place in such a view, it is expressive rather than constitutive: a way of articulating our hopes, rather than making factual claims.

TILLICH'S APPROACH

Existentialism is about 'ultimate concern' – to use Tillich's term – it is about personal commitments, about what we hold to be of supreme value and importance. So, from an existential perspective, God is as much about our 'ultimate concern' as 'Being itself.' This shaped Tillich's way of doing theology.

He started by pointing out that human beings naturally ask 'existential' questions, and are frustrated that empiricism and science can give no answers to them. We cannot prove that life either has or is devoid of meaning; it's just something we find for ourselves. However, Tillich suggested that religious language offered symbols that could offer an answer to such questions. In other words, existentialism sets the agenda, while religion provides hints at an answer. Unless you feel the need to ask what life is for, you are unlikely to be impressed by any religious answer, or even that of atheism. And, for Tillich, there is a reciprocal relationship – religious symbols enhance and give depth to existential questions, but in turn those religious symbols are given significance by being aligned with our existential questions.

So, to put it simply, the idea of a loving God will only be relevant if we are already aware a need for meaning and direction. Without the question, the answer becomes irrelevant.

From the atheist standpoint, the problem is that religious beliefs are presented as though they are external, fixed and able to be empirically justified. Whereas, as cultural creations, devised to give a sense of meaning and purpose, they enhance rather than threaten rational thought. In other words, for both theist and atheist, the purpose of enquiring about the meaning of things is fundamentally existential.

PRACTICAL SPIRITUALITY

One female minister with whom I discussed these things, presented a practical approach that seems influenced by existentialism. Faith, for her, was more a matter of the heart than of the intellect, seeing theological attempts to define belief as having a negative impact and therefore self-defeating. Christian liturgy, she argued, used visible symbols of spirituality, and presented the idea of God as an inward experience. For her, Jesus was seen as a radical humanist and a universalist, with socialism as part of the Christian legacy.

Her aim was to build a community of those who share and promote spiritual and moral values, while sitting lightly on intellectual questions about God. As we shall see, moving into the debates of the latter part of the 20th century, the old questions of God and atheism have little significance for those who adopt this personal, existential and practical view of religion. Their views of life are fully compatible with some forms of atheism, in that they do not depend upon traditional theistic arguments, nor depend on traditionally 'supernatural' ideas. What they think of as Faith, is an experience and a set of convictions about life, rather than a set of propositions or hypotheses about the nature of things.

It therefore seems to me not only possible, but essential to develop a spirituality that is not linked to superstition or the supernatural. At its heart, spirituality is about developing a sense of inner confidence and direction, growing a sense of identity, appreciating the world of which one is a part, and attempting to live by the moral and social implications of one's personal vision. For many people, that cannot happen with integrity if they are expected to be looking for an external or supernatural explanation for life, rather than simply engaging with life as it is experienced.

After all, superstition generally involves beliefs and practices that are irrational or unfounded, relying on luck, omens or supernatural forces, suggesting that everything depends on some external chance intervention. It is based on an unpredictable and unstable relation between self and world. By contrast, a spirituality that is not linked to supernatural ideas can be based on personal confidence and a realistic view of the world as it is, a view that can be honestly shared with others, whether they call themselves believers or atheists.

The third of the Buddha's 'universal truths' is that all life involves *dukkha*, a word that may be best translated as 'unsatisfactoriness' – that life does not live up to our expectations. Because everything is constantly changing, the world cannot fit into our particular hopes or schemes. To seek a spirituality based on the Buddha's teachings, one therefore has to take this element of change and chance into account, as a normal feature of human life. Getting a disease, or dying, is not seen as an external punishment, or 'the will of God', but a natural feature of life. One may struggle against illness and death; that is natural. One may use human ingenuity in the form of medicine or palliative care to enhance and prolong life; that too is natural. But there is absolutely no point in simply crossing your fingers or praying that things will be different; life is not open to such manipulation.

Spirituality without superstition is, I believe, key to using the best of the intuitions and insights offered by culture and religion as a guide for enhancing one's rational and emotional life. This does not preclude what some believers will refer to as 'grace', since all that we have comes from beyond ourselves, and all life is an acknowledgement of what is received, as much as what is generated by our own efforts.

Spirituality does not come ready made, but develops in the course of thoughtful and positive living, by being open to receive and learn from the changes that life brings, and accepting a measure of personal responsibility that has always been the hallmark of existentialism.

However, reality was rather lacking the curious corner into which the Philosophy of Religion seemed to have got itself in the years following World War Two, so it is time to explore its nonsense.

Chapter 12

Philosophical Nonsense

And if you would know God, be not therefore a solver of riddles.
Rather look about you and you shall see Him…
The Prophet, Kahlil Gibran

The main danger to theism today comes from people
who want to say that 'God exists'
and 'God does not exist' are equally absurd.
'*The Existence of God*', J.J.C. Smart

For the later years of my working life, the coming of summer was greeted by large grey packages of examination scripts on the Philosophy of Religion, waiting to be marked. It was an interesting, but frequently depressing task, watching so much intellectual effort produce so little by way of positive results.

More often than not, the questions presupposed that religious beliefs could answer the riddle of life by fancy intellectual footwork. But in truth there is no riddle. Life stands before us as it is; we either embrace it or hide from it.

There is a long tradition – from the mystics of the Western religions to the spiritual implications of Eastern thought – that sees our perception of life as too cluttered with our thoughts, fears, hopes, arguments and memories to see clearly what lies before us. De-cluttering would be particularly useful if it could rid us of much of what passes for the Philosophy of Religion as an academic subject.

HOW DID IT COME TO THIS?

I'm not sure who is more to blame: Bertrand Russell or Father Copleston. Perhaps it was just the context of the BBC's 'Third Program' intellectualism in the immediate postwar period. Their debate about God, broadcast on 28th January 1948, set an agenda for students of the Philosophy of Religion for decades, its famous protagonists seen as exemplifying humanist atheism and traditional theism.

Their debate went horribly wrong right from the start. Copleston, recognising the need for a provisional agreement on the meaning of 'God', says 'I presume that we mean a supreme personal being – distinct from the world and creator of the world' and Russell agrees. While Copleston thinks the existence of God can be proved philosophically, Russell is agnostic. So far, so disastrously 'hybrid', from a Catholic theologian steeped in Aquinas, who certainly did know better. My guess is that, being 'on the radio' he thought to simplify matters for the ordinary 'Third Program' listener.

Copleston then suggests that 'if God does not exist, human beings and human history can have to other purpose than the purpose they choose to give themselves…', adding later that if there is no God – in other words 'no absolute Being' – there can be no absolute values, to which Russell responds by pointing to alternative ways of establishing moral value.

Then, after launching into a discussion in which Copleston presents the cosmological case for God that has been mainstream since Thomas Aquinas and Aristotle, Russell cut back with:

> Well, certainly the question "Does the cause of the world exist?" is a question that has meaning. But if you say "Yes, God is the cause of the world" you're using God as a proper name; then "God exists" will not be a statement that has meaning…

That really is the crunch point. People have always asked and pondered about the source of values or the cause of the world. There's no problem there, it has have been the driving force behind much philosophy, art, culture and so on. It is a basic quest to understand both who we are and our relationship with the world around us. But to ascribe to it the name 'God' appears to be linking the open question to a very specific and pre-understood answer – an answer open to misinterpretation.

The fact that Copleston sees God as both distinct from the world and its creator sets the whole debate towards stalemate, for it suggests – although it does not state – that God is in some way 'outside' the universe. In terms of empirical evidence, 'distinct' implies 'separate from'. Things 'exist' if they stand out against a background (the origin of the term 'ex-istere' may be to do just that). Therefore it is easy to conceive of the God being spoken of as standing out against the world. The argument is doomed from that point, and so is 'God.' If only Copleston had started by saying that God does not 'exist' in the sense that other things exist, the misunderstanding might have been avoided. As it is, Russell presses on to say that the world is as it is and requires no cause, in other words no separate cause. But God never was that, not for the Early Fathers, nor for Aquinas or Anselm. Alas, even the best of Thomist scholars was trying to defend a position that was open to caricature.

ATHEIST PHILOSOPHY OF RELIGION?

Although I was not aware of it at the time, the Philosophy of Religion I studied at college in the 1960s was fundamentally atheist. It was based on the assumption that language about God, and claims about his nature, could be subject to logical scrutiny – intuition would not do, poetry would not do, fiction would not do, even abstract art would not do. Yet if beliefs need rational and empirical justification they exclude God, for such justification implies that God – if he exists – is part of the known universe. That assumption is not only false, but has been known to be false for more than two millennia.

So, for example, we looked at John Wisdom's 'Parable of the Gardener' and struggled, along with one of the two explorers who had come across a clearing in the jungle and assumed it to be a garden, to show that the arrangements of weeds and flowers could logically require an external gardener. Wisdom's conclusion was that, once you had done all the tests and found no evidence for the gardener who might come to tend the 'garden', you accept that the hypothesis of the gardener dies 'the death of a thousand qualifications'. Inevitably so, for the notion of God as a gardener is self-contradictory. God cannot be both an individual who acts in particular ways (i.e. tends this garden) and also an eternal, infinite being.

Logical positivism sought to reduce all language to factual, claims. Influenced by that approach, much of the philosophy of religion therefore sought to find intellectual wriggles that would allow religious belief to have meaning in terms acceptable to radical empiricism. It was a philosophical dead-end, because it argued, in effect, that God could only be shown to exist, if he were part of a world in which, by the assumed definition of 'God', he could not exist.

That approach suited both the theist and atheist sides in the debate. So, for example, in his book *A Defense of Atheism*, 1957, Ernest Nagel (1901 – 1985) the American philosopher of science, presented atheism primarily as a critique and denial of the claims made by theists. That narrow definition of what is involved in the theism/atheism debate continues to infect the Philosophy of Religion to this day.

Academic courses in the Philosophy of Religion also included the experiential approach of Schleiermacher and Otto and the existential approach of Keirkegaard, in an attempt to flesh out the significance of God, but the damage (from religion's point of view) has already been done. With reason as judge and jury, God could not exist, unless he could be re-defined as an abstract term for reality, and that, it was assumed, would never satisfy religious believers.

Stalemate!

If you think my comments here are harsh, consider this from Kai Nielsen in *Wittgenstein's Fideism*, 2005:

> ... I have little time for the standard philosophy of religion business. It is too complacently rationalistic and stuck with either a metaphysical realism or anti-realism or the dogmatism of Reformed epistemology. I think of the philosophy of religion as the slum section of contemporary philosophy and this considered judgement of mine has nothing to do with my atheism. This at least putative state of the philosophy of religion is all the more saddening given the human importance of religion. (p98)

The key point is in that last sentence. The philosophy of religion had become an intellectual game detached from the practice of religion, but it was what students studied, giving them the false impression that it was what religion is about.

However, Nielsen argues that post-metaphysical conceptions of God reduce to a moral core. That is too narrow. The moral dimension of religion is largely a response to a sense of wonder, meaning and purpose in life, to which moral views are only one form of response.

POSITIVE CONTRIBUTIONS?

Only two things are required in the philosophical assessment of religion – internal consistency and external compatibility. The first is required if believers are to find that their religion offers an integrated view of life, which is largely what the religious quest is about anyway. The second is necessary because, if religious ideas are incompatible with the majority of things that people hold to be true, accepting them will

191

cause a certain amount of duplicity, or what we tend to call 'cognitive dissonance'.

In theory, philosophy should be a useful tool in sorting out both the internal and external compatibility of religious claims. As it is, it has long been dominated by arguments that are frankly nonsense. They are outdated, in the sense that they have been substantially answered long since, and they provide an unwelcome distraction from any serious attempt to get to grips with what religion is, what it offers, and why it has survived so many intellectual and cultural attempts to eliminate it.

In *Atheism: a very short introduction*, 2003 the English philosopher Julian Baggini pointed out that what most atheists deny is much broader than the narrow questions about God's existence, including everything to do with the supernatural or the transcendent. His assumption is that, if you reject the idea of God, you are likely to reject all the rest as well. Belief in God is not a standalone idea; it is the focus of a much broader view of the way the world works. But demolishing arguments for the existence of God is not in itself going to remove the reasons why many people continue to be religious.

There is an additional problem: the mismatch between a philosophical approach and the experience of 'believers'. This was clearly set out in a lecture given in Adelaide in 1951 by the philosopher J. J. C. Smart, and reproduced in *New Essays in Philosophical Theology*, originally published in 1955 and used by many generations of theological students:

> In order to acquire the concept of an electron we must find out about experiments with cathode-ray tubes, the Wilson cloud chamber, about spectra and so on. We then find the concept of the electron a useful one, one which plays a part in a mass of physical theory. When we reach this stage the question 'Do electrons exist?' no longer arises. Before we reached this stage the question 'Do electrons exist?' had no clear meaning. Similarly, I suggest,

the question 'Does God exist?' has no clear meaning for the unconverted. But for the converted the question no longer arises. The word 'God' gets its meaning from the part it plays in religious speech and literature, and in religious speech and literature the question of the existence of God does not arise.

This mismatch corresponds to the shift in Wittgenstein's thinking, from his early view of meaning as based on empirical evidence, to his later one of meaning given by use. For Smart and many later theologians, the meaning of 'God' is the use that word has in the practice of religion.

If that really is the case, then the stalemate between theists and atheists about the existence of God does not matter. Philosophy and theology adopt very different perspectives, and it is therefore perfectly possible to be atheist with respect to the arguments for the existence of God, but yet find the idea of 'God' a useful one in religion and culture.

More than that, the failure of the philosophy of religion contributes to my original thesis that atheism can come to the rescue of God, because it shows clearly that 'God' is a cultural construct rather than an existing entity. And that remains true even if you, personally, find the idea of God an inspiring one or one that helps to make sense of your life.

In 1984, Keith Ward – an Oxford Professor known for his traditional but well-articulated approach to Christian ideas – published a modest book entitled *The Living God*. In it he sets out to explain that we need to rid ourselves of the literal idea of God as a separate being, existing somewhere beyond our experienced world. So far, so orthodox and traditional But then, as we go on through the book, he starts to say of God that 'he knows,' 'he directs,' that his wisdom is 'expressed in' the world, and so on. Now, it is clear that Ward does not mean this language to be taken literally – that would imply a crude, physical idea of God – but the fact that he speaks of

God as expressing intelligence, preferences, and taking action to direct things, gives a linguistic context in which the imagination is led to see God as a separate, intelligent, willing agent.

In other words, he has switched from the more philosophical way of speaking to one that reflects culture and narrative. He is telling a story and describing a person acting within it. He is cautious in doing this, however. In talking about religious experience, he is able to say that those who do not believe in God may also have experiences that point to what God means (page 75). But a little later, speaking of worship, he asks 'So why does God want us to praise him?' (page 80).

What Ward does here, in his careful and measured way, is to allow philosophy to slip into cultural narrative. He moves from *logos* to *mythos* without explaining why. As a result, those who do not notice that the move has happened, assume he is arguing philosophically and either accept a literal idea of God or reject his conclusions entirely. At this point, the thoughtful atheist is probably nearer to the idea of God than the superficial believer – a view endorsed by Karl Jaspers, Paul Tillich and others..

I also have reservations about two serious attempts to relate religious ideas to our usual understanding of the world...

The first is that of Stephen Jay Gould, who – in a range of books on science and religion – takes the view that they have non-overlapping magisterial (NOMA). In other words, science deals with empirical facts, which religion deals with values and metaphors, and therefore that there is no overlap between their two worlds. In my view, that will not stand scrutiny, because the practice of science and technology has profound ethical and human significance. Science may use empirical methods, but the values by which it operates, and the decisions about where funding should be provided for research are very much based on values, religious or secular. Similarly, the worldview of religion shapes society, and hence gives impetus (or otherwise) to the scientific endeavour. The two magisteria overlap most of the time.

The other is the position of Alvin Plantinga, who sees belief in God as 'properly basic'. In other words, he considers that such belief is the basis upon which other beliefs are founded, but which does not itself require further evidence. This foundationalism – called 'Reformed Epistemology' after the views of the reformer, John Calvin – regards God as just there, unchallengeable. Clearly, some value or intuition about reality is going to be experienced as basic – unless you enter the heady realm of postmodernism where any view or truth is as good as any other. But why does that have to be God? An atheist might say that 'God' here is a symbol pointing to a particular quality of human relationships – for example love – so only the latter is basic.

And alongside this, I am haunted by a phrase of Richard Dawkins (in *Out of Eden*, 1996) that the universe shows 'blind, pitiless indifference', a characteristic that we would expect if there is no god. The question that needs to follow that observation – and one I considered in my earlier book *Home: a Philosophy of Personal Space* is: How then can we manage to feel positive and 'at home' in such a world?

The essence of religion is to provide a way of interpreting life and providing it with value. So the question becomes: As you engage with life, do you see in all around you signs of the invisible, undetectable hand of God, acting alongside the ordinary world perceived by the senses? Or do you see all that happens as an expression of a vulnerable and changing reality, sufficient in itself and the bearer of values? Can you, like Nietzsche, say 'yes' to life, whatever happens? A non-theist may argue that all life is vulnerable, and therefore that suffering – in the sense of the inevitability of illness, old age and death – is inevitable. Life does not pose a question, but a challenge.

THE POINTLESSNESS OF ARGUMENT

The Buddha argued that attempting to rationalise and explain life is pointless. What matters is what one does, and how one sets about creating happiness and avoiding suffering; from this perspective, overthinking the issue may be a distraction.

If all our seeing and understanding is coloured by our experience and the culture within which we live, is there any point whatsoever in trying to argue about these things?

Theologians start from the standpoint of religion and examine issues that arise from it. That's their job – and we see it in the work of Plantinga, Swinburne, William Lane Craig and a host of others, including the Catholic radical Hans Küng, or the Protestant radical Paul Tillich, along with social and political theology, where Christian teachings are applied to practical situations. All this is good and positive, showing both the relevance and the intellectual coherence of religious claims, using both 'natural theology' (beliefs that are supported by reason) and 'revealed theology' (supported by the interpretation of scripture). They work from *within* religion.

The experience of religion is a mixture of emotional commitment, existential hope and engagement with the religious narrative. It generally includes some intellectual propositions, but these are seldom brought to the fore. They are tokens of religious commitment, but not its driving force. The only time most religious people find themselves defending arguments for the existence of God is when they engage in debate with those who do not believe.

Hence, any philosophical debate between theist and atheist, is likely to be unsatisfactory. Each side defends its overall experience of life, but does so through the proxy of a discussion about whether or not there is a Supreme Being. Minds are seldom changed by such argument. Although I say it with a heavy heart, it is just a form of academic Sudoku.

If you feel comfortable using religious language to express your experience of reality, feel free to do so. You will benefit from language and rituals honed over centuries. But if you do not, it is equally healthy to declare yourself atheist because, even if you want to retain the values expressed in religion, you do not need to use God-language to express them.

THE SLIPPERY SLOPE

What counts as acceptable belief varies against the current background of ideas, and in our largely secular society there has been a slippery slope in terms of religious doctrines.

Probably the first to go was the literal idea that the end of the world was nigh. By the late 20th century that had more or less gone from the religious agenda, except for a minor blip as the millennium approached. Next came disease as caused by demon possession. It too became a fringe interest. Miracles were mainly interpreted in symbolic terms, and then became limited to those performed by Jesus and related to healing. The miraculous crossing of the Red Sea, manna in the desert and turning stocks into snakes, had long been demythologised.

What remained were the miraculous events that seemed crucial to the Christian message – including, of course, the virgin birth and the resurrection of Jesus. Fundamentalists continued to argue that creation took place as outlined in Genesis, but a majority of believers saw the narrative as showing the significance of creation rather than a description of how the world started. Evolution became acceptable.

One of the most clearly slipped beliefs was what happens after death. The Greek idea that people had immortal souls was originally seen as incompatible with the Christian idea that the dead would – at the Second Coming – be raised up and given a new, spiritual body, so 'the resurrection of the body' remained in the creeds, even if seldom defended, and often regarded as naïve.

In a postgraduate Philosophy of Religion seminar at King's London, at the end of the 1960s, I found myself getting irritated by an argument claiming that the natural immortality of the soul was a fundamental requirement for Christian belief. At the end of the paper, I modestly asked how such a view related to the Christian idea of the resurrection of the body. By the look on the face of the learned professor who had just delivered the paper, you might have thought I had audibly farted! "That's just nonsense!" he said, and the matter was closed. Now, I thought it was a reasonable question since, as undergraduates, we had been taught that the resurrection of the body had been a fundamental feature of early Christian belief. However, the resurrection at the end of time came from a worldview so distant that the professor no longer saw it as a feature of Christian thought. To me, that showed what the Philosophy of Religion had done to the range of ideas that were acceptable as religious beliefs. Those compatible with early Greek thought, or with reason and evidence, were in, while those from the more colourful spectrum of supernatural ideas were out.

That was quite different from what I had experienced out in the world of Anglican parishes. There, people wanted to believe because they loved the worship, the ancient buildings, the hymns and the traditional readings. That was more real than any intellectual debate. They were engaged with a community of like-minded people, a set of moral values, and a sense that religion could make the world a better place.

Intellectual arguments may have seemed pointless, but a few years before my frustrating seminar, they had the effect of prodding the Church of England into recognising that what was popularly believed in the pews of its churches was rather out of step with ideas being explored in academia. For many, the issues came to a head in 1963, with the newspaper headline 'Our Image of God must Go!'

Chapter 13

A Belated Funeral?

Our Image of God Must Go
The Observer, Sunday March 17th 1963

Be with God as though God did not exist.
Dietrich Bonhoeffer

'God' is a word that belongs to the past.
Paul Van Buren

Sometimes the debate following a book's publication can be more enlightening than the book itself. That is largely the case with John Robinson's *Honest to God*, published by SCM Press in March 1963. Within months, not only had it sold hundreds of thousands of copies – remarkable for a book about religious belief – but it sparked a major controversy within the church and society.

Robinson, the Church of England bishop of Woolwich, with time on his hands while recovering from back trouble, decided to write about the challenges to Christian doctrine, which he sought to guard and defend. He did so, as he made clear in his Preface, because 'I am convinced that there is a growing gulf between the traditional orthodox supernaturalism in which our Faith has been framed and the categories which the 'lay' world (for want of a better term) finds meaningful today.' He was also against the tendency of orthodox believers to brand as 'enemies' those who do not share their views. So, fearing that he may not have been radical enough, he introduced the laity to theologians who had long been accepted within the world of academic theology, but were relatively unknown to lay believers: Bultman, Bonhoeffer and Tillich. The book was his reflection on the fact that the Church was becoming increasing ignored by the population it was called to serve. Coming from a bishop, however, the book was explosive.

And in a quiet corner of Essex, for this doubting 17-year-old, the book came as a breath of fresh air. It reassured me that I was not alone in questioning the supernatural and, more importantly, it introduced me to the work of Paul Tillich, who inspired me to read theology, convincing me that I could now do so in good conscience and with integrity. My parents caught me reading it and, by their reaction, it might as well have been pornography. Perhaps, for them, as unquestioning, loyal churchgoers, it was just that.

THE CONTROVERSY

A few months later, SCM press followed their blockbuster with *The Honest to God Debate*, by John Robinson and David Edwards, gathering a wide range of comments and reviews.

Reading it again recently, I am struck by how little the academic community appreciated why there was such a fuss. Bonhoeffer, Tillich and Bultman were theologians who had been studied extensively and were appreciated within the academic world. Yet for those who held a traditional, supernatural perspective, Robinson's argument that 'our image of God must go' came as a shock. Yet all he had done was to set aside the caricature of the 'hybrid' god, in order to reinstate theism.

One of the contributors to that book has already been introduced. In 1948, the sharp and youthful Frederick Copleston had taken on the venerable Bertrand Russell, in the debate that set much of the sad agenda of Philosophy of Religion. Now, as I sat at his feet in King's College, London, Copleston had himself become venerable, with a multi-volume history of philosophy to his credit and a reputation as a sound and balanced thinker with a distinctly conservative and Thomist cast of mind. Here, in *The Honest to God Debate*, Copleston states clearly that he never had - nor should anyone else - considered God to be 'up there' or 'out there', or located in any other way within the universe. The God whose image Robinson declared to be in need of change, had never existed.

At the same time, there was fury among many readers that God was being dethroned and that the faith within which people had been brought up was in jeopardy. There were calls for the Bishop to resign from the Church whose foundations he appeared to be trying to demolish. It was a clear indication that the theological errors to which Robinson was pointing were long established and deep-seated.

One of the newspaper headings featured on the cover of the *Debate*, under the claim that 'Bishop's book will shock thousands' was 'God is not a daddy in the sky.' To which one should only say 'of course not, and never was'. The true shock was that thousands were shocked by this new revelation.

From a Catholic standpoint (in the journal *Blackfriars*, July/August 1963), Herbert McCabe sums up the problem of dealing with the question of 'God.' Critical of Robinson's presentation of the 'traditional' idea of a God 'up there' or 'out there', he comments:

> A very great deal of work has been done, and vastly more books have been written, on the problem of how to speak of the existence of a God who is not part of reality, who is neither a particular thing nor yet an 'abstraction', who is not any kind of thing at all and who cannot be defined or described. The book [*Honest to God*] contributes nothing towards the solution of these ancient problems but it does

considerable service in reminding people that the problems exist.

In some quarters, the situation has not changed substantially in this regard. Whereas theologians and a majority of thinking Christians do not think that God 'exists' in any such literal sense, that is not the impression given to those outside the orbit of the three monotheistic religions. In particular, the image of God dismissed by Robinson continues to be used in philosophical debates and in the popular writings of the 'New Atheists.' It is sometimes presented as the 'genuine' image of God, as opposed to the more subtle ideas of theologians. In this way, a narrowly focused atheism continues to challenge a long-discredited form of deism.

Hence the central importance of examining whether 'God' can be rescued from crude literalism The misunderstanding of the nature of God, as it appears in popular discussion of arguments for and against the existence of such a God, does a double disservice. On the one hand, its caricature insults those who take belief seriously; on the other, it encourages people to dismiss the whole idea of God, leaving a gaping hole, not just in the way we express human aspirations and hopes, but in the appreciation of so much Western culture.

In his contribution to the debate, Alastair MacIntyre, combining humour with cutting logic, starts by saying that Robinson is clearly an atheist, and that Protestant theology, of the sort represented by Tillich, Bonhoeffer and Bultman, is also atheist because it follows Feuerbach in translating theological statements into human ones. He concludes:

> The difficulty lies in the combination of atheism in the practice of the life of the vast majority, with the profession of either superstition or theism by the same majority. The creed of the English is that there is no God and that it is wise to pray to him from time to time. (p227f)

What I find extraordinary is that MacIntyre and Copleston could come to such different conclusions. From within the world of traditional Christian belief, nothing in *Honest to God* was really new – at least not among the ranks of the academic theologians. But from the world of the philosophy of religion, which had been focused on arguments that related to the 'hybrid' god, Robinson and his radical theologians seemed to be supporting atheism. What Robinson was actually doing was attempting to rescue God from a deist caricature and reinstate a broader, more thoughtful theism.

THE DEATH OF GOD?

Over the years, many thinkers have declared God to be dead – from Thomas Hardy and Friedrich Nietzsche in the 19th century to the 'Death of God' theologians who emerged into public consciousness in the 1960s and 70s, following the debates initiated by *Honest to God*.

The approaches taken by radical theology in those days are many and beyond the scope of this book. Some took an incarnational approach, which insisted that the only way to speak about God was to speak about Jesus, the political and religious radical from Nazareth. Others that religious language was no longer a valid way to describe reality, and that 'God' in all his forms, was a word that belonged to the past. All were opposed to the 18th century hybrid god of popular caricature. Hence, my conclusion then (and now) was that the supernatural god had to be shown to be bogus, if the best of religious ideas were to be of use in a secular world. It is no longer helpful for either side of the atheism/theism debate to be stuck with an idea that was never credible.

In *Confessions of a Buddhist Atheist* Stephen Batchelor describes the experience of writing about an existentialist approach to Buddhism in 1980, which had the effect of clarifying and stimulating his thought. He then says...

I saw myself, arrogantly perhaps, as a participant in a groundbreaking experiment to redefine traditional religious thinking in a way that transcended sectarian boundaries. This experiment was neither Christian, Jewish, nor Buddhist: it was an attempt to humanise and secularise religion, to free is from the prison of metaphysics and supernatural beliefs, to allow it to speak out in a lucid, impassioned, and committed voice. (p59)

This is exactly what motivated me to write my first book, *Cancer and the God of Love*, and I felt an immense sense of relief at having said something positive about getting beyond supernatural beliefs: that love was real, and that God was no more than an optional way of describing that reality. Without denying the value of the idea of God for other people, I was free to come out as an atheist. The world felt more real, more immediate, more open, but at the same time there was a depth and a beauty in religious symbolism and liturgy that I was to miss terribly.

For a while I had already been cheating; let me give a single example. For me, the most intimate and wonderful moment was to give the bread and wine to those who come up to the rail for communion at the Eucharist. In a moment of quiet reflection, each person's hands opened to receive the tiny wafer – a moment of commitment, simplicity, shared with all the others who are kneeling along that communion rail. I said what I was expected to say: 'The Body of Christ,' but what I thought immediately before that, but left unsaid, were the words 'You are...' That was theologically sound. The people sharing the Eucharist were exactly that – members of the body of Christ – and in that moment they were touching the most intimate source of personal meaning. They were, to use the traditional term 'becoming God' (*theopoesis*). In that way, reality had taken over from optional supernatural language. That, for me, was also a kind of 'death of God' – the religious words evaporating to leave a more basic reality. It got me into trouble, but that's another story.

However, as I soon found (as no doubt did Stephen Batchelor) the world moves on, carrying its old weight of supernatural problems, having simply by-passed the for-all-time answer that one arrogantly assumed one had provided.

But who had really killed God?

When Pope John Paul II published *Crossing the Threshold of Hope* in 1994, he sought to identify the culprits who appeared to have killed off God. One might have assumed that the Pope would point the finger at the likes of Nietzsche or Marx, followed by the Logical Positivists or Existentialists, but no. In his view, the blame lay with Descartes and the thinkers of the Enlightenment. Why? For exactly the reason we have been examining in this chapter: that Descartes and his followers, insisted that everything depended upon reason and evidence, and thus God was excluded from the normal way in which people were to examine the world. In contrast to the earlier view, in which God was imminent in the world, and thus a way to interpret the world, he was relegated to an external hypothesis. Hence the development, as the Pope saw it, of inadequate ideas of God, and particular of deism.

I never thought I would end up agreeing with a Pope, but in this I believe he was entirely correct. It was the Enlightenment mind-set that made God unbelievable and transcendence limited to a subjective longing or a positive view of human culture. If only Descartes had not concluded his battle against a demon deceiver with the defensive and limiting 'I think, therefore I am', but instead had taken the positive and self-affirming 'I am, therefore I think' we could have been spared much philosophical and theological grief.

Robinson might have encouraged the idea that 'Our image of God must go!', but actually that image of God had died several generations previously. It was as if theologians of the mid 20th century had suddenly woken up to the implication of the work of Nietzsche, Feuerbach, Durkeim, Shleiermacher and Marx. The popular idea of God had been wrong, and wrong for at least two hundred years. Not only were they catching up with 19th century thinking, but they were equally looking back to the 13th century and even the 3rd and 4th. The Early Fathers, struggling to engage with Hellenistic thought in order to make Christian teachings intellectually acceptable, as later did Aquinas and Anselm in their day.

The traditionally pious of the mid-20th century may have been upset by attempts to proclaim the death of God, but most other people just shrugged their shoulders and moved on.

MOVING ON?

Since then, things have moved on and the theologians of that era seem as quaint as their contemporary hippies with their flares, hair and flowers. Nevertheless, it was a heady time for theology, with the possibility of a secular form of Christianity, indeed what was termed 'Christian atheism' seemed possible. Emphasis shifted from supernatural claims to the secular features of religion, the universal quest for love and peace, and – following the example of Jesus – a critical distancing from formal religion.

In *But That I Can't Believe*, 1967, John Robinson asked 'Do we need a God?' By way of illustrating his answer, he cited what was then a recent survey of religious belief in England, in which 84% of those surveyed claimed to believe in the existence of God, against only 2% who definitely did not. The equivalent percentage of believers in the USA at the time was given as 97%! More remarkably, 45% claimed to pray regularly. However, he commented that, when their other views were taken into account, most of that 45% were 'practical atheists', and he therefore concluded that the traditional question about whether or not God existed had ceased to be relevant.

Now, 58 years later, the situation is quite different. Today, a minority of people in both East and West are regular, practicing members of religion within their cultures. Atheism, and secular humanism are respectable intellectual positions to hold. Indeed, to avoid cognitive dissonance, they are the only positions to take on most issues and enquiries. Almost half the population claim to have no religion, and a substantial but smaller percentage are prepared to declare themselves to be atheist. But the legacy of religion remains, giving depth and richness to life in literature, art, architecture and music. Its stories and its values continue to nourish.

Something significant has happened over this last half century, but it's not what the theologians of the 1960s expected. Their exploration of the 'death of God' that Nietzsche had proclaimed a century earlier, was something of a belated funeral for a deity that had been in serious decline for most of the first half of the 20th century. They spoke as though the moment had arrived when 'God' was about to change beyond recognition, the Church was to become an agent for secular change, and we had all come of age. It didn't quite work out like that.

In my view, one of the finest surveys of religious thought and its engagement with atheism and secularism in the 1970s, is contained in two books by the Swiss theologian Hans Küng (1928-2021). In *On Being a Christian* and *Does God Exist?*, Küng, a devout but radical Catholic priest and thinker, takes a long and deeply argued position of the way Christian thought can relate to the modern secular world. Needless to say, any form of deism is rejected in favour of a god who is encountered within reality itself. My only hesitation with the second of those books is that he is all too ready to identify atheism with nihilism. So, whilst he claims that there can be no definitive way of arguing for either theism or atheism, he sees that as parallel to the commitment to a sense of meaning as against a broadly nihilist view, while my view is that it is quite possible to take an atheist view while at the same time taking a very positive view of life and human commitments.

But theology and philosophy moved on, each in its own direction. In *The Existence of God* (Clarendon Press, 1991), Richard Swinburne argued that, although religious experience cannot in itself be conclusive with respect to the existence of God, it adds to the *probability* that God exists, and that we must assume that most of the time most people do in fact experience what they claim to experience. That, of course, is nonsense of many levels, as we have already seen. To claim to experience God is an interpretation of an experience, rather than an objective account of what it experienced. The argument from religious experience should be about the convictions that arise from such experiences, rather than about the claim to have experienced 'God'. The problem is that a philosophical question is being addressed, rather than religious or existential one.

Thinkers such as D.Z.Phillips and Don Cupitt took a non-realist approach. This argues that religious claims do not correspond to a state of affairs, but rather are initiating a 'form of life' to use Wittgenstein's term. They form a set of beliefs that have internal and personal coherence. As with any non-realist approach, the key thing (as with Gareth Moore, *Believing in God*, 1988, himself a Catholic theologian), is that religious truths are made rather than discovered. In other words, within their 'form of life' a religious community will create a system of ideas and values.

As Peter Vardy has pointed out (*Routledge Companion to the Study of Religion*, 2005, p93), the key point is that for non-realists, language about God 'does not refer to any reality or state of affairs beyond itself' but that 'it is true because it is accepted and used by those within the community of faith'. In other words, the idea of God is a cultural construct, rather than an objective entity.

But these discussions do not even touch on the development of political theology – especially as Liberation Theology developed in South America – or urban theology, or the other ways in which religious ideas have been explored and applied in a practical and ethical context. There is more to language about 'God' over the last half century than has ever met the metaphysical eye.

But while theology has generally been getting more 'incarnational' – in other words, looking at the secular, practical and moral implication of Christian thought – philosophy of religion has, if anything turned in the other direction, and continued to show the metaphysical failures of religious belief that few religious people still hold. That led to the endless examination scripts I used to mark, and also to the sadder phenomenon of the 'New Atheists' of the early 21st century, and all the superficial nonsense that has proved to be such a distraction from the real issues of religion and the quest for meaning.

A BELATED FUNERAL?

God seems to have been given far too many funerals. Some, as Nietzsche, think they have come too early, and that God's death is still some way off. Hardy observed the funeral in despair during the years before the Great War. Others, like the 'Death of God' movement of the 60s and 70's are certainly belated: the death they proclaimed had come decades earlier, probably on the battlefields of that Great War. Fashionable theologians were merely catching up with what had been a reality for a majority of people for decades, even if the churches had continued to plod on with dwindling congregations and a positive willingness to do good.

Thinking they saw a twitch in the corpse, the New Atheists of the first years of the 21st century were determined to drive a stake down through its heart, forever ridding the world of its pernicious influence. Unfortunately, for them, their efforts did little to enable God to have a proper funeral. If anything, the superficiality of their attack only strengthened the case for God, albeit in a more liberal and reflective form.

A funeral tends to be the time to take an overview of the deceased's life and to celebrate his or her achievements. For good or ill, the explosive interest in God in the 1960s and 70s, against a background of radical politics, flower power, dreams for a better future, and – for the Beetles and others – the discovery of Eastern religion and meditation, was the appropriate time for the funeral of the hybrid god, after its 200 year life. Since then, both within the Church and outside it, there has been little excuse for not being aware of the ambiguity of the word 'God'. The narrow innocence of 19th century hymn-writers or 20th century Logical Positivists was no longer a valid option for those who would attempt a serious look at religion.

But, from within secular culture, the world was busy devising other stories to give comfort and direction, which were embedding themselves in society, replacing the former hegemony of religion and becoming what Nietzsche referred to as the 'Shadows of God'.

Chapter 14

Meaning, Home
and the Shadows of God

*The greatest task for any person is to find
meaning in his or her own life.*
Viktor Frankl

God is dead... Yet his shadow still looms.
Friedrich Nietzsche

*And the people bowed and prayed,
To the neon God they made*
The Sound of Silence, Simon & Garfunkel

God would appear to be optional; the quest for meaning is not. A sense of identity, of meaningful engagement with life, and of a world in which one can feel 'at home' is fundamental to human happiness. Their lack engenders both selfishness and a sense of emptiness.

If you have followed my argument thus far, you will know that I despair of debates between theists and atheists and the naïve literalism of some who claim to believe in God and others who do not. Why despair? Simply because the question of God threatens to be a distraction from the fundamental issue for which language about 'God', at its best, has always been a proxy: the quest for meaning.

LOGOTHERAPY

It's all too easy to quip that the secret or life is that there is no secret, but that morphs all too easily into the more sinister view that the meaning of life is that life has no meaning. Few have been content without meaning which, at its most basic, is found in our relationships, our work, our projects, our beliefs (in the original sense of that word) and our sense of identity through home, locality and nationality.

Nietzsche feared that the death of God would lead us to drift in a meaningless, darkening universe. But in practice that has not been most people's experience. If the meaning provided by religion is removed, people simply find alternatives – the 'shadows' of God that Nietzsche saw as his replacements.

In his book *Man's Search for Meaning*, 1946, the psychotherapist Victor Frankl developed techniques to help people find purpose and direction even in the most challenging of circumstances. These included mentally focusing on others, rather than oneself, the benefit of friendships and social support, the value of creativity, and a general acceptance that the world is not fair. Key to his approach is the assumption that meaning is something that people choose and generate for themselves; it is not simply 'given' from outside. Frankl argued that the quest for meaning was our main motivating force – a view that set him at loggerheads with both the Freudian and Adlerian approaches to psychotherapy, and led him to develop 'logotherapy' as an alternative.

For those who might think his 'will to meaning' is unrealistic, it might be worth recalling that Victor Frankl survived four years in Nazi concentration camps during the Second World War. His father had died in Theresienstadt, his mother and brother in Auschwitz and his wife in Bergen-Belsen. Logotheraphy was not a theory born of new age fancy, but in circumstances that might be expected to destroy any sense of meaning and purpose. Any positive view of life that survives Auschwitz needs to be taken seriously.

For Frankl, we are free to choose how we respond to our circumstances and having a sense of meaning and direction can be an aid to survival. His work adds an interesting, practical and therapeutic dimension to our discussion. The cultural aspects of religion have always included both creativity and community – with people inspired by ritual, literature, art, architecture and the sense of belonging to a place of worship. But, if Frankl is right, this cultural benefit operates independently of specific beliefs and therefore does not depend on a traditional idea of God.

HOME

In my earlier book *Home: a philosophy of personal space* I argued that the quest for a sense of home reflects a deep human need and lies behind much of the religious impulse and the idea of God. It can't be wrong to want to feel at home in our world, and everything we do to enhance our sense of belonging improves the quality of our life. But that is a human task, made even more necessary as our knowledge of the dimensions and impersonal nature of the universe has increased.

Believing in a loving God who has concern for your personal welfare is going to be comforting. Belonging to a religious community, within which you have a part to play and bonds of loyalty and friendship, is reassuring. Believing that you can engage with the creative force of the world through prayer, and thereby receiving guidance and inspiration, is positive in terms of your sense of identity. Practising a religion can therefore offer a great deal in terms of personal direction and meaning. That is part of its attraction, and no doubt accounts for why religions and religious beliefs have survived.

The fundamental question therefore: can you feel 'at home' in the universe as an atheist? In challenging and questioning religious doctrines and beliefs, does atheism automatically deny the sources of comfort that religion traditionally provided?

Society, is seems, cannot easily dispense with myth, for it remains the driving force behind social cohesion, morality and creativity. Some story with a positive ending is required. If there is to be no religion, and no mythology, life remains at a very thin, superficial level. Culture requires and therefore generates myth. The idea of the self as a separate, creative, choosing entity is itself a form of myth.

In the absence of God, surrogates become all the more important, attempting to fill the gap that – as the old quip goes – is 'much needed'. Here the atheist, agnostic and humanist fraternities who seem to cling on most determinedly to myth – whether it is evolution, or growth, or humanity, or scientific understanding, or creativity – for, in the absence of some metaphysical claim to give direction and meaning, humankind must set about creating an alternative or two.

For the supernaturalist, 'home' is likely to be elsewhere – in a heaven that awaits, or in a spiritual realm that is distinct and separate from the physical universe – but for an atheist, there is no such option. For the atheist, any feeling of being 'at home' is related to this world. It is, of course, also true of the intellectually liberal approach to theism – for God is that 'within which we live, move and have our being', the common 'home' for all.

Without vision, people perish – not immediately, but by the death of a thousand dissatisfactions. The problem: how to re-gain the sort of inspirational direction given to life by religion, without letting go of one's integrity. My sense is that atheism is a constant and valuable reminder that home is here, not in some external paradise. But to make that real we need both intuition and culture; home cannot be built on science and logic alone.

CAN WE BE HONEST AND STILL DREAM?

We look at things, intuit meaning and value them. We use our imagination to think of their use, their future and our relationship to them. We design; we create; we entertain dreams and hopes for the future. We dwell, inhabit and shape our environment. We know how we would like things to be, even if we do not know how to change them.

With success, our dreams become reality. We express ourselves and are pleased with the result, whether it is a business, a practical job that needed to be done, a work of art, or perhaps something we have bought, or a new friendship established. Without intuition and imagination, none of these things would have come about. They are the product of the relationship between our minds and the world around us; they are our culture.

Sometimes, of course, reality shatters such dreams, as we encounter failure and death, or prolonged suffering, or frustration at human folly, both our own and that of others. We despair and lose hope, or perhaps become desperately and unrealistically optimistic in order to defend our dreams. Dreams are a necessary push against the limitations of life; kill them and only despair remains.

And within society, we share and celebrate, we identify within groups, social and political. We have moments of ritual: the hug or kiss on meeting, the open-handed wave; the celebratory meal offered and shared; the act of defiance, the demonstration, the march, the saluted flag.

All this, and much more, is what I refer to as human culture. It is all that human beings do and cultivate, it is their personal and shared world. It is held in a kind of tension – between the physical limitations of our limited and brief place in the world, and the dreams that go way beyond the present and the now, shaping our dreams and our creativity. But consider the dangers if that tension is allowed to becomes one-sided: to dream without recognising the physical limitations of life is to take leave of the senses and live in a world of make-believe, where wanting it to be so is mistaken for reality.

On the other hand, to give up dreaming and focus only on material facts, is to live hollowed-out, devoid of all the richness of human experience. It is a 'thin' and sad world limited entirely by reason and evidence, colourless and causally determined, untouched by dreams or creativity.

If 'God' is to make any sense, that word needs to be related to this profoundly human need to find overall direction and meaning. But equally, if 'atheism' is to make sense, it needs to provide an alternative. People cannot live in an ideological vacuum; they will always fill it with something.

THE SHADOWS OF GOD

Nietzsche never lacked vivid metaphors. The quote at the head of this chapter is from his 'New Struggles' aphorism, and he follows it up by saying. 'God is dead; but given the way people are, there may still for millennia be caves in which they show his shadow.' The shadows of God are the ideas that seek to replace him and occupy the place he once held within human thought. There have been many; whether they will survive for millennia is another matter.

Nietzsche's immediate point is that to think of the universe as having purpose, nobility or beauty is to anthropomorphise what is essentially impersonal and chaotic.

This takes us right back to the fundamental mistake of the 4th century, as far as the West is concerned. Aristotle's prime mover, and the Logos of the Stoics – both ways in which we anthropomorphise the universe – was identified with the God of religion. God emerges from stories that ennoble life and give it direction, to become a universal creator and designer. Religion moved from being a cultural phenomenon, to a theory of everything. Then, and only then, recognising how different such a divine world was from that in which we habitually move, did the separation of the 'real' and the 'apparent' come about. Only then did the projection of God onto the universe become the nonsense of a 'real' world above and outside our own. Hence, Nietzsche wants us to de-deify nature, but is that possible?

Are the 'shadows' of God adequate to the task we ask of them?

PROGRESS?

Before the rise of science and the Enlightenment, the world of the Christian West was one in which humankind was seen as playing a part in a cosmic drama – from the creation of the world by God, through sin and the Fall, through redemption in Christ and finally the prospect of a second coming, judgment and the establishment of the rule of God on Earth.

Seldom taken literally in recent centuries, it remained 'true' for those who experienced it, and it became the framework for Christian spirituality.

As we have seen, much of this was challenged by the new way of thinking that took root in the 17th and 18th centuries, but what was not challenged was the need for some sort of intellectual and emotional framework. Thus there emerged a commitment to the future of humankind, to progress, and to the perfectibility of human life and society. Humanism, with a view of the progress of humankind became the secular equivalent of the older theistic myths of redemption and the Second Coming.

As Peter Byrne pointed out in *Natural Religion and the Nature of Religion: The legacy of deism*, 1989, the Enlightenment saw religion as a natural phenomenon, dismissing its supernatural elements, and this went hand in hand with a very positive and progressive view of humankind. Herbert of Cherbury (1583 – 1648), an early figure in English deism, opposed the idea of the depravity of men and women, which he saw as a feature of traditional Christianity. People are not inevitably sinful or deserving of punishment, but are naturally positive and able to develop and grow. In 21st century guise, one might think of the work of the popular Dutch philosopher Rutger Bregman, whose *Humankind* points to progress in moral behavior, or the Israeli intellectual Yuval Harari, who surveys both the history of humankind (in *Sapiens*) and it's potential future (in *Homo Deus*). The Enlightenment project lives on in terms of positive thinking and human progress.

A similar view of progress can sometimes be found in the traditionally religious. The Jesuit scientist Teilhard de Chardin (1881-1955) believed that humankind was evolving along an axis that led towards a single personal point of fulfilment: a point he called Omega, and identified with Christ. Although his theory is open to serious challenges, both theological and scientific, the fact that he somehow wanted to integrate the two loves of his life – science and religion – says something important about his existential need to feel that life has meaning and direction.

Progress implies change, but how does that relate to the idea of a changeless spiritual reality?

In *Seven Types of Atheism*, John Gray comments:
> Like the Christian monotheism from which it sprang, secular humanism is a garbled mix of Jewish religion and Greek philosophy. For Plato – the fountainhead of Gnosticism in western philosophy – the world of passing time is a veil that conceals a changeless spiritual reality. The Bible suggests a different view. In the Old Testament, contingency – the arbitrary fact that things happen as they do – is an ultimate reality. God created the world, and intervenes in it as he pleases. (p28)

This is the real divide: between an eternalism that has an unchanging 'God' or 'Form of the Good', and a view of reality as a sequence of contingent events. The former was a philosophical idea, the latter an experience of value in and through change – sometimes referred to as 'incarnational' theology, since it saw the ultimate in meaning and value as embodied in Jesus and in his followers.

Ideas of progress, often linked to an unchallenged need for growth in the economy, remain – particularly in the political world – one of the least questioned shadows of God.

LIBERAL DEMOCRACY?

Progress may be expressed through liberal democracy, in the commitment to a better future for humanity, or to a cleaner environment, or to a recognition of the interconnectedness of all living things, or universal justice.

Such liberal, secular commitments fill the gap left when the deist god becomes an optional extra and the supernatural enchantment of the world gives way to scientific materialism. Far from atheism denying all values and direction, it is now clearly possible to engage with ultimate values, global in scope and entirely positive, without necessarily linking them to traditional supernatural beliefs.

Looking back to the Enlightenment, individuality and democracy were in the intellectual air, but were seen as dangerous substitutes for religion. Voltaire wanted to keep discussion of atheism from the servants, for fear that they might go on the rampage; John Locke, in helping to set up the constitution of the Carolinas, made belief in God compulsory; Rousseau, in *The Social Contract*, suggested that it would be necessary to banish or put to death anyone who did not believe in 'the existence of a powerful, intelligent, prescient and providential Divinity, the life to come, the happiness of the just, the punishment of the wicked'. Between them they illustrate just how repressive liberal thought could be, especially the need to keep the lower classes in order by the hope of heaven or the fear of hell.

Meanwhile, the world continued to search for an overall metanarrative to establish meaning.

The most obvious and most devastating were the political religions of the Fascism and Marxist Communism. Both provided what religion was no longer supplying for most people – a sense of identity and national or international revival, a set of rituals and ceremonies, flags, slogans, pride in giving oneself for a cause. When you look at the images presenting both the Nazi and the Communist worlds, you see people looking up into the distance, displaying pride in being a member of the Hitler Youth, or the communist workers holding aloft the red flag. To see oneself as part of a great revival, moving towards a better world, giving life for something transcendent – a future, a hope, a sense of direction. Both ideologies demanded commitment, divided people, and led to atrocities of an unimaginable scale. They displayed the very worst aspects of religious zeal, and their advocates were true zealots.

At the other end of the scale, the ideals of equality, justice, democracy, social provision for the poorest and mutual respect, were promoted by Christian groups, who saw them as reflecting fundamental Christian values. For some, socialism and engaged Christianity went hand in hand. The crucial thing to recognise here is that the values promoted may indeed have been fundamental to Christianity, but they were shared by the secular majority who saw them as a straightforward expression of altruism and common sense. The value of Christian social action, did not depend on metaphysics, but on commitment to a way of life based on the teachings of Jesus. Even if done in the name of religion, the overall focus was secular.

IN THE SECULAR REALM

There are many god-substitutes within the secular realm, as outlined by Charles Taylor and other sociologists: growth, capitalism, freedom, self-development. Today, images of the good life persist in the supplements and lifestyle sections of weekend newspapers. They offer ways of getting a better body, at a time when obesity is becoming almost the norm; of relaxation and insight through meditation and mindfulness, when stress has become the norm. Those looking for meaning and progress do not lack suggestions and images of their possible future.

The quest to understand who we are takes many forms: art, music, drama, ritual, moments of quiet observation, a sense of oneness, the desperate longing for love. They are usually inconclusive and unending. Equally, the quest to avoid the pain of meaninglessness takes many forms: the power of money, or prestige, or status, or exclusivism, the need for beliefs and certainty, the sense of control. Most give little more than temporary respite, to be honest.

Against this background of secular gods, the old discussion between theists and atheists seems anachronistic and irrelevant. Both appear to offer hypothetical structures, rather than life itself. In the secular realm, religion can be seen as a lifestyle option, or as a bastion against the threat of meaninglessness. It claims to have something positive to offer, even in a material world that is inherently meaningless and directionless. Religion therefore retains existential power, rather than explanatory power.

Clearly, you do not need 'God' in order to discover meaning, or to create value, as Eastern religions testify. Atheists do not live in a state of permanent disorientation and despair, but promote human self respect, value reason, and hope for a better world: an approach championed by the likes of Bertrand Russell in the 20th century, backed up my moral

221

seriousness. Among believers, the greatest fear of atheism is that – as Nietzsche's madman pointed out – it suggests we are forced to experience ourselves as drifting in a directionless void, and hence to nihilism. In the face of this, meaningful stories need constant repetition.

The social aspect of this was shown back in the 19th century by Durkheim in *The Elementary Forms of Religious Life*:

> There is something eternal in religion which is destined to survive all the particular symbols in which religious thought has successfully enveloped itself. There can be no society which does not feel the need for upholding and re-affirming at regular intervals the collective sentiments and the collective ideas which make its unity and its personality. (*op cit* p347)

Durkheim may have been a sociologist rather than a theologian or philosopher, but surely he is right in this. The need may manifest in society and culture, but it is deeply ingrained. We cannot sustain coherence in society without some way of affirming who we are and what we believe.

But that need does not automatically justify particular beliefs – whether theist of atheist. What it does point to is the relevance and the need. Can that need be met without belief in God? Clearly it can. Can it be met without some form of religious culture? That is more problematic. What happens to society if there appears to be no single set of beliefs to give identity? These questions are fundamental, but apply equally to theist and atheist views of society.

Part of the task of atheism, as a corrective to belief, is to show that it is quite possible for humankind to observe the world honestly, and to commit to values that make life worthwhile. This should not be difficult. After all, Buddhism starts with three universal features of existence: that everything is in a process of change; that nothing has a fixed or inherent existence; and that the inevitable result of this is that life will always be somehow unsatisfactory, never quite what we imagine it might be, and always under that shadow of sickness, old age and death. In other words, Buddhism suggests that, if you seek happiness, it is best to start by getting real, and looking directly at life as it is, not as we might wish it to be.

Coming at the same situation from a different angle, but equally providing meaning and direction, is the idea of the Tao, the natural flow of life, or in the Vedanta tradition of Hinduism, where the Atman and Brahman, the self and the impersonal reality of all, are identified. None of these religious traditions requires a God, but all provide a sense of meaning, identity and direction.

The situation today is rather different from that of earlier centuries, simply because of global awareness and blending of cultures. We are able to explore and engage with different religious traditions. The world is no longer divided between 'God fearers' and 'infidels', except for those who wilfully choose to see it that way. Human spirituality is now available as a global phenomenon, and with that comes a balance between the atheist and theist ways of interpreting human culture.

JAPAN

Japan offers an interesting example of the shift from religion to the cultural embodiment of spirituality. In 1868, the Meiji empire was restored and with it came the promotion of State Shinto. It emphasised purity of living offering worldly benefits, but along with this personal aspect came the national and political. The Emperor was seen as a human-god and became the source of all authority. Shinto gave a sense of national identity, and in this way politics itself took on a religious character.

Before this, Japan had a great variety in its religious traditions, including Buddhism and Confucianism, and its Shinto was often expressed in terms of the kami of local shrines, giving a sense of locality to religious observations. State Shinto tried to suppress the local shrines – focussing everything on the national. After 1945, however, State Shinto went into severe decline, and the Emperor – the embodiment of that religion – declared himself to be merely human. The era of Japanese imperial religion was over.

So what has happened to Japanese society since then? One might expect secular materialism to dominate, and so it does to some extent. But today there is a return of the traditional variety of religions. 108 million Japanese identity their religion as Shinto, and 96 million as Buddhist – so the older traditions have emerged from under the State's control. There are also 2.1 million Christians. 77% of the population (in a survey in 2003) said that they did not participate in organised religion, but five years later 40% said that they had belief in the Buddha, and used religion for social and family events.

So religion has largely re-emerged in the form of culture. In the chapter 'The Secular and the Spiritual in Contemporary Japanese Society' (in *Making Sense of the Secular*, ed R. Ghosh, Routledge, 2013), the author comments:
> … Japanese religious life is coterminous with cultures both in the sense of higher culture and popular culture (p178)

So culture has, in a sense, come to sacralise Japanese society or, to put it another way, secular civil society in Japan exists rather like a faith. It gives the identity as being distinctively 'Japanese', and its many forms of spirituality and aesthetic appreciation are part of that. The question remains whether secular and cultural spirituality can provide a positive alternative to traditional religion.

There are many non-religious ways of committing to meaning, as there have been demonic alternatives like the Nazi ideal of the Third Reich, or the dictatorship of the proletariat underpinning atrocities in the Soviet Union.

Choosing of an ideal as a guide to life is dangerous because it is empowering and can lead to disaster if it proves inadequate.

THE THEOLOGY OF CULTURE

In 1959, Paul Tillich published a book of essays entitled *Theology of Culture*, in which he explored a question that would be anathema to many philosophers today. He argued that the question of the nature of being (ontology) should be related to existential questions about life, asked most often within the discussion of religion and culture. He suggested that the questions with which theology deals – the nature of reality ('being-itself') and that which is of the most profound existential concern ('ultimate concern') – are raised from within art, literature, drama, religion and other cultural products. In practice it meant that the theological agenda is set by the existential questions that people ask – What is the meaning of my life? What is worth doing? What can give my life purpose or make it worthwhile?   Such questions are inescapable, and are about our 'ultimate concern', to use Tillich's term. They are asked equally by theist and atheist, because they are feature of being human. They are about exploring the depth of life.

What Tillich (being a Christian theologian) then goes on to say is that the answer to such questions are given through the symbols of religion – the images and stories that religion presents. In other words, if you engage with those stories or images, you may find in them a way of addressing your personal, existential questions.

That is an activity that is equally open to theist and atheist. It does not require prior accepting of metaphysical ideas, no credulity, nor superstition. It simply requires a willingness to ask questions. Might this continue as a universal option, even after the old images of God are dead and buried?

It's not that we don't have gods anymore. We are manufacturing them at a faster rate than ever. Just pick up a weekend newspaper supplement and they are paraded: the cult-like emulation of influencers, or of those who have risen to fame via an invisible trajectory; the fashionable paths to liberation via food, fasting, or mindfulness; the stories that inspire; the icons created. Music, sport, drama – they are constructing gods all the time; projections of all that is best, most athletic, more stylish. It's not gods that we are short of, but the critical ability to see that they are projections, rather than reality. If atheism engages with the old metaphysical pantheon and shows it to be a projection, it serves as a necessary corrective, making religion a human construct but one that is valuable, perhaps necessary for civilised life. But atheism needs to put its corrective skills to use in examining and offering a critique of the many gods of our new cultural environment.

If we need to secularise some traditional religious ideas and practices, we also need to hold back the easy divinisation of their secular equivalents. Enthusiasm for 'religious' ideas in the past has proved deadly, but so can the mini-deities of consumerism, or political simplicity, or superficial success.

The quest for meaning and the Shadows of God were features of Modernism, a period of thought that took itself seriously against a background of social and political upheaval. Today that era would appear to be over, and the world is faced with a threat that would dismiss both the serious atheist and the believer – Postmodernism.

Chapter 15

Are We Stranded in Postmodernism?

> *If I want the door to turn, the hinges must stay put.*
> Ludwig Wittgenstein

> *The Almighty can survive tragedy, but not absurdity.*
> *As long as there appears to be some immanent sense to things,*
> *one can always enquire after the source from which it springs.*
> Terry Eagleton

Please don't ask me to define postmodernism; it is too diffuse and nebulous for that. It is a mixture of styles and attitudes, in literature and the arts, which tends to reject general theories and absolute claims, regards every truth as limited by its time and place of origin, and tends to parades images and ideas from the past as thought they were consumer objects. It is a garish shop-front, where nothing has more than cash value, and everything is of equal significance or none. It is the antithesis of seriousness and has become the curse of our present age. It rejects any attempt at foundationalism, and particularly the commitment to reason and science and the anticipation of progress. Like atheism of old, it tends to be described in terms of what it rejects, so we need to start by looking at modernism.

MODERNISM AND POST-MODERNISM

Modernism is not a single school of thought, but the view of human life and creativity that spans, literature, philosophy, art and music. It developed partly as a response to the Enlightenment, with its emphasis on the individual and freedom of thought and expression. Within modernist thought, people are free and encouraged to explore a sense of meaning and direction.

Modernist painters broke away from attempting a lifelike reproduction of their model and tried to 'say' something, by defying tradition and exploring new styles and angles. Think of formal Tudor portraits, then think of Picasso. In literature, modernism strains to find meaning in a world where nothing in guaranteed. In philosophy, it embraces existentialism, the ontology of thinkers such as Heidegger, and the theology of Paul Tillich. It strives to find meaning in this world of chance, to give a story that will make sense of life.

Following on from our last chapter, modernism embraces and explores the 'shadows of God'. Humans long to make sense of their life, even if they are frustrated in the attempt to do so. In his novels, Albert Camus sees the world as 'absurd' simply because it fails to meet what we ask of it – and that asking is fundamental to the modernist way of thinking.

Modernism has something of the tragic about it, since we live in a world where meaning is not guaranteed. Nietzsche saw the death of God as tragic, with the world floating free of any mooring that could give it stability. Similarly, in modernist works of all sorts – dramatic, literary, or philosophical, musical even – there is a sense of yearning for meaning, even if that meaning is simply the creation of the individual. To use Tillich's term, modernism seeks 'depth'.

But post-modernism rejects all that. Its roots go back to the scepticism of Ancient Greece via Nietzsche's challenge, demolishing the grand narratives that tried to make sense of life in previous times. Beyond the writings of thinkers such as Jacques Derrida (1930 – 2004) whose subversively deconstructed readings of other philosophers suggested their inherent instability, or Jean-François Lyotard (1928 – 1998) who provided a political demolition job on all the 'grand narratives' that had previously shaped society, it is a form of sceptical relativism that has seeped into every aspect of our culture.

Everything is exactly what it is; nothing more. Everything is equally true or false, valid or invalid. It is post-truth, in that fictions may be presented as truth and serve in its place. I am whatever I choose to present as myself. Postmodernism is proud to be shallow. Depth and meaning are Modernist illusions and all truth is relative. There is no fundamental distinction between image and reality: a business is its website; an individual is the image he, she or they choose to present on social media. Everything has a price; everything can be marketed. Religion too can be presented as a commodity, an optional form of life enhancement. Don't ask if it's true, just enjoy it if you wish, leave it if it no longer suits.

That may be a caricature, but I believe it captures something of what postmodernism is about. Postmodernism had serious origins in the nihilist fears of Nietzsche, or the relativism of Protagoras in Ancient Greece, but it has been given extra significance by those 'shadows of God', the faith in progress, rationality and science that have became the hallmark of Western thinking since the Enlightenment. If the 18th century endorsed the idea of a rational and purposeful universe designed by a creator-god, postmodernism rejected the premise of rationality and thus brought down any plausible reason for there to be a deity.

In true modernist style, Paul Tillich spoke of 'depth' as an alternative way of articulating what God was about. He suggested that only those who could say that life had no meaning or depth – that it was surface only – could be truly atheist. My younger self found great comfort in that argument. I don't think he was fair to atheists, but we'll come to that later.

Gavin Hyman (in *The Cambridge Companion to Atheism*) argues that atheism, as we know it, is closely bound up with modernism. If modernism finally disappears, it is likely to have implications for both atheism and theism. So what has the coming of postmodernism done to the depths that both God and atheism sought to probe?

If society is dominated by anti-rational, relativist and superficial ways of thinking, then the 'Enlightenment' project' that has largely sustained both religion and principled atheism for more than two hundred years, is finally over. Or perhaps not…

BEYOND GOD AND ATHEISM?

In *Culture and the Death of God* (2014), Terry Eagleton explains that postmodernism, with its denial of the tragedy that comes with the quest for depth and meaning in life, is perhaps the first true atheism, in that it denies not just God, along with transcendence and the idea of metaphysics, but also the surrogate forms that dominated the 20th century, in humanism and a sense that humanity had purpose and direction.

For postmodernism, the main function of human beings is to consume. If we see themselves as creators, we can still sense (if we wish) that we participate in that activity alongside a creator God. But, if we see ourselves only as consumers, we arrive at something close to pure nihilism. In terms of the debate between God and atheism, both sides are equally threatened by such postmodernism.

Some 70 years earlier, in trying to find words that could indicate the true nature of God as 'Being-itself' and our 'ultimate concern', Tillich said that one understood God if one knew what it was to speak of the 'depth' of life, and therefore that the only true atheist was one who could say that life has no depth. At the time he presented that argument, and even when it was repeated again in the debates of the 1960s and 70s, the assumption was that no thinking person would say that life had no depth, meaning or purpose. That assumption no longer holds.

For postmodernism nothing is lost by the absence of God, since it lacked any awareness of the reality to which 'God' pointed. As Eagleton puts it:

> [Postmodernism] is too young to recall a time when there was (so it is alleged) truth, unity, totality, objectivity, universals, absolute values, stable identities and rock-solid foundations, and thus finds nothing disquieting in their apparent absence.

Postmodernism, in general, sees religious ideas as an individual preference, subjective and culturally generated. What you believe depends on the history of that particular idea (its 'archaeology' to use Michel Foucault's term). There are no absolute truths, for all truth emerges in particular places, cultures and situations, and is grasped by individuals in their own way. Even to talk about the development of the word 'God' therefore implies a postmodernist assumption.

Both God and atheism are rendered irrelevant by the postmodernist ways of thinking, because both are ways of describing the world as a whole and both assume that it is possible to give a true description of reality. Even the 'shadows' of God only work for those who are seeking some overall meaning to life.

But what of non-theistic worldviews? Buddhism suggests that everything as in a state flux, that nothing has a permanent or inherent existence, and that the transient nature of life inevitably means that we need to accept some measure of loss or unsatisfactoriness in life. But nevertheless, in spite of these 'universal truths', as they are called, the Buddha exhorted his followers to 'strive on' – to make an effort to develop wisdom and compassion, with the intention of helping all beings to achieve happiness and avoid suffering. In this way, Buddhism promotes a commitment to give life meaning and direction, even in a universe that provides neither. It therefore has the potential to survive radical postmodernism.

A postmodernist may accept that, in earlier times, people found it helpful to live according to myths about creation, redemption and judgment, about a loving God and a crafty Devil, about heaven and hell. That story might have been helpful or destructive, but either way, it was just a cultural fabrication. Accepting it as true could still be an option, if you happen to like that sort of thing. Equally, for a postmodernist, as explored in Ray Billington's *Religion without God*, religious figures, such as Jesus, can be seen as visualised ideals – much as Feuerbach saw God as a projection in the 19th century.

In a world in which we are always being offered dreams – by those who advertise holidays, homes, health regimes or impossibly good investments – we are tempted to become suspicious of any package that is presented as a panacea. Hence both religion and atheism languish in a postmodernist culture. A postmodernist need not bother to argue against them; the whole thing is just not worth the effort.

Perhaps that explains the confusion about God in this postmodern age, or the variety of views we outlined in the Introduction: God is whatever we choose to make him, or find sufficiently plausible to accept. If nothing is foundational, he is just an option, like any other.

ETHICAL IMPLICATIONS

If any view is as good as any other, any news dismissed as 'fake', or any incredible story presented as though fact, it is not just our intellects that are mocked, but our sense of morality.

Just as beliefs need some foundational point of reference – some point of certainty from which we can survey passing ambiguities – so our ethics need some kind of foundational value, if they are to be consistent and credible. In a secular world, utilitarianism is popular because it seems to reflect common sense; we should always aim to do what will achieve the maximum happiness for the maximum number of those people affected. As any quick unpacking of that claim shows, it begs a good number of questions, including how we define happiness and whether our goals are short or long-term. Nevertheless, it provides a starting point for reflection.

It is sometimes argued therefore that atheism cannot establish an adequate basis for ethics, since it lacks the foundational idea of God, who can underwrite the values that should motivate our action. That simplistic claim, of course, has long been seen as inadequate, since unaided human reason has long been capable of questioning divine commands or suggesting qualities that offer a positive benefit to humanity.

Given that there are few certainties in the postmodernist world, one might be tempted to think that atheism does not help when it comes to discussing moral issues. As I have already argued, I do not take a nihilist view of atheism, and find that it can indeed provide a credible set of values by which to life. In his contribution to *Philosophers and God*, of which he was co-editor, Michael McGhee tackles the question 'How to be a good atheist?' He suggests that the quest for understanding the reality to which the term God has traditionally been applied in the thinking of traditional theologians such as Thomas Aquinas or Karl Rahner, can persist, even if the superficial and inadequate concepts of God adopted by some naïve believers and dismissed by equally naïve atheists, are sett aside. His argument, which includes reference to Wittgenstein and D.Z.Philips, cannot be adequately summarized here, but deserved serious study.

Both theism and atheism can support ethics; its main threat comes from the fundamental postmodernist view that denies any logical quest for truth or universal value. Towards the end of his life, Ludwig Wittgenstein produced what was to be the third phase of his thinking, a form of foundationalism, set out now in his *On Certainty*. In it, he makes a simple observation in the quote that heads this chapter: in order for a door to open and shut, it is necessary for the hinges to be securely fixed (proposition 343). Without a fixed point from which we can gain perspective, our world falls flat the moment we reach out and give it a push. So it is with postmodernism.

THE DEMYSTIFIED WORLD

The 'death of God', through its many forms in the 19th and 20th centuries was largely the product of a modernist framework of thought. Since Kant, it has been regarded as normal to divide up knowledge into sense experience on the one hand (always subject to change, vulnerable and changing) and a priori reason on the other. Science gives us information about the objective world, reason decides how we interpret that information and the values by which we live. This leads to culture being regarded primarily as subjective – how we live, what we create, the values we adopt and the visions that inspire us, are all seen as human constructs. As part of culture, religion therefore becomes an optional, subjective activity. Value and morality are not to be discovered, but created. The apparent simplicity and obviousness of utilitarian calculations masks its underlying assumption that all value is related to human needs and desires.

From Durkheim to Charles Taylor, sociologists see the modern world as disenchanted. The enchantment has been removed to large measure because the encountered world has been evacuated of the value and inspiration that it held before the rise of science. Romantics seen to celebrate wonder, yet for the likes of Feuerbach that wonder is a projection of humankind, not something inhering in the world itself.

In *Mind, Language and Society*, 1999, the philosopher John Searle includes a section entitled 'Beyond Atheism'. What he has to say there is absolutely relevant to the problem caused by the 17th century legacy of a hybrid God.

In discussing the ultimate reality of the world in terms of physics and chemistry, he then comments that someone will say 'What about God? If he exists, then surely He is the ultimate reality, and physics and all the rest are dependent on God...' He points out that writers such as J S Mill and Bertrand Russell wrote attacks on traditional religion, but he says 'Nobody bothers, and it is considered in slightly bad taste even to raise the question of God's existence' and that matters of religion are seen as personal matters of taste. He then asks what has happened to bring about such a change. He points out that, although there has been a decline in religious faith among the more educated sections of the populations of Europe and North America, he suggests that the religious urge is as strong as ever. But the point he wants to make is that the world has become demystified – in other words, we do not link the mysteries of the world, as we see them, with the supernatural. He points out that we no longer think of odd occurrences as signs of God acting miraculously, simply that they are things we do not understand. Also, if God were shown to exist, he would simply be yet another fact of nature.

In other words, what has changed is not the religious urge, or the sense of mystery, but the tendency to move from mystery to some supernatural explanation. His conclusion:

> The fact that the world has become demystified to the point at which religion no longer matters in the public way that it once did shows not so much that we are all becoming atheists but that we have moved beyond atheism to the point where the issues have a different meaning for us. (*op cit* p36)

Although I would not necessarily explain things in the way he did, I think Searle has pointed to a crucial fact. What was seen as a traditional belief in God, and therefore what sustained much religion, was linked to supernatural claims that simply do not retain credibility in a demystified world. He does not dismiss the sense of wonder, nor does he claim that there are no mysteries in the universe – but he simply notes the decline in the assumption that the unknown can be explained by what amounts to an external, deist God.

We therefore need to ask about the significance and purpose of atheism and theism in the secular culture within which we live. What difference, if any, does the debate between them make? Is there any situation in which the result of that debate can contribute to the overall welfare of humankind, if that is to be taken as our ultimate value? But, of course, if we are stuck with postmodernism, it is not a question it makes any sense to ask.

ALTERNATIVE NARRATIVES

In July 2024, President Donald Trump, on the campaign trail, was addressing a rally when shots rang out. Trump turned his head at exactly the moment for the bullet to miss its target and do no more than take out the top off his ear. It was a terrible incident, in which one man, crouching over his family to protect them with his own body, was shot dead, and another injured. Trump emerged bloodied but defiant and went on to win a second term as President.

But notice the reaction. The sniper was immediately shot dead and both the Secret Service and local police were questioned about how he had been able to gain access to the roof and therefore to get himself in line of site to the then former President. That sort of event should never be allowed to happen. It was someone's fault. The shooter's background was investigated to see if anything in his past could account for his assassination attempt. It is assumed that there are rational, or psychological explanations for both; we live in a world where everything should be explained.

Trump survived because he turned to point to a chart about illegal immigration, a reasonable movement to make given what we was saying as the shots were fired. But... Social media soon displayed an image of Jesus standing behind Trump and guarding him, and Trump himself claimed that God had spared him by causing him to move at exactly that moment. The event had become a sign of divine blessing and protection, and hence – to his followers (Trump's, rather than God's) – an endorsement of his campaign.

Two entirely different narratives come out of that event. Almost everyone accepts the physical one, whatever their view of the outcome, but some add the story of supernatural intervention and through it re-evaluate the incident, giving it a spin in Trump's favour. God is presented as playing a part in such narratives, but how many would give that any credence? Quite a few, if social media is to be believed.

But equally, this being a postmodern world, there were alternative stories. Within hours, it was claimed that the whole thing was staged, or that the blood coming from Trump's ear was faked. Before the identity of the shooter was known, it was claimed that President Biden had given the order to assassinate Trump. All these theories were shown to be false, but in a postmodern world, being false does not prevent a story from being presented as true.

If there is no absolute truth, any lie, repeated sufficiently often, becomes 'true'. What matters is what is presented, not what is true, and thus, in this postmodern world, all that sustained both theism and atheist humanism is undermined. When there is a dramatic event, a frenzy of speculation may be unleashed; ordinary explanations are seldom enough.

THE CHALLENGE

Today, it is not so much debates for or against God that characterise our society, but a wide denial or at least disregard of the significance of religion and philosophy. The post-modernist tendency to reject any meta-narratives, or any foundational or ultimate concepts, leads to a superficial acceptance whatever appears fashionable.

I think it is important to be atheist, in order to hold at bay the bogus deities that so easily crowd in and colonise one's thoughts and feelings. It is also important because the temptation to define God as an objectively existing being (never the option for serious theologians, of course, but a popular one), is fundamentally wrong. Taken literally, such a belief would cause any amount of cognitive dissonance. Happily, many deeply spiritual people are content to sit lightly on the mythology within which religion is wrapped, and enjoy the deeply personal engagement with life that religious insights can bring. But stating the positive contribution of atheism is a good first step.

However, I think it is equally important to remain 'religious' in the broad sense of the word, keeping open the dimension of human spirituality that has been at the heart of so much culture and offering an underpinning for values and morality. Combining it with atheism is not as easy within a Western culture as it would be in the East. It's a matter of keeping a balance between two very different aspects of human experience – the *mythos* and the *logos* of Ancient Greece. It is equally essential both to be analytic and rational, and also to remain open to intuition and emotion, sensing what enables us to be 'at home' in this world, but also what challenges us to explore the depths of our being and the reality that goes beyond the passing flotsam of life.

Throughout the modernist period, whether acknowledged or not, atheism has been the norm, with theists generally on the defensive, attempting to show that their beliefs are logical and compatible with the assumptions of our age. But in doing so, they have sometimes found themselves defending an inadequate concept of God; one that would have embarrassed the likes of Anselm or Aquinas.

But that was yesterday's response to yesterday's challenge. The issue now is the extent to which both theism and atheism can retain their respective quests for truth and 'depth' in the face of a postmodernist culture. The American postmodernist philosopher Richard Rorty (1931 – 2007) argued that nothing is final but everything is part of an on-going conversation. Since all our language is shaped by our historical context, all our arguments and assumptions will be temporary. This applies as much to the language or science as any other; theories are related to the situation in which they are produced. The implication of this – seriously argued by Rorty and difficult to dismiss – is that it is not just particular beliefs that are determined by our social and political situation, but truth itself. We cannot step outside our situation to describe eternal verities.

The 'shallow' nature of some postmodernist language, presenting the unlikely as equal in value to the broadly established or well argued, creates an environment in which neither atheism nor theism can flourish easily. However, it may accidentally provide an opportunity to set opposites alongside one another as alternative ways of approaching the same issue – hence the possibility that theism and atheism, seen as absolute opposites within a Modernist era, may be set side-by-side in a postmodernist one, as two equally valid ways of engaging with reality, with each serving to sharpen focus on the other.

The background challenge, however, is expressed succinctly by Terry Eagleton in his magnificent and impassioned *Culture and the Death of God*:

The real enemy, going forward, is a kind of materialist nihilism, where the valid acceptance of post-modernist cultural variety, without the willingness to explore the transcendent within it, can lead to a spiritual vacuum.

And so to our final question: Can God and atheism rescue one another from irrelevance in the potential 'spiritual vacuum' of which Eagleton warns?

Chapter 16

Can Atheism Rescue God?

(and *vice versa*)

> *God is not an object to be known*
> *But the principle of our thought.*
> Spinoza, *Short Treatise on God*, 1661

> *It is as atheistic to affirm the existence of God*
> *as to deny it. God is being-itself, not a being.*
> Paul Tillich

If atheism is to rescue God, and God atheism, two absolutely fundamental questions need to be addressed. The first is whether it is possible, in this postmodern age, to find value and meaning within the secular world. The second is whether it is possible to do so without drawing on one or other of the great metanarratives, both religious and secular, which have shaped our cultural heritage.

If the answer to the first is 'Yes', then atheism does not inevitably lead to nihilism, as some theists fear, and we do not need to use 'God language' in order to explore 'Being Itself' and lead a meaningful and moral life. For reasons I've given earlier in this book, I think this to be true. It also implies that postmodernism does not have the last word, and that the quest for the deeper significance of things is a valid one.

The answer to the second is more problematic. The myths and worldviews that have shaped human culture contribute a rich heritage of insight and experience, but they need to be handled sensitively and not mistaken for naïve or implausible factual statements. They offer a depth of experience that logic, reason and science cannot replace. Hence atheism needs to be rescued from a reductionist interpretation and the tendency to neglect, or even deny, the validity of culture, intuition and creativity. However, it is also indubitably the case that the 'religious' quest does not necessarily require metanarratives or supernatural beliefs, but can be based on a thoughtful appreciation of experience, as Buddhism and other meditative traditions have shown.

In his book *The Secular Age*, Charles Taylor points out what any history of religion demonstrates, namely that the beliefs of each era do not come in isolation, but are integrated into the whole pattern of experience and language of their time. We have seen that in the background to Greek religion and philosophy, but also in the early development of Christian doctrines, in the Enlightenment, the traumas of the 20th century, and again today in an age which is largely secular, but within which religion, in its many forms, continues to thrive against all the intellectual odds. The God in which believers place their trust today cannot be described in the same way as the God of the Enlightenment, or of the Early Fathers. As the world moved on, it produces its own, ever-changing cultural background within which we seek to understand and express life's overall meaning – or to despair if we find it has none. Like it or not, the word 'God' changes.

So it is appropriate to ask whether the culture within which we find ourselves today is such that belief in God, as traditionally defined, can still make sense. I have suggested that, taken literally, God certainly does not 'exist', and hence that it would seem natural for most people to identify as atheist. But that is not the whole story, for we have seen that this literal God was never considered by serious religious thinkers as more than an idol, a crude representation of that which is beyond concepts and words.

Sixty years ago, in *The Religious Significance of Atheism,* the philosopher Alasdair MacIntyre commented:

> Theists are offering atheists less and less in which to disbelieve. Theism thereby deprives active atheism of much of its significance and power and encourages the more passive atheism of the indifferent. (*op cit* p24)

If atheism serves to highlight the irrational nature of the hybrid or deistic God, it actually supports theistic religion by removing an incredible impediment to adopting it as a reasonable view of life. Whether it makes it any more relevant is, of course, another matter. My hunch, looking back to the debates of the 1960s, is that the advance of atheism since then has indeed been in terms of indifference and the willingness of many people to put 'none' when asked about religious affiliation.

When the 1960s radicals spoke of 'religionless Christianity' they meant nothing of the kind. What they were proposing was a Christianity that was profoundly 'religious', in that it constituted a whole view of life, but one shorn of supernatural trappings, formalized worship and – most of all – the creeds. It is unfortunate that the bishops from the 4th century, acting as civil servants on behalf on an empire determined to establish a universal religion to integrate its diverse population, were forced to come up with forms of words to define the indefinable. Like a government saddled with the promises upon which it fought the last general election, the Church is stuck with 'beliefs' that it was forced to impose for political reasons. Their evaporation would not change its religious quest and would improve its credibility in the eyes of those who have a naturally agnostic approach to life but not a cynical or nihilist one.

ALL OR NOTHING?

In 2007 Louise Anthony, an American philosophy professor, published a collection of very personal pieces by philosophers who did not believe God. Entitled *Philosophers Without Gods*, it showed that being atheist did not necessarily require rejection of all that religion might have to offer.

Some of the contributors had been brought up either as Orthodox Jews or as Christians. They looked back over their earlier life and tried to articulate the positive things that religion offered them, as well as the reasons why they could not believe as once they had. The book attempted a rare balance between the contributions of religion and the attractions of atheism. However, what struck me particularly is that the faith that those serious thinkers had rejected had not been able to keep up with their developing philosophical enquiry. Yet, what they were rejecting, and the arguments they gave for having abandoned their former beliefs, were seldom informed by equivalent developments in theology. What some of them had moved away from was not far removed from a naïve form of religious belief that is also set aside by open-minded believers.

When, in the introduction to this present book, I cited *vox pop* responses to the question of God's existence, some might regard that as no more a caricature of religious belief, as opposed to the more sophisticated views of liberal theologians. But in Louise Antony's book we have a collection of personal journeys and reflections by those who teach philosophy. Hence, the mismatch between religious beliefs and the views of many who would describe themselves as humanist, atheist, agnostic or non-theist, is by no means confined to an unreflective or superficial approach to life.

The residue of belief, presented in a literal and uncritical way, still informs most people's view of religion. The world will be the poorer if the legacy of religion cannot escape the confines of that supernatural worldview.

244

SANTA

No doubt the demise of any cherished beliefs can be traumatic. A report, published around Christmas 2023, suggested that children start to doubt the existence of Father Christmas at about the age of 8 or 9, although their parents often try to keep the fantasy going for a few more years. Most learn of Santa's non-existence from other children. Others work it out for themselves, given the impossibility of riding a sleigh through the sky, descending chimneys and leaving presents for millions of children worldwide on a single night. Nevertheless, plenty of parents put out sherry and a mince pie, and are happy to display proof of Santa's nocturnal visit by the empty glass and crumbs on the plate.

Personally, I never discussed it with my parents. I simply recognised it as a fantasy out of which I did rather well. But, for some, learning that Santa does not exist can be disturbing. It reminds the child that his or her parents have been deceiving them. And if Santa is dismissed, how much longer before they admit that babies are not delivered, ready formed and wrapped, by a stalk!

What do we do, we grown-up children, in a world where stalks do not fly in with babies or where Santa's sleigh bells can't be heard on Christmas night? Mostly, it seems we are content to explain to children about the real arrival of babies at a fairly early age, to accustom them to the more wonderful reality of the child growing in the womb. Stalks were never really convincing anyway, since there seemed to be no explanation of where they had collected the babies in the first place. With Santa it's different; it's part of a fantasy that sustains serious retail opportunities. In terms of the investment involved, Santa has eclipsed the birth of Jesus as a feature of the season of goodwill.

I've played along and taken children to his grotto. One year my rather precocious granddaughter, being told by Santa that his real name was Saint Nicholas, demanded to know where he came from. She had been to the Netherlands and knew the story. Embarrassingly, for Santa, his training had included no historical background to the part he was to play and he was at a loss to know how to answer her. As it is, the story of Saint Nicholas, moving from Turkey, via Spain and the Netherlands to the rest of the world, is part of human culture. It's a good moral tale, with Saint Nicholas throwing gold coins out of his window to help a poor widow who is thereby enabled to find husbands for her daughters. Saint Nicholas was an early adopter of the principles of gender equality.

Hopefully, at the simplest level, the generosity of Santa may emerge from the narrative and survive his literal demise. How to achieve that in the case of God may be more problematic.

THE CHOICE

At the beginning of this book, I suggested that there were broadly two views of atheism and two views of God and that a healthy and positive view of life required one of each. By now it should be clear which options I am recommending.

If God is seen as a supernatural being of any sort, remote from the world, especially in the form of the hypothetical creator of Deism or the 'hybrid' compromise, then – for reasons of intellectual health – he is best discarded. The positive option is to use the word 'God' as a shorthand term for the reality within which we all, theist and atheist alike, live. We need to ask questions that stretch beyond the immediate and the empirical; existential questions about the meaning and purpose of life. For some – and it is only for some, not a universal recipe – the use of the term 'God' for this reality may be useful. For others it may not. It is not only possible but intellectually healthy to hold a view of the world that includes the sense of the transcendent, or Being-itself, without resorting to literalist supernatural beliefs of that sort.

For atheism there is a parallel dilemma. It is possible to be atheist – in the sense of not having belief in a God or gods –
246

without thereby denying that life has inherent value or moral sense. Atheism can be liberating and challenging, in that responsibility for one's view to the world and establishing one's place within it, is down to the individual. Morality is no less significant because it lacks supernatural backing. However, it is always possible for atheism to slip into crude scientism and display a lack of appreciation of the cultural richness that transcends simple materialism. It may well be, as the atomists of Ancient Greece claimed, that the universe is nothing but atoms in a void. Indeed, in the physical sense, that is clearly the case, although our understanding of atomic structures is now rather more sophisticated. But that is not the whole story. It does not take into account what the Ancients assumed, namely the value of culture and society. While the Epicureans took an atomist view of the nature of the material universe, they also established a serious set of aims in terms of the good life, promoting happiness and simplicity.

Assuming that we choose a liberal use of the word 'God' and a critical, positive and non-nihilist view of atheism, then atheism may indeed be able to rescue God, and *vice versa*, but *should* it?

THE BENEFITS OF A RESCUE

Purging religious liturgy and theology of deism, would create a more positive basis upon which religious ideas can contribute to the self-understanding of today's largely secular world. Indeed, that has been a feature of liberal religion for the last half century, with revised liturgy and more accessible language. In this way, religion is largely rescuing itself by its evangelical efforts. However, there is still something of a gulf between such accessible religion and the atheism or indifference of a majority of the population.

We cannot imagine a world without science and technology, but few would want to live in a world without culture. To escape the supernatural God, is to restore the profound and serious issue of 'God' in the broader sense – the quest to engage with and appreciate the meaning of life, and to take responsibility for the future of the planet. That may be going on, but it remains largely invisible; a sensitive atheist still registers as atheist.

One might also argue that God is already being rescued by atheism. In a recent on-line survey of Anglican theology, it was acknowledged that, broadly speaking, theologians are unlikely to attribute specific events to the agency of God, nor blame God for tragic events when they happen. The assumption – and one finds this in so many situations where religion comes as a solace in difficult times, or in funeral orations – is that what happens in this life is the result of natural causes or accidents, but that God cares and supports people whatever their situation.

This view of God's role is so obviously religious that one would not even start to refer to it as atheism. But look more closely at what it implies. At one time, belief in God was inevitably supported by miracles, and people were expected to pray for God to intervene and put a stop to the natural hazards to which human life is universally vulnerable. Atheists and agnostics deny the existence of such an interventionist God. But gently, subtly, that crude idea of God's action is evaporating within the context of liberal Christianity, as it has within the liberal traditions in Judaism and Islam. Common sense atheism is helping Christianity to focus on what matters in terms of comfort and support, rather than using every sad occasion to justify the specific plans of a deity. 'Why did God allow this?' is a question to which few appear prepared to give a detailed, supernatural answer. At most, they retreat into admitting that God's will is inscrutable and his purposes a mystery. That's common sense atheism struggling with inherited beliefs.

At the other extreme, those who insist on demon possession or the justification of terrorism in the name of God may claim

248

justification for their views in terms of their scriptures, but are now largely seen as a deluded minority. There are religious leaders in all the monotheistic religions who promote a more subtle and nuanced idea of God, free from literalism or the factionalism to which it gives rise.

What has caused this quiet shift in the idea of God? In my view, it has come about because of the general, atheist assumptions that lie behind both modern science and culture. This view, free from any tendency towards supernaturalism or superstition, has provided the common sense view of life that pervades society. Slowly and gently, the idea of God is being shorn of its supernatural trappings and is being used as a word for the reality 'within which we live, move and have our being'. In other words, God is being rescued from the clutches of fanatics and fundamentalists, and this can only be to the benefit of those both inside and outside the circles of conventional religion.

Feuerbach saw the idea of the deity as a projection of the best of humanity – a form of projected anthropology. When his book *The Essence of Christianity* was published in 1841, is was a huge success, and very influential, appealing to a wide range of people, both religious and non-religious. He argued that:

> In religion man seeks contentment; religion is his highest good. But how could we find consolation and peace in God, if God were an essentially different being? How can I share the peace of a being if I am not of the same nature with him? ... Thus, if man feels peace in God, he feels it only because in God he first attains his true nature...

The only thing I would point out in this approach is that what is projected is not humanity as it is, with all its finite limitations, but as we would wish it to be. It is the ideal, the goal, the final aim and the intuition of our potential. To live without any such intuition is to be very sad.

A similar point is made in the definition of God given by the late Don Cupitt at the end of his book *The Sea of Faith*:

God is the sum of our values, representing to us their ideal unity, their claims upon us and their creative power.

One can argue that both Feuerbach and Cupitt were sensitive to the role played by 'God' in religion, but both benefit from an overall view influenced by atheism.

And *vice versa*?

For some of us who take a broadly atheist view, there was nothing more embarrassing than the rants of 'New Atheists' who argued against a God who never existed anyway, and whose pitch was made entirely against religious extremists. In the early 21st century, they came, waved their flags, thought of themselves as 'brights', and attempted to refute theological ideas of which, from their publications, they appear to have had no more than the most superficial understanding and little historical context.

Atheism need not be identified with that perspective, and needs to be rescued from it. The more the monotheistic religions adopt a more subtle view of God, the more atheists, and non-theists will find common ground with 'believers'. The non-theistic traditions of Taoism and Buddhism have spiritual traditions that are not so far removed from the mystical traditions within the monotheistic faiths, and the social and environmental campaigners in secular society find common cause with religious people with similar aims.

A positive, mutual interaction between atheism and theism may thus enable each to rescue the other from the danger of narrowness and partisan arguments. Theists and atheists inhabit the same world, live and die alongside one another, and confront the same challenges; they have much to contribute to one another.

SO WHERE NOW?

Religion is unlikely to disappear any time soon. If it were simply a matter of logic, it would have gone long ago, with the mockery of the Ancient Greek playwrights, the Hellenistic philosophers, the Renaissance, the rise of science, the European Enlightenment, the arrival of explanatory ideas in evolution, psychology and sociology. It should have died the death after the horrors of The Great War destroyed the hopes of previous generations. But no, religion is still with us. Its social standing and influence may have diminished over the last half-century, but you only have to look on the web, or engage with social media groups, to be aware that it is fully alive and kicking.

It is still a very mixed phenomenon, from the respectable to the utterly crazy, but I don't think the New Atheists were right in blaming it for all the evils of humankind, since secular regimes seem equally adept at cruelty and self-deception. Religion deserves serious consideration, if only because it continues to carry a huge load of cultural creativity and insight. We just need to allow it to escape the clutches of those who would use it as a divisive tool, applying its doctrines with a literalism that renders them clear, precise, defiant and wrong.

One of the things that most impressed me when I encountered Buddhism was its ability to identify simple goals (e.g. the recognition that all beings seek happiness) and then offer basic steps in order to help bring it about. It is able to do that because it is not encumbered by the need to get a philosophical grasp of the overall meaning and direction of life before it starts on its path towards making life better. There is an old story, ascribed to the Buddha, about a fool who, having been shot with a poisoned arrow, refuses to have it removed until he is shown who shot the arrow and how it was manufactured. The prime task in life is to remove arrows, understanding them is secondary.

Theism and atheism, like a pair of old sparring partners, continue to damage one another in a match that has ceased to interest most onlookers. Neither has landed a decisive blow on the other; each camp lives on to fight another day, to the utter frustration of the other. Perhaps they will do simply go down together, unwilling to compromise or acknowledge their desperate need of rescue one another from fundamentalist religion or valueless materialism. Meanwhile, the more immediate task is to explore what atheism and theism have in common – the attempt to see life as it is, without the distortion of prejudice.

We live in a culture that is largely non-theistic. Its ethics are mainly utilitarian, and it maintains a broad consensus about human rights. There is also a broad consensus, shared by those of any religion and none, about what constitutes the good life, and particularly where there is a failure of humane and rational behavior. Could those who survived the trench warfare and devastated landscapes of the Great War, hoping that a new world order would emerge from that carnage, ever have imagined that, more than a century later, we would be watching the equal horrors of Gaza and Ukraine on our screens? We know all too well what happens when reason and basic altruism fail, but the recovery of humanity from such failures requires a consensus, based on reason and compassion, that goes beyond any division between religious and secular, theist and atheist.

In *Systematic Theology*, Paul Tillich, summarising his discussion about the nature of God, comments:

> Thus the question of the existence of God can be neither asked nor answered. If asked, it is a question about that which by its very nature is above existence, and therefore the answer – whether negative or affirmative – implicitly denies the nature of God. It is as atheistic to affirm the existence of God as to deny it. God is being-itself, not *a* being. (*op cit*, volume 1, page 262),

For me, that gives closure on any crude interpretations of theism, and illustrates the folly of deism. Neither the attempt to identify God with the structure of the world, nor to set him outside it as its external creator, can be justified rationally. The one is irrelevant; the other is self-contradictory. Atheism opposes this trivialised idea of God that, as a partisan and capricious supernatural agent, whose intentions people claim to know, and whose punishments they seem willing to enact.

The promotion of a secular spirituality does not denigrate the value that people find in religion, so I'm not saying that people should cease to believe in God, if they find that helpful. I simply encourage them to see their faith as part of a broader quest for meaning, in which atheists are fellow travellers. If there is any dualism in the world of ideas, it is not between God and atheism, nor between matter and spirit, but between the deep and the superficial.

The Dalai Lama frequently makes the point that all religions are fundamentally the same, in that they seek to develop a kind heart and selflessness. Although he does not believe in a creator God, he does not denigrate theistic belief and accepts that what suits one person will not suit another. In this disarmingly simple way, the Dalai Lama presents exactly the sort of 'rescue' I have in mind. He does not treat religious doctrines as facts to be debated, but as part of religious traditions that are judged by whether or not they help people to develop a kind heart. His atheist perspective protects him from becoming enmeshed in theological debates, but enables him to cut through to what is essential.

Over the years, I've moved from being a theist with huge intellectual reservations, to being an atheist with a serious appreciation for the personal, social and cultural benefits of religion. Hence it is my conviction that God needs to be rescued from literalism by a healthy dose of atheism, and atheism needs to be deepened by recognising the value of that to which the word 'God points.

Some find the idea of 'God' helpful, others do not. I belong to the latter camp, but have respect for those in the former. If it is a means of getting human life into perspective, and of cultivating qualities of wisdom and compassion, a rescued 'God', shorn of its supernatural trappings, may yet have a role to play, even in this secular age.

Neither atheism nor theism need conform to their caricatures; together they offer a balance of rational and cultural subtlety that is far richer than either can offer on its own. And that richness finds its expression in the natural desire to create, to celebrate and to love.

A Personal Postscript
or Accidental Prologue

Fifty-six years ago, in the radical days of the late 1960s, students of King's College, London who wanted the additional qualification of 'Associate of King's College London' (AKC) had to write an essay under examination conditions.

That warm summer afternoon in the examination room, I turned over the paper and scanned down the list of essay titles. Most seemed predictably barren, but there was one that appealed: 'Secularisation: friend of foe of religion?' I sat staring at it for a moment, wondering if I dare be honest. I was anyway in two minds about whether I should get ordained, so I decided that, since this was an opportunity to go public, I'd throw down the gauntlet to those holding the conventional, supernatural beliefs with which I had struggled for the previous three years, and write exactly what I thought.

I straightened the sheets of lined paper, lowered my head, took a deep breath and for two hours poured out all my frustration about supernaturalism, suggesting that the values expressed in the biblical narratives were not pointers to impossible supernatural beliefs but an open exploration of the values by which people could live within the world here and now. I scribbled until my wrist absolutely ached, and handed in the paper thinking "That's done it; they'll never accept me for ordination now." I was angry, relieved and exhausted.

As tradition had it, a couple of weeks later, a shortlist was posted of those of those who had taken the AKC essay paper. It named the candidates who were required to appear in person before the examiners. Mostly they would be those whose papers were considered borderline, but one would be the winner of the Tinniswood Essay Prize for the year. We sat on a row of chairs, waiting to be summoned, desperately rehearsing our excuses.

I was left sitting alone; the last to be called. Both examiners made it clear that they utterly disagreed with my conclusions, but neither seemed keen to end their afternoon by disputing them with me. The Tinniswood Prize took the form of a modest pile of books, freely selected, each eventually bearing a bookplate, denoting the prize for that year. I still have those volumes and will never part with them. In some ways, this book is a continuation, after more than half a century, of that essay.

Bibliography

Most books, including classic texts, have been referenced directly in the text, and their authors listed in the Index. However, in addition to these, I have found the following books (many of which are also mentioned in the text) of particular interest:

Antony, Louise M. (ed), *Philosophers Without Gods*, OUP, 2007.

Armstrong, Karen *A History of God*, Heinemann, 1993; *The Case for God*, The Bodley Head, 2009;

Baggini, Julian *Atheism: a very short introduction*, Oxford, 2003

Barnes, Schofield and Sorabji (eds) *Articles on Aristotle*, Duckworth, 1979 (see article by G. Patziq, 'Theology and Ontology in Aristotle's *Metaphysics*')

Batchelor, Sephen. *Confessions of a Buddhist Atheist*, Spiegel & Grau, 2010

Billington, Ray *Religion Without God*, Routledge, 2002

Bullivant S. and Ruse M. (eds) *The Oxford Handbook of Atheism*, OUP

Byrne, Peter *Natural Religion and the Nature of Religion: The legacy of deism*, Routledge, 1989

Calhoun, Juergensmeyer and VanAntwerpen, *Rethinking Secularism*, OUP, 2014.

Cornwall, J. and McGhee, M. (eds) *Philosophers and God*, Continuum, 2009

Dawkins, Richard *The God Delusion*, Bantam Press, 2006.

Dawkins, Richard *Out of Eden*, 1996

Eagleton, Terry *Culture and the Death of God*, Yale, 2014

Firth, Raymond *Religion: a humanist interpretation*, Routledge, 1996

Ghosh, R *Making Sense of the Secular*, Routledge, 2013

Gray, John *Seven Types of Atheism*, Allen Lane, 2018

Griffiths, Bede *A New Vision of Reality*, Collins, 1989

Hick, John *God and the Universe of Faiths*, 1993

Homiac, Marcia *An Aristotelian Life*,

Hussey, Edward *The Pre-Socratics*, Duckworth, 1972

Kenny, J. P. *The Supernatural*, Alba House, 1972

Küng, Hans *On Being a Christian*, Collins, 1974

Küng, Hans *Does God Exist?*, Collins, 1980

MacIntyre, Alasdair and Ricoeur, Paul *The Religious Significance of Atheism*, Columbia, 1966

Martin, Michael (ed) *The Cambridge Companion to Atheism*, CUP, 2007

Martin, Michael *Atheism: a Philosophical Justification*, Temple U P, 1990

Mohr, R. D. *God and Forms in Plato*, Parmenides Publishing, 2005

Nielsen, Kai and Phillips D.Z. *Wittgenstein's Fideism*, SCM, 2005

Nietzsche, Friedrich The Gay Science, CUP, 2001, edited by Bernard Williams

Pleins, J. David *The Evolving God: Charles Darwin on the Naturalness of Religion*, Bloomsbury, 2013

Robinson, John A. T., *But that I can't believe*, Collins, 1967

Robinson, John A. T., *Exploration into God*, SCM, 1967

Robinson, John A. T., *Honest to God*, SCM, 1963

Robinson, John and Edwards, David *The Honest to God Debate*, SCM, 1963

Searle, John *Mind, Language and Society*, 1999

Smart J J C contributing to *New Essays in Philosophical Theology*,

Smart, Ninian *Beyond Ideology*, Collins, 1981

Swinburne, Richard *The Existence of God*, Clarendon Press, 1991

Swinburne, Richard *Faith and Reason*, 2nd ed, Clarendon Press, 2005

Taylor, Charles *A Secular Age*, Harvard U P, 2007

Thrower, James *Western Atheism: a short history*, Prometheus, 2000

Tillich, Paul *Systematic Theology* (in 3 volumes, various editions)

Tillich, Paul *Theology of Culture*, 1959

Van Buren, Paul *Theological Explorations*, 1968

Ward, Keith *The Living God*, SPCK, 1984

Whitmarsh, Tim *Battling the Gods: atheism in the ancient world*, Faber & Faber, 2016

Index of Names